D0240822

Understanding Primary Science

Third Edition

MIC LIBRARY
WITHDRAWN FROM STOCK

Education at SAGE

SAGE is a leading international publisher of journals, books, and electronic media for academic, educational, and professional markets.

Our education publishing includes:

- accessible and comprehensive texts for aspiring education professionals and practitioners looking to further their careers through continuing professional development

- inspirational advice and guidance for the classroom

- authoritative state of the art reference from the leading authors in the field

Find out more at: **www.sagepub.co.uk/education**

Understanding Primary Science

Science Knowledge for Teaching

Third Edition

Martin Wenham and Peter Ovens

Los Angeles | London | New Delhi
Singapore | Washington DC

Coláiste
Mhuire Gan Smál
Luimneach

Class	372.35
Suff	WEN
M	15000491

Third edition © Martin Wenham and Peter Ovens 2010
First published 1995
Reprinted 2002, 2003
Second edition published 2005
© Introduction Lynn D. Newton
Reprinted 2005, 2006
Third Edition published 2010
Reprinted 2012

Apart from any fair dealing for the purposes of research or
private study, or criticism or review, as permitted under the
Copyright, Designs and Patents Act, 1988, this publication
may be reproduced, stored or transmitted in any form, or by
any means, only with the prior permission in writing of the
publishers, or in the case of reprographic reproduction, in
accordance with the terms of licences issued by the
Copyright Licensing Agency. Enquiries concerning
reproduction outside those terms should be sent to the
publishers.

The CD-ROM may not be reproduced for use by others
without prior written permission from SAGE. The CD-ROM
may not be distributed or sold separately from the book
without the prior written permission of SAGE. All material
is © Martin Wenham and Peter Ovens 2010

SAGE Publications Ltd
1 Oliver's Yard
55 City Road
London EC1Y 1SP

SAGE Publications Inc.
2455 Teller Road
Thousand Oaks, California 91320

SAGE Publications India Pvt Ltd
B 1/I 1 Mohan Cooperative Industrial Area
Mathura Road
New Delhi 110 044

SAGE Publications Asia-Pacific Pte Ltd
3 Church Street
#10-4 Samsung Hub
Singapore 049483

Library of Congress Control Number: 2009924394
British Library Cataloguing in Publication data

A catalogue record for this book is available from the British Library

ISBN 0 978–1-84860–118-5
ISBN 0 978–1-84860–119-2 (pbk)

Typeset by Dorwyn, Wells, Somerset
Printed in Great Britain by the MPG Books Group
Printed on paper from sustainable resources

MIX
Paper from
responsible sources
FSC
www.fsc.org
FSC® C018575

CONTENTS

ABOUT THE AUTHORS

Martin Wenham originally trained in plant biology and forestry, becoming a teacher in 1967, after four years in full-time research. His teaching experience has included work in secondary, primary and special schools, with pupils of all ages from 5 to 18. Between 1989 and 1998 he was a Lecturer in Primary Education at the University of Leicester, specializing in science and art.

Peter Ovens is Principal lecturer in professional and curriculum development in the School of Education and a specialist in primary science education at Nottingham Trent University. His area of study includes writing and research concerning the philosophical, curriculum and pedagogical aspects of science learning, teaching and assessment in early years and primary school settings.

Lynn D. Newton is Professor of Primary Education and Head of the School of Education, University of Durham. Previously a primary teacher and advisory teacher for primary science, she has extensive experience of researching and writing on science issues for primary teachers. She is the author of *Co-ordinating Science Across the Primary* (1998) and *Meeting the Standards in Primary Science* (2000), both published by Routledge Falmer, and has edited *Teaching for Understanding Across the Primary Curriculum* (Multilingual Matters, 2003).

FOREWORD

IMPROVING PRIMARY SCIENCE TEACHING

by Lynn D. Newton

The wide ranging Education Reform Act of 1988 prepared the way for massive curriculum change in primary schools. The Act required science to be taught as a core curriculum subject for all pupils between five and sixteen years of age. It was to be on equal terms with English and mathematics in the National Curriculum.

Today, although science is meant to be a core subject in schools, it is rarely afforded an equal status with English and mathematics. As successive government education departments have focused on the quality and quantity of literacy and numeracy to the potential exclusion of all else, science has languished. After a time of promise when the National Curriculum for Science was introduced, the amount of time given to it in primary schools has often declined. In the time given to science, teachers tend to teach scientific vocabulary and facts, and avoid causal explanations and teaching for understanding. For instance, teachers may ask which fabric is best for keeping the water warm in a cup but not ask why. They often acknowledge the value of 'investigation' but use it only to follow a procedural recipe or to check facts, not explore ideas or develop explanations. For example, primary children often test different kinds of threads to find out which thread is the strongest but they are not encouraged to think about why one is stronger than another. I accept that scientific explanations are hard to grasp, but I am not talking about teaching thermal conduction to seven-year-olds or tensile strength to ten-year-olds. But seven-year-olds are able to grasp the generalization that thick fabrics are more likely than thin fabrics to keep a cup warm and ten-year-olds can grasp the idea that some materials have more strength than others, that thicker thread is generally stronger than thinner thread and, in combination, this can explain their results.

Science lessons are the main source of children's experience of causal explanation (the water in the cup stays warmer longer *because* the wrapping is thick; the thread X takes more weight before it snaps *because* it is thicker than the other threads of the same material; at the same time, thread X takes more weight *because* it must be made of stronger material than the other threads of the same thickness).

Most of the rest of the week, they talk about purpose and intention, why people do things and what things are for. Vocabulary and facts are important in any subject, but in science the opportunity to work with causal explanation should not be missed. This is all part of the richer tapestry that helps them to begin to develop their argumentation skills in science.

Why does causal explanation not receive the attention I believe it should? One reason could be that some teachers do not feel confident enough in science to explain or draw out explanations from the children. They may play safe in their lessons, filling them with facts and avoiding reasons. Practical work is given to the children but it lacks a press for understanding procedures and conclusions. Certainly, such teachers talk much less with the children about the science. Another reason could be that some teachers see science as being about facts. For these teachers, understanding in science will amount to grasping the words and descriptions, a misconception reinforced by the focus of many of the questions on the annual Key Stage 2 tests, the SATs. Others may know that science is about *explaining the world* but see such explanations as beyond the comprehension of younger children. Children are, however, capable of understanding physical causation from a very early age. When adults think of scientific explanations, they tend to think of them as they are generally expressed by scientists. But there is a lot of science out there that can be taught in a way that generates cognitive engagement and leads to the construction of understandings on the part of young children, with meaningful causal explanations, as was illustrated above.

One approach to improving primary science teaching is to accept that this is the way the teaching world is. To make it better, teachers should be given the 'right' materials and trained to open them at relevant pages. According to this model, what teachers know or do not know does not matter. Point them at the class, turn them on and watch the learning build up. This factory model of teaching, of course, ignores the human element, both in the teacher and the children. A teacher with particular conceptions of science and science education will consciously or unconsciously shape his or her teaching in line with these conceptions. For example, if teachers believe that science is about facts and descriptions, this is what they will emphasize and give marks for. The danger is that this, in turn, will shape the children's conceptions. Even the most perfect teaching materials can be bent into other shapes, even by well-intentioned users. Then there are the children. No 'right' materials can allow for their infinite variety. What if one of them asks an unanticipated question? And what if it is the dreaded 'Why?' question? And, of course, what is 'right' for one teacher and one child at one time may not be right for others at that time or for anyone at another time. Very quickly, the situation dissolves into the real world where the teacher has to draw on his or her own resources. The point is, that you cannot beat knowing and understanding the subject. This is the view taken in an alternative approach.

The alternative approach is to help teachers construct worthwhile lessons that suit the needs of particular children. This means you would expect to see one lesson on, say, simple circuits in one school and a different lesson on the same topic in another. While the lessons would probably have things in common, the teachers would have tuned them to the needs of the particular children in each school. But teachers need to know enough science to produce and tune lessons to the needs of their children. Not the least part of this is being able to lead discussions that include modelling the explanation process, answer questions and help the children construct scientific explanations.

However well intentioned, there is an inherent danger in 'official' schemes and lesson plans, like those of the government-endorsed Qualifications and Curriculum Authority (the QCA) Scheme of Work for Science. Although it may not have been the intention, their origin induces teachers to adopt them and follow them closely, perhaps believing that Office for Standards in Education (Ofsted) inspectors will approve their office's products. The danger is that hardpressed teachers use them without due thought, that science lessons become the same everywhere, and that development and creativity in primary science teaching (both the teacher's ability to plan a creative lesson and the children's opportunities to be creative in their explanations and investigations) is stifled. From the point of view of the classroom teacher, the last point stands repetition. A joy of teaching is in the creative opportunities it presents. A lesson, personally crafted for the occasion, taught with interest and enthusiasm, can make the day worthwhile. The ability to craft that lesson needs a teacher who does not follow blindly the plans of others. It needs one who knows what the subject is about, who understands the science that he or she is teaching. Teachers need to grasp three important things about science, namely, that it involves:

- products (the body of scientific knowledge, facts, descriptions and *explanations* of the world);
- processes (ways of thinking and working scientifically, explorations, investigations and experiments); and
- people (science is a human enterprise that has bearing upon both those who engage in it and those who live with it).

Although preparation to teach science is compulsory on initial teacher training courses, such courses are generally too short. The breadth of science (biology, chemistry, physics, geology and astronomy) is such that there is not the time to cover everything. How to teach primary science is exemplified but the teaching of every aspect of every subject is impossible – everything cannot be covered. New teachers must inevitably meet science topics and cross-curricular themes that they must plan for themselves. At the same time, even the model lessons they have seen in school and tried for themselves are limited and need to be adapted for different occasions. Experienced teachers may also be keen to further develop their expertise. Yet the current focus on literacy, numeracy and information and communications technology has resulted in very little opportunity for continuing professional development support in science.

This state of affairs could well continue with the implementation of the recommendations of the most recent 2009 Independent Review of the Primary Curriculum, the Rose Review. The Review identifies *Science and Technology* as one of the six areas and provides potential for some wonderful opportunities for primary science through its emphasis on cross-curricular opportunities and problem solving and creativity. However, the disappointing emphasis on literacy, numeracy and ICT skills and the equally disappointing lack of significant reference to science are likely to do little to re-balance the current situation. While the encouragement of cross-curricular approaches is to be applauded, those who have worked for many years as primary teachers and in the field of science education will recognise the risks this poses for science. First, not all desirable science experiences fit neatly into cross-curricular opportunities and so there is a risk that some may be diluted or avoided altogether. Second, there is a degree of confidence and competence needed to plan and organise cross-curricular teaching. This is something that most primary teachers are good at. However, this rests on a basis of understanding the opportunities available within each subject to integrate it into a cross-curricular theme. Past experience suggests that primary teachers who lack confidence and competence in science and science teaching may not recognize such opportunities. In addition, and disappointingly, the review seems to attribute problem-solving opportunities to the area of mathematical understanding and creativity to arts. This sends a message that science (and its application in technological contexts) does not provide opportunities for problem solving and productive and creative thinking. Of course it does, but only if teachers have the necessary skills, knowledge and understandings of science to recognize such opportunities.

Evidence from educational research and school inspections indicates that effective primary science teaching involves:

- a security that comes from having a sound understanding of science;
- control of the science material being taught;
- careful planning that tunes lessons to the needs of particular children;
- well organized and managed activities (mental as well as physical);

- a high level of oral interaction (teacher and children talking about the science);
- clear responses to questions and provision of high-quality scientific explanations; and
- the use of the assessment of progress to set clear targets.

Training courses tend to focus upon subject application. This means that teachers are expected to draw upon and develop their own subject knowledge to a significant extent. But, of course, their own prior knowledge of science can lack breadth as well as depth. Many current trainees' experiences of science teaching may have been adequate to pass elementary examinations but itself has failed to give them an adequate conception of the breadth of science, science as products, processes and people, and of science as explanation. Nor do they appreciate what counts as understanding or productive thinking in science. This makes it difficult at times for trainees to develop the above attributes.

This book is intended to help you teach science successfully, whether you are a trainee teacher acquiring the basic skills and knowledge or an experienced teacher who wants to become more effective. It offers you the knowledge of science to enable you to plan good lessons that will engage the learners in your care with confidence. If successful, it may halt the marginalization of science and return it to its proper place among the core subjects in the primary school.

Lynn D. Newton

Professor of Primary Education
Durham University, 2009

INTRODUCTION

LEARNING SCIENCE SUBJECT KNOWLEDGE FOR TEACHING

Using this book to maximize your learning

If you have been successful in learning science subject knowledge for passing examinations such as GCSE, then you may have developed a particular approach to learning. For example, you may have put a heavier emphasis on memorizing the knowledge than on understanding it. Perhaps your intention was to remember the fixed, static knowledge just long enough and well enough to pass the test or examination, and little more. But **learning subject knowledge for teaching** is fundamentally different. It has the more complex purpose of providing you as a teacher with an adaptable, dynamic understanding that can be used in different ways and fitted to different situations.

One of the joys (and challenges) of investigative teaching of science is that we never know what children may ask, what they might think, what words and expressions they may use, or what 'funny' ideas they may have. In order to teach well, we need to be able to respond to their ideas with accurate scientific understanding that is **adapted to their situation**. You need to be able to **apply** your science subject knowledge to unpredictable situations that arise spontaneously. We need to be able to talk about relevant knowledge and understanding with **personalized and contextualized language** that matches their thinking and interest at that time. So, when you are learning science subject knowledge for teaching you should aim for understanding much more than memorizing. Your learning should also include practising the application of the knowledge to investigative situations like those in children's learning activities in classrooms. **We best learn science subject knowledge FOR TEACHING when we are thinking about how to apply it in our teaching.** We need to link our science knowledge of all three kinds (1.3) to what children do in their investigations and how we will talk with them about their ideas and experiences.

There is a rational sequence for **planning teaching** that may look sensible in theory. It advocates a series of separate stages like: choose the content that needs to be 'covered', define precise aims and objectives, find some relevant learning activities and plan the practical resources. Aims are supposed to be thought about separately from the means to achieve them. Checking the accuracy and depth of understanding of the relevant science knowledge probably happens near the start. In practice, teachers' thinking about planning may be a blend of this rational plan and a more intuitive and creative process of flitting backwards and forwards between aims and ways of achieving them, including what the accurate meaning of a particular science idea might be. The plan might start off with what seems to be a good idea for some exciting investigative projects using new resources. Clarifying the science ideas and pinpointing the precise objectives may best occur after the sequences of lessons have begun, so as to be responsive to what the teacher discovers to be the children's current ideas and interests and be adaptable to the emergent objectives and targets that need to be set.

The ideal teaching resource provides authoritatively precise accounts of the science knowledge with plenty of tried and tested learning activities, so that one can be thought about with quick and easy cross-reference to the other. With this book you have a CD-ROM which provides practical ideas for many **Investigations in Science**. Refer to the relevant activities where the book shows the symbol ☉ and a reference number, as you learn your science subject knowledge for teaching from this book. Have both sources open, as you prepare some teaching, to help you to link scientists' ideas with how children might talk and understand them as part of their investigative experiences. **This will help your teaching to aim for Sc1 objectives simultaneously with the Sc2 (or Sc3 or Sc4) objectives** (see the National Curriculum perspective in 1.1.1). Advice about how this links with a topic approach to planning is provided in section 1.4.

Taking full advantage of this approach helps your confidence to teach science. Sometimes teachers say they lack confidence because they perceive that they do not know enough about the subject matter that they want the children to learn. They may be correct, but they may also think this because they have an outdated idea of what science is. They feel that successful science learning is mainly getting the children to learn science facts, names and theories (*knowledge that*, see 1.3). So the teacher feels confident only when s/he has learned *that* kind of subject knowledge well. However, a teacher with a modern view of science is aiming to help children to **become scientific** about the area of experience that they are learning about. This is less concerned with children learning conceptual knowledge alone, and more about integrating it with a rich experience of learning resources and activities. The teacher is careful about the language in use (1.11.1), arouses children's curiosity, and is adaptable and responsive to their questions and ideas. This embraces *knowing that, knowing why* and *knowing how to* (see 1.3). Successful science learning is shown by the children thinking, talking and writing scientifically. So the teacher's confidence is about knowing how to help them to do this. Looking at it this way, subject knowledge for teaching can be seen as not just knowing the scientific facts, names and theories, but also knowing how they link into the pedagogical, practical and other aspects of teaching, learning and assessment. This book and its CD-ROM provide a comprehensive resource for all these aspects of teaching science well.

PROGRESSION IN CHILDREN'S LEARNING TO BECOME SCIENTIFIC

As teachers we have an awesome responsibility for the progressive, personalized learning of every child in the class. The better we get to know each child, the more we realize their uniqueness. We find ways to recognize this wonderful variation in human qualities and help them all to progress. Creating an effective match between 'where a child is' and the learning activities that offer the best opportunities for progress is at the heart of good teaching. We need to attend to difference as much as we can. However, we also need to use general guidance about what kinds of progress it is reasonable to expect our pupils to achieve. The National Curriculum specifies **levels** for learning in science that can provide one source of general guidance.

Using the metaphor of a series of *levels*, there are statements about what kind of knowledge, skill or understanding can be expected from a child at a particular point in their progression in each area of the National Curriculum. Across Key Stages 1 and 2, there are six levels of progress, and at each one, for each Attainment Target, a statement is provided. When using these statements, a teacher needs to apply their professional judgement in several ways. There are inevitable differences between the statement and what a particular group or child seems to be learning. Also, the statements represent a summary of the general trends in children's progress, gained from experience rather than the result of systematic research. They are loose descriptions and are not meant to be accurate predictors of any individual child's progress in learning. Using *levels* in planning for progression in our teaching can be helpful. As we accumulate our experience of children's learning of science, we can refine our practice so as to guide progression more wisely, avoiding any inclination to allow them to straitjacket our expectations for individual children.

In the CD-ROM, the level statements are summarized and presented in ways that will help you plan. This is to facilitate the teaching of the science ideas and understanding through investigative learning approaches.

FINDING YOUR WAY AROUND THIS BOOK AND THE CD-ROM

There are a number of ways of finding what you want or need.

1. There is detailed list of sections in the **Contents** of the book.
2. At the beginning of each of the four main parts of the book, there is an **introduction** to the relevant Attainment Targets of the Science National Curriculum. For example:
    BECOMING SCIENTIFIC on page 6
    LIFE PROCESSES AND LIVING THINGS on page 31
3. Go to the **Quick Guides** in the CD-ROM showing links between each part of the Attainment Target at Key Stages 1 and 2 and the relevant parts of this book. This enables you to find the subject knowledge more quickly.
4. There are many links between different parts of the National Curriculum, which are shown in this book by **cross-references** to other sections. For example on page 28 we read:
    "We can describe the way it was moving as something that changed. Then we can explain that forces which were out of balance were acting on it (11.5)".
    This refers you to section 11.5, FORCES OUT OF BALANCE on page 199, for more information.
5. There is an **Index** of subjects and topics at the back of the book.
6. There are many links between each part of the book and the many **practical learning activities** on the CD-ROM. Look for the symbol ☉ and the Activity or Section number. For example:
    ☉ *Activity 4.2.3 is about how to investigate flowers* on page 73 – Go to *200 Science Investigations* on the CD-ROM and open up Activity 4.2.3.
7. For each Attainment Target, there is a relevant part of the CD-ROM which summarizes the kind of **progression in children's learning** that you can use as a guide to planning and assessment.

To use the CD you may need to download Adobe Acrobat Reader. If you do not have this on your system you can download it free from the Adobe website – go to www.adobe.com and click on Get Acrobat Reader on the first page. You can search the pdfs for activities using the Find function on the Edit menu, or using the Go To function from the View menu.

PART 1

DEVELOPING SCIENTIFIC KNOWLEDGE

The title of this book, *Understanding Primary Science,* indicates that it is partly about the conceptual knowledge that scientists have developed: the ideas about plants, animals, materials, energy and so on. However, the book is also about understanding science itself, and how this relates to young children who are learning to become scientific. Helping children to become scientific is a much more interesting and enjoyable part of being a primary school teacher than just teaching them scientific conceptual knowledge. It is about inducting children into one of the most significant ways of thinking and learning in our cultural heritage.

This book is a vital resource for primary teachers teaching science, and this is its most important chapter. It explains how teachers can harness a wide range of young children's **investigative** learning experiences (which are provided in the rest of the book and the CD-ROM) as sources of **evidence** from which to learn about the **ideas** of science by **becoming scientific**.

This section sets out what you need to know and understand in order to teach Sc1.

1 HELPING CHILDREN TO BECOME SCIENTIFIC

1.1 BECOMING SCIENTIFIC

This phrase is meant to convey a particular way of thinking about learning science which involves the whole person of the learner, what s/he thinks, feels and does. It acknowledges the parts played by learners' personal interests, their previous experiences and how they perceive themselves as learners. Becoming scientific involves many things, including learning about what scientists know and think, how they have come to believe in their sometimes strange ideas, and why they do science. Young children can best learn this by developing scientific knowledge and thinking at their own level of understanding, using increasingly complex scientific ways of finding out, following their own purposes and interests and learning about the purposes and interests of scientists. When children are becoming scientific, they playfully explore new experiences, think about previous ideas and develop new ones to extend their knowledge. They progress by focusing their curiosity more sharply and making their ideas and evidence more scientific through critical discussion and deeper investigations.

Scientific knowledge on its own is not science, any more than a collection of paintings and sculpture is art. To know facts and concepts in biology, chemistry and physics is not to be scientifically educated, any more than to know the names of monarchs and the dates of their reign is to be historically educated. *Being scientific* is a way of knowing, doing and thinking which is distinct from being artistic or being historical. It involves thinking about one's own ideas, how they are tested against experience in scientific ways and comparing them with scientists' ideas and evidence.

1.1.1 The National Curriculum perspective

The Science National Curriculum programme of study in science has the following statement about knowledge, skills and understanding: 'Teaching should ensure that *scientific enquiry is taught* through contexts taken from the sections on life processes and living things, materials and their properties and physical processes' (emphasis added). This underlines the central importance of Attainment Target 1 (or Sc1 for short) which is then specified under two headings:

1. Ideas and evidence in science
2. Investigative skills

This means that whatever ideas we are teaching from the other Attainment Targets in the National Curriculum (Sc2, Sc3 or Sc4) whether they are to do with seeds, magnetism or rusting, then **how** we teach them should involve learners in thinking about the **ideas** in relation to **evidence,** in the investigatively skilful ways that are specified by Sc1. **This should apply to all learning of science.** The other Attainment Targets specify **what** is to be learned, while Sc1 specifies **how** the science is to be learned. This chapter is about understanding why Sc1 is so important in learning science.

The phrase 'Ideas and evidence' is meant to convey that at the heart of science itself there is an expectation that when we are thinking scientifically, the ideas we use to try to understand or explain what we experience about the world need evidence in the form of observations and measurements to enable us to decide if the ideas are valid. Equally, when observing closely or measuring carefully, we need good ideas to explain or understand or apply to our thinking. It is these kinds of interactions of ideas and evidence that we can look for in children's thinking that we call scientific.

It may be helpful to compare the relationship between Sc1 and the other Attainment Targets in the science national curriculum, with the relationship between the official curriculum and the *hidden curriculum.* The official curriculum is **what** we intend to teach. We may define this as subjects such as English, mathematics, history, etc., or as cross-curricular topics such as *The school's environment.* But, **how** we intend to teach such subjects or topics should include consideration of our *hidden curriculum*: our values and beliefs about how we want children to learn them. In science, **what** we teach in Sc2, Sc3 and Sc4, **provides the context** for **how** we help children to gain what we value in being scientific. This includes developing the skills, attitudes and ways of working that express our scientific values such as curiosity, collaboration, scepticism, imagination, questioning, tolerance to uncertainty, etc.

1.1.2 Wider educational perspectives

The Sc1 part of the Science National Curriculum also implies that a teacher needs to be aware of how their teaching of science is related to wider perspectives. This includes what we are aiming for in children's education, and what we understand about how children learn.

To be clear about our aims, we need to deepen our understanding of what it means to **be scientific**. Some argue it is a quality that is fundamental to what it means to be human. Frank Smith, a Canadian professor of education, says that being scientific is also a fundamental quality of how we learn.

> In some areas of research it has become customary to talk of 'the child as an experimenter' or 'the child as scientist'. But I do not think that these analogies do sufficient credit to children. They suggest that children are precocious, and raise the question of where children might get the specialised skill which among adults seems to be largely restricted to scientists. I think the analogy should go the other way. When scientists are conducting experiments they are behaving like children. Scientists, in the discipline of their professional activities, do deliberately and consciously what children do naturally, instinctively and effortlessly. *The 'scientific method' is the natural way to learn displayed by us all in our early years.* The problem as we get older is that we give up the basic requirement for learning by experiment – tentativeness. As we get older we become dogmatic about what we think (I tentatively propose). But in childhood the very basis of our learning is a willingness to look for evidence that might lead us to change our minds. (Smith, 1978: 91–2, emphasis added.)

We are all born with a capacity to become scientific which we can develop.

If our teaching of science is to contribute to the achievement of wider aims of education, then we need to bear in mind that science is a human endeavour that is an increasingly important part of the cultural inheritances that we are handing on to the next generation. Scientific learning is one of the most recent aspects of our civilization to develop, historically. More and more people use existing scientific knowledge and engage in scientific ways of finding out new knowledge as part of their working lives. Teachers need to have a modern image of science and its place in society and this should inform how we understand and use Sc1 in our teaching. A Victorian image of science, for example, which regarded science knowledge as fixed and certain truth, would be consistent with a didactic method of teaching, with little need for learners to engage in genuine, whole investigations of their own. But a modern image of science, as described briefly here, is consistent with constructivist approaches which involve learners in whole, real investigations. Teaching is better when it is guided by a thoughtful understanding of how children learn in different ways and how a teacher enables their best learning. Theories of learning are helpful in guiding our teaching of children's thinking abilities and attitudes that are important to their achievement of Sc1. For example, behaviourist approaches to the teaching and learning of Sc2, Sc3 and Sc4 may match the limited intentions of *teaching to the test* in a Y6 class preparing for SATs, but constructivist approaches are more helpful to a teacher who is aiming for children to develop their thinking about scientific ideas through investigative activity.

1.2 THINKING ABOUT SCIENTIFIC KNOWLEDGE AND INVESTIGATION

Science is a way of exploring and investigating our world. The aim is to learn more about and understand better, the objects, materials, living things and phenomena we experience. Science combines the ability to investigate scientifically with the growth of knowledge and understanding. They are like the opposite sides of a coin: in looking at one or the other we mustn't forget the whole thing. Science is not only a way of knowing: it is also a way of doing, and each shapes the other. Understanding the nature of science helps us as teachers to understand not only what scientists do, but also to understand and encourage children's investigations much better.

In a modern view of science, the facts, concepts and theories which make up scientific knowledge are neither permanent nor beyond dispute. They are much more like a report on progress so far, which future investigators will modify and even, maybe, contradict. Any scientific theory is, to put it simply, the best agreed explanation which scientists have produced up to the present. Theories are not final, and certainly not true with a capital T: they are provisional, and are used until something is observed which contradicts them or which they cannot explain. When that happens to an important and influential theory, something rather like a scientific revolution occurs: an old theory may be discarded and a new one is invented, tested, discussed, negotiated, refined and eventually accepted, or rejected, by the scientific community. Large-scale scientific theories such as the theory of evolution can never be proved true beyond all doubt. Older views of the nature of science held that the strength and reliability of scientific knowledge and its claim to be highly regarded were based on its certainty; on the way it had been tested and proved true. It was as if the 'scientific method' could infallibly find a way to know for sure. Newer ideas take almost exactly the reverse view.

Today, the strength of science can be thought to lie in its openness to criticism and correction. Science is regarded as a powerful and influential activity precisely because the truth of scientific knowledge cannot be taken for granted and because it is always open to question. Like other human activities, science is fallible. This does not mean that science is simply guesswork or that 'anything goes'. On the contrary: whether in the research laboratory or the primary school, no observation, idea or theory should be accepted until it has been tested in as fair and as thorough a way as possible (1.10), while remembering that testing ideas and theories cannot prove that they are true. Testing may be essential, but it can do no more than help us to decide whether our answers and explanations are good enough to accept *for the time being*, until they obviously need correction or a better idea emerges.

How then can there be any measure of the reliability of scientific knowledge? Because when it is used in research, technology or everyday affairs, it is constantly being tested against experience and what can be observed in the world. Of course all this is not necessarily *directly* applicable to our teaching in the sense that we tell children about all these ideas explicitly (although we can, in some situations) but indirectly, an appreciation of the uncertainty of science is helpful to teaching science investigatively because we can reassure ourselves, as teachers, that tolerance to uncertainty in our own and our children's learning is a feature of science itself.

1.3 THREE KINDS OF KNOWLEDGE

Becoming scientific includes developing three kinds of knowledge, which have been called knowledge 'that', knowledge 'why' and knowledge 'how to'.

1.3.1 Knowing 'that'

Knowing 'that' is the knowing of facts, events and changes. It is the kind of knowing which grows out of, and enables us to answer, factual questions beginning with **what**, **where**, **when** and **how**. **Becoming scientific involves learning more scientific facts**. Examples of knowledge 'that' are that *muscles only pull and do not push* (3.5), that *if steam is cooled it condenses into liquid water* (6.2.2) and that *steel is a magnetic material, but brass is not* (12.3). Knowing 'that' is important because it gives us an account of how the world is thought to be, and helps to frame our expectations about what we may see or what may happen in the future. For example, if a child knows that when sugar dissolves in water, it does not disappear but mixes with the water, she is likely to expect the solution to taste sweet, whereas if she does not have this knowledge the sweetness is likely to come as a surprise. Surprises are particularly important in both scientific research and education. We feel surprise when we experience things that do not happen as we expect. What we expect has grown out of what we know and understand. A surprise may signify that the new evidence is challenging our existing personal theory. This means that **surprises should always call for investigation** both in what we know (knowledge 'that') and in our understanding of it (knowledge 'why').

1.3.2 Knowing 'why'

Knowing 'why' is concerned with identifying causes for what has been observed (1.3) by seeking explanations and by gaining understanding rather than gaining factual knowledge. It is the kind of knowing which grows out of, and enables us to answer, questions beginning with 'Why ... ?', and which can be summed up in statements beginning with 'Because ... '. Knowledge 'why' is usually more complex than knowledge 'that', because it starts with the facts and seeks to explain them. **Becoming scientific involves learning explanations and understanding**. Most established scientific theories are highly developed and tested examples of knowledge 'why'. For example, why does the Sun seem to move across the sky during the day? It seems to move because the Earth is spinning and we are carried round with it, so the angle from which we see the Sun changes through the day. This is an explanation which grows out of the theory that the Sun is at the centre of the Solar System and the Earth is in orbit round it (14.2.1). The nature of knowledge 'why' is explored further in section 1.7, in relation to the making of hypotheses.

Scientific knowledge is commonly thought of as knowing 'that' and knowing 'why', but the third kind of knowledge, knowing 'how to', is just as important. Science is not only concerned with knowing and understanding: it is also concerned with practical investigation, and the ability to investigate effectively is particularly important in primary science, where theories of learning advise us that children's learning depends as much on personal, first-hand experience as on being told about things or reading about them.

1.3.3 Knowing 'how to'

This is an essential part of becoming scientific. There are two main kinds. One is concerned with knowing how to do investigative processes and procedures, including 'fair' tests for ideas and theories (1.10). For example, investigating scientifically whether a parachute with a small hole in the centre is better than one with no hole depends on knowing how to set up and carry out fair and thorough testing. The other kind of knowing 'how to' is about making things work practically in a controlled and predictable way. It is often on the borders of science and technology. Most testing of scientific ideas and theories involves knowing 'how to' of both kinds. For example, if children want to find out which of a collection of play-balls is the bounciest, they have to carry out a fair test. This will involve not only knowing how to conduct a fair test by identifying and controlling variables (1.10), but also the practical knowing how to devise and use a method for measuring accurately how high each ball bounces.

An important point needs to be made here about the use of Information and Communication Technology in helping children to learn science. It is increasingly easy to find visual ways of indirectly experiencing scientific ideas on a screen, some of which may give opportunities for the teacher to demonstrate cause and effect relationships. They can help children to gain 'knowing that' and 'knowing why' in science. However, children can only develop 'knowing how to' by doing their own practical investigations and gaining direct experience of the challenges of finding out for oneself. This is when they best feel that they are becoming scientific and it is where technology can be immensely helpful in making better measurements and records to strengthen the evidence base for testing ideas.

Scientific investigation makes two important contributions to primary education. First, it helps children develop the ability to perceive problems, think up possible answers, find out whether their ideas stand up to testing and communicate their findings clearly. Second, it develops a critical awareness of science and its influence within the community. As far as anyone can predict, the lives of children who are in primary schools today will be affected even more by science than the lives of their teachers and parents are at present. There is an obvious need for as many people as possible not only to understand something of the scientific knowledge and theory which affects their lives, but also to be critical of scientists' claims. Critical evaluation of any kind of knowledge or discovery is impossible unless one knows how the results were arrived at. This is because, **in any kind of investigation, results and ways of working depend on and shape each other.** What is discovered depends not only on what is investigated, but also on the methods used (1.5) and the ideas, knowledge and experience of the investigator. This means that first-hand investigations are relevant and valuable not only because they develop knowledge, understanding and the ability to investigate competently, but also because they help to give children a more realistic insight into how science works, its achievements and (equally importantly) its limitations.

1.4 THE TOPIC APPROACH

Becoming scientific is largely concerned with investigating through first-hand experience which helps children to understand the world around them. This presents the teacher with great opportunities, but can also raise problems. One major problem when trying to develop a science education based on first-hand experience is that it is impossible for children to investigate everything in their lives, so choices have to be made. Another is that real-life situations are usually much more complex than the artificially simplified world of the science laboratory. A third is that the experience which children bring to school, and the learning opportunities offered by each school's locality, are as varied as the localities and life itself. The topic approach used in several parts of this book offers one way to overcome such problems: to exploit local conditions and resources effectively and to help ensure the relevance of science investigations to children's lives and experience. This is consistent with the current curriculum planning advice, for schools to develop their own interpretation of the National Curriculum, contained in *Excellence and Enjoyment*.

There are two main ways of using the topic approach. The first is for planning in which the science component is focused on particular resources and opportunities. For example, if there is a building site near the school it could, with good liaison, act as a focus for work on the properties of materials, and physical and chemical change, which would fit easily with related work in most other areas of the curriculum. The second use of the topic approach is relevant to teaching about complex aspects of science such as living things and the environment where a great variety of animals, plants, environmental conditions and climate are involved. It offers a means of reducing such complexity to manageable proportions. For example, instead of trying to investigate a range of ecosystems (5.7), a topic could be focused on one or two (preferably small and simple) habitats. Using expert help where necessary, the animals and plants can be identified, conditions measured and an understanding of each ecosystem built up, which can be related to general theories and principles. Using this approach, children are likely to gain a greater insight into, and respect for, areas which they might previously have ignored as trivial. It has the added advantage that information, understanding and expertise can be accumulated over a period of time, so that the burden of preparatory work becomes less as the quality of experience for the children increases. The topic approach is also recommended when children are learning and investigating in the context of large-scale scientific theories such as adaptation (5.5, 5.6) or chemical change (6.3.2) when the teacher chooses one or two examples as case-studies, researches these in detail and helps the children to see, through their own investigations, how these relate to the broader scientific ideas.

1.4.1 Children's questions

A teacher's planning for children to become scientific using a topic approach can draw upon a hugely powerful resource: the children's own questions and problems. The first national curriculum project in primary science stated that:

> We concluded, and believe very strongly, that a child should raise his/her own scientific problems, partly because isolating a problem is an important

part of scientific thinking, partly because the ever increasing body of knowledge makes it increasingly ridiculous to prescribe what any child should
know, but mostly because we do not believe that anyone can ask a completely significant question for someone else. This would demand a complete
appreciation of the person's ability, and the extent and quality of previous
experience, and *only the individual him/herself can ask a question which takes all
that into account.* (Wastnedge, 1968: 642, emphasis added.)

A topic can begin with a visit to a building site or an interesting habitat near the
school, or with making a classroom display or collection of interesting things that
relate to the topic, e.g. shiny things that prepare for learning about reflection of light.
This **experiential starting point** arouses children's curiosity, scientific thinking and
discussion about what they already know and want to learn next. Then their teacher
can help them to express their curiosity through questions, and help them to sort out
which of their questions are investigable ones. Until this point is reached, the teaching objectives in the plan are broad ones, but now it becomes possible to define
specific objectives and personalized targets for particular children and groups. This
is done when the teacher elicits children's investigable questions or problems and
negotiates with them over which ones lead to appropriate practical investigations
and how to seek answers or solutions. The point made in the quotation above is that
a teacher cannot know with sufficient detail or accuracy everything that is crucially
relevant to each child's next step in their learning, to plan what to do. However, children's own questions and problems, which are intuitively based on their own
starting points for learning provide the first step in achieving the topic aims.
Therefore the topic plan should elicit and respond to children's questions and problems. Children who are enabled to share control over their learning in this way
become more fully learning partners with each other and with their teacher.

1.5 PATTERNS IN SCIENTIFIC INVESTIGATION

Another important implication of a modern view of science (1.2) is that science
can, to some extent at least, be demystified. Scientific investigation and research
are often seen as very complex, but it is possible to see how they are rooted in, and
grow out of, the common-sense sort of investigations which people use in everyday life. Although scientists have sophisticated ways of working and testing ideas,
and they use special materials, equipment and methods, there is no 'scientific
method' which is right for all kinds of enquiry and which always leads to the discovery of the truth if it is properly applied. This more open and flexible view of
scientific investigation is particularly important for primary education because it

makes it possible for teachers to see a clear relationship and progression from children's exploratory play in the early years, through increasingly well designed investigations as they grow older.

Scientific investigation grows out of human exploratory behaviour as a whole. What makes it scientific is not a special method, but the fact that it is carried out in an agreed and thorough way. It is applied to questions and problems which scientists find interesting and significant, using existing scientific concepts and theories which are tested by being used in this way. Very similar kinds of investigation are carried out by many people – historians and archaeologists, for example – but their work is not science because their purposes are different. Children become scientific in their thinking and learning when they too apply scientific ways of investigation to the questions and problems which they find purposeful.

1.5.1 Purpose and curiosity

Children do investigations to answer a question or solve a problem about what they perceive as relevant to their personal and social interests. As teachers, we need to honour children's interest as the motivational drive for their learning. We need to do all we can to stimulate their curiosity, and nurture its expression in the questions and problems they raise. All that follows in the rest of this chapter is founded on an assumption that scientific skills and processes occur in the context of whole, real investigations that link closely to questions and problems originated by the children themselves as their purpose for learning. If we think about B. F. Skinner's claim (1964: 94) that 'education is what survives, when what was learned has been forgotten', then maybe our greatest aspiration as science educators is that even if our children forget some of the science knowledge they learned, then at least they will have been educated to be scientifically purposeful and curious, and know how to go on inquiring scientifically into new knowledge.

1.5.2 Variety and style in learning and investigation

Although scientific investigation is not governed by a rigid formula and a precisely defined method, this does not mean that there are no patterns and sequences in answering questions and solving problems. One of the most fundamental patterns in any investigative activity is the integration of two apparently opposing qualities: creative imagination and strict criticism. In science, the ability to come up with bright ideas has to be allied to the logical thinking, thoroughness and practical ability as an investigator which are needed to test both one's own ideas and those suggested by others. Strict standards and fairness are useful in understanding how scientific ideas are tested and criticized, but the process by which a person actually creates the ideas themselves cannot be described in this way. It is not that there are no patterns in the ways that ideas, knowledge and possible solutions to problems (see hypothesizing 1.7) are arrived at. Quite the reverse: there are so many patterns that it is impossible even to attempt to describe them. As much as anything else, it is a matter of personal style.

Different children and adults trying to learn and solve problems are likely to look for knowledge and possible solutions in quite different ways. The two extremes of learning style can be represented by the following two models:

- *Knowledge first*: facts, concepts and theories are taught, and the learner integrates them with remembered experience and existing knowledge. Later, they are made meaningful, extended and modified by being applied to observation, interpretation and prediction of real-life situations.
- *Experience first*: hands-on experience, coupled with existing knowledge, is provided by the teacher to develop a new idea. Learners then verbalize, communicate and make it meaningful by modifying or extending their existing knowledge.

In practice, no-one seems to rely solely on either of these models. Any person's learning is likely to be a complex interaction of both, but individuals may show a marked preference for one of these styles of learning and dislike the other.

Some topics in science may also lend themselves more readily to one style of learning rather than the other. For example, when learning about basic plant structure (4.2), the 'knowledge first' approach is likely to be helpful. Basic and partly familiar concepts such as stem, leaf and bud can be introduced and related using a diagrammatic plan (Fig. 4.1) as an 'advance organizer' before children try to identify and interpret the varied forms of real plants. In contrast, children can arrive at concepts of magnetic and non-magnetic materials and magnetic poles (12.3 and 12.4), through exploratory play. Their ideas can then be verbalized and shared in discussion, brought into line with accepted scientific terminology and consolidated by being used in further investigations.

1.5.3 Creativity and criticism

When we watch children being scientific, their ideas develop, like ours and scientists' do, from a combination of imagination and criticism. When we see children who seek safety in plodding through all the possibilities methodically we can encourage them to guess more boldly and take a bit of a risk. On the other hand, some children just make a wild guess and stick to their idea come what may, so we need to encourage them to think if it makes sense and fits all the observations. Through guessing, criticizing and testing ideas against experience, everyone can learn that ideas can be changed and improved. A really useful and testable idea is often arrived at in several stages, each one getting nearer to the final idea by eliminating what can be shown not to fit the evidence, or adding some new evidence. Once a testable hypothesis (1.7) has been arrived at, stricter rules and patterns of activity have to be followed in order to test it properly, involving the identification and manipulation of variables (1.10).

1.5.4 Investigative skills

Although there is no precisely defined scientific method, different authors identify different sets of skills, processes and 'process skills' that are used in scientific investigation. By watching and talking to children when they are being scientific, we can learn about how children use them in their investigation. In the National Curriculum, Sc1 refers not only to the importance of *ideas and evidence in science* but provides lists of *investigative skills*. The meaning of both is defined with increasing depth and detail at each Key Stage. Here, investigative skills and processes are presented in the rest of this chapter in five groups: observing, hypothesizing, predicting, experimenting and fair testing. They are the scientifically most important ones to understand and to use in teaching primary science.

1.6 OBSERVING

Scientific observation can use any of the senses, but because vision is for most people the most important of the senses in scientific investigation, we will focus on observing through sight. However, as teachers, we can encourage children to learn through experience by using all relevant senses. If there are risks, particularly in using taste and smell to investigate, then we must take appropriate action to manage such risks. Observation is a well recognized feature of very young children's scientific learning, but tends to be an undervalued part of being scientific with older primary school children.

Vision is not simply a matter of opening our eyes and allowing light into them. It is a complex process, involving the eyes and the brain, by which we carry out an exploration or investigation of the world around us (3.10). Our brain directs the scanning of our eyes in response both to the information reaching it, and what we know or remember. The result is that what we see usually depends very much on our prior knowledge, understanding and experience. A rare or unusual plant, for example, is likely to attract the attention of a knowledgeable person, whereas someone who knows little about plants may not even be aware of it, even though both are looking in the same place. As scientists use the term, however, observation implies something rather more than simple recognition: it can usefully be thought of as *seeing-with-understanding*.

I can say I have observed something in the scientific sense when I have both perceived it and realized something of its importance or significance. For example, most trees have green microscopic plants (algae) growing on their trunks and branches, but when we see the trees, only a few of us are likely to be aware of the algae, or to observe that on most trees they grow in particular patterns. (More algae grow in parts of the bark where there is shade or the sunlight is less strong and also where there is more moisture.) Also, if I say I have observed the pattern, it does not necessarily mean that I can explain it, but it does imply that I have realized that there is something to be explained. Once a pattern of this kind has been investigated and understood, it is much more likely that similar patterns will be observed elsewhere, on walls and buildings, for example. **In science, observation and understanding reinforce one another: the more we know and understand, the more we can observe, and the more we observe, the more we will learn.** In primary science, children need to learn in the same way.

Like the other processes and skills, observation rarely if ever takes place on its own, but is rather part of a purposeful activity. If I wish to observe how woodlice behave when they are given a choice between damp and dry conditions, for example, I will concentrate on the pattern of their movement and activity rather than on the details of their structure, even though those details are there to be observed and, in other circumstances, might be what I want to learn about. So observation is a very disciplined activity and for most children, learning to concentrate and observe in this purposeful way is a very gradual process, requiring patience and skill from the teacher as well!

In many scientific investigations, observation is accompanied by measurement, requiring the development of a complementary range of skills related to numeracy and computational ability on the one hand, and manipulative skill on the other. Here again, the experience and judgement of the teacher are likely to be fully exercised to ensure that the kind of measurement, the scales used and the accuracy required match both the nature of the investigation and the understanding and skill of the pupils.

Before moving to another aspect of being scientific, it is worth bearing in mind the earlier point about the importance of children's curiosity. A teacher who was describing (a little unkindly?) how closely one of her children was observing the spiders in the tree outside the classroom said: 'Now, she watches them laying eggs and sees the eggs hatch, but before she wouldn't have seen the tree!' The teacher had not directly taught this child to observe, but had encouraged the child's curiosity for ideas and experience. As soon as curiosity appeared, the teacher fostered it by modelling close observation and asking the child questions to provoke more and better observations, such as: 'What is it like? What can you notice? Does it always do that? Does it change? How is it similar/different from X?'

1.7 HYPOTHESIZING

Before asking what a hypothesis is, let's begin by asking what part it plays in a scientific investigation. Like children, scientists carry out investigations in order to answer questions or solve puzzles and problems. Hypotheses are simply the guesses or tentative answers or untried solutions to these questions or problems. They are guesses which we want to test, to see if we are right. For each kind of scientific knowledge – knowing 'that', knowing 'why' and knowing 'how to' (1.3) – there are corresponding kinds of scientific hypotheses.

1.7.1 Descriptive and predictive hypotheses

These relate to knowing 'that'. They are either statements about matters of fact (descriptive hypotheses) or simple predictions about what is expected to happen (predictive hypotheses). They are a very common starting-point for children's hypothesizing.

Examples of hypothesizing may occur when children are investigating rolling cars down a ramp. They may make a descriptive hypothesis such as 'The steeper the ramp, the further the car goes across the floor' or make a predictive hypothesis, such as 'If we raise the end of the ramp, the car will go further', which is a different form of the same idea. Other examples include: 'The red car will go further than the green one', 'This ball bounces better on the floor than on the carpet' and 'This paper towel absorbs the most water'. All these are quite straightforward descriptive or predictive hypotheses. They claim to say something about a part of the world which the child has experienced and is investigating, but they need to be tried and tested to see whether or not they are true. Unlike the more complex causal-explanatory hypotheses (see below), there is usually a simple way in which this testing might be done. Predictive hypotheses and some kinds of predictions are very similar.

Descriptive-predictive hypotheses play a valuable part as children's investigative ability develops, because they can often lead directly on to more complex learning such as causal and explanatory hypotheses. For example, quite young children may hypothesize that: 'All balls bounce better on hard surfaces than on soft ones' and children with more investigative achievement may go on to guess why.

1.7.2 Causal and explanatory hypotheses

These are guesses **why** something happens as it does. Scientists are rarely if ever content with factual knowledge (knowing 'that'): they also seek understanding (knowing 'why'). There are usually two aspects to scientific understanding. The first is to identify the **cause** for what has been observed; the second is to seek an **explanation** of it. For example, if I run fast, my pulse rate increases. The cause of this is that my heart is beating faster, but identifying the cause does not explain why it happens (see 3.9). This is usually more difficult, involving scientific knowledge, understanding and previous experience, and much of this book is devoted to providing scientific explanations for commonly observed objects, events and changes.

When we seek causes and explanations, to develop our knowledge 'why', our hypotheses are different from descriptive-predictive hypotheses. For example, a child observes that when a candle is first lit, it often burns with a small flame, which becomes much bigger after a few minutes. S/he may learn to predict that this will happen routinely. Then s/he might wonder why this happens and guess that: 'The flame gets bigger because the wick gets longer'. This is a causal hypothesis: it identifies the cause of the change but does not explain it. To do that, an explanatory hypothesis is needed, which might be, 'Because the wick is longer, melted wax is vaporized and burnt at a greater rate, so the flame is bigger.' (8.3.2).

If children make a statement, whether a spontaneous guess or something more considered, which could be rephrased as: 'I think it may happen because …' they are almost certainly making a causal or explanatory hypothesis. Once we as teachers are able to recognize this kind of statement, we notice that most children are generating them all the time. Most of their intuitive theories about the world and themselves are ideas of this kind; for example, the idea that seeing consists of sending out a ray from the eye to the object which is seen (13.4). The teacher's role is to help children identify causes and think up possible explanations using their observations, their prior experience and their existing scientific knowledge and understanding. Learning to do this is likely to be a long, gradual process, so we need to support its development patiently.

Sometimes explanatory hypotheses can be generated easily. For example, children watching woodlice disappear into damp leaves are likely (among other, less testable ideas) to hypothesize that they do it 'Because they don't like light' and 'Because they like damp places'. Often, however, causal and explanatory hypotheses have to be arrived at by longer and less direct thinking involving ideas and evidence. When trying to find out why some seedlings grow more than others, for example, or why an electric lamp is dimly lit, it may be necessary to identify causes by eliminating possibilities: 'It can't be the water because we watered them all the same', or 'It's not the battery because we tested it with another lamp'. This kind of thinking is allied to the scientific meaning of fair comparison or fair testing (see below). Perhaps the greatest challenge facing teachers is to help children to develop this way of thinking without stifling their spontaneity and creativity.

1.7.3 Procedural hypotheses

These are guessed ways of how to find out and how to make things work better, using and developing knowing 'how to' that is concerned with the procedures and practicalities of experimenting and fair testing. Procedural hypotheses are concerned with setting up fair tests (1.10). For example, if we want to test the (descriptive) hypothesis that the weight of a person affects how easily a trainer shoe slips on the floor, we need to test it in ways that are scientifically fair. If we are not sure how to carry out a fair test, we may have to imagine an untried method of testing. This is the procedural hypothesis. We may try out a procedure in which we put different metal weights on to a trainer shoe and measure how much force is needed to make it slip. Any possible solution such as this to the procedural problem of how to test the original idea, may have to be modified if it is found to be unfair. Our knowing 'how to' is developed through repeated practical investigations in which we realize that there is a factor which has not been properly controlled or our observations or measurements are not reliable. Talking and planning are no substitute for practical experience in gaining the know-how and ingenuity to make things work and take reliable measurements, neither is a computer-generated simulation or demonstration.

Children who are testing the 'strength' of magnets by attraction, or comparing the tearing strengths of different papers, have to invent some device to carry out the test. It is most unlikely that they will achieve this without a process of testing and modifying. During the development process the children are likely to go far beyond what they have expressed or could express in words or drawings, through what they actually make and test and the intuitive know-how that they gain. Also, their quality of understanding will be way beyond what they could gain from passively watching a computer presentation of the same ideas. It is practical experience of the devices themselves which are the trial solutions to the problem; the procedural hypotheses. Like other hypotheses, they have to be tested. Do they satisfy the requirements of fair testing and do they work reliably?

Here is a summary of the three ways of scientific knowing and the related kinds of hypothesizing:

Kind of knowing	Examples of each kind of knowledge	The related kind of hypothesizing	Examples of each kind of hypothesis
Knowing that: Facts, events, changes	Muscles only pull and do not push. If steam cools it turns into liquid water. Steel is a magnetic material, but brass is not.	Guessed **description** or prediction of **what** will happen.	The red car will go further than the green one. The ball bounces better on the floor than on the carpet. The paper towel absorbs more water than the piece of plastic sheet.
Knowing why: Identifying causes, explanations, understanding	The reason **why** the Sun seems to move across the sky during the day is because the Earth is spinning, and so the angle from which we see the Sun changes through-out the day.	Guessed **cause** of what happens or a guessed **explanation** of what happens.	The red car may go further because its wheels have less friction and turn more easily than the wheels on the green car. The ball may bounce better on the floor because the floor is harder than the carpet. The paper towel may absorb more because it has tiny spaces in it where the water goes, that the plastic sheet doesn't have.
Knowing how to: Carry out scientifically investigative processes and procedures, making things work	**How to** test the idea that a parachute with a hole in the centre is better than one with no hole, means changing the independent variable, measuring the dependent variable and keeping all the other variables the same each time.	Guessed **procedure** for how to find out or a guessed method of testing.	If I put different weights on the same training shoe and measure how big a force is needed to make it slide across the same surface at the same speed, then I may be able to find out if a heavier weight on the shoe makes it slide more easily or less easily. If I slowly move a magnet closer to a paper clip and measure the dis-tance between them just as the clip jumps on to the magnet, I may be able to do this with several magnets, to find out hich one is the strongest.

1.8 PREDICTING

Predictions are statements about what we expect to happen in the future. They are used in scientific investigation in two ways.

The first form of prediction is the predictive hypothesis (1.7.1), which young children especially are likely to make in the form of a simple guess, such as 'If you load the trolley with Plasticine it will go further'. The ability and willingness to predict in this way (and risk being wrong) is of great importance in developing an awareness and understanding of the links between causes and effects. Children can develop this awareness if we encourage them to look for patterns emerging from their observations and measurements and predict future observations and measurements. For example, children who are investigating the effect of hanging weights on rubber bands may observe a pattern that if the weights increase, then the bands get longer. We could ask them to record this by drawing and we could ask them to write down measurements of the length of the elastic band for one weight, and predict what the length will be when a different weight is added. Maybe adding a weight that is twice as heavy will make the increase in the length of the elastic band twice as big. The ability to predict in this way can be used to sharpen observation and help in the search for explanations wherever predictable patterns are to be found.

The second form of prediction is more complex. It becomes important when a causal or explanatory hypothesis is being tested. We need to make a prediction based on our hypothesis and find out, by observing or experimenting, whether it is true or false. For example, if children hypothesize that the bending of plants towards a window is caused by light coming from one side, it could be predicted that if the plants are turned through 180° they will straighten up, then bend towards the light again, and this prediction could be tested.

Although strict logic requires us to make a prediction when a causal or explanatory hypothesis is being tested, both children and adults often do not state the prediction explicitly because we tend to go intuitively from hypothesis to testing by observation or experiment. Children who hypothesize that woodlice do not like light, for example, will usually set about devising some kind of choice-chamber to test their idea. This does not mean that they have no clear idea of what they predict will happen, but that they have not made their prediction explicit. If things go as the children expect and their hypothesis is upheld, this does not matter, but if their implicit prediction is wrong and the unexpected happens, it may be necessary for the teacher to backtrack and tease it out with some questions such as, 'What did you expect to happen?' and 'Why did you think that would happen?'

1.9 EXPERIMENTING

'Experiment' is a much misunderstood word. It may be used popularly to refer to any practical experience that is perceived to be scientific in some way, including playful exploration. It may be used to refer to a practical way of showing a scientific principle or idea. Although this is a valuable way of teaching, it is a demonstration, not an experiment. The term 'experiment' is also used quite often when what is really meant is investigation by trial and error. For example, children making, testing and modifying parachutes to find out which designs and materials work best, could be described by many people as 'experimenting', whereas they are doing something much wider and more varied. Experimentation is only one part of an investigation. To confuse the two is to risk failing to notice all the other skills and processes (such as hypothesizing and predicting) which are being used as part of the overall activity.

The strict scientific meaning of **experiment**, is to devise a practical test of a hypothesis. If I hypothesize that the amount of water used to mix concrete has an effect on its strength when set, I have to set up a special test situation, under strictly controlled conditions (1.10) in order to find out whether the idea is true or false. It is this special test situation which is the experiment. Many hypotheses cannot be tested by setting up experiments. For example, if I hypothesize that the pattern of green micro-plants on a tree is related to water supply, I have to test that idea by controlled observation, interfering with the natural situation as little as possible.

Young children may switch from a broad investigation (How to make the best parachute) to a much more focused enquiry involving systematic experiments (How does a hole in the middle change how a parachute works?). It is useful to be able to identify this switch, because children may begin experimenting without being entirely clear as to what idea it is they are testing; in other words, with an unstated hypothesis. As with unstated predictions (1.8), this may raise no problems, but if the experimental procedure becomes too complex to manage or the children find it difficult to communicate their findings, it may be necessary for the teacher to go back and help them make clear to themselves exactly what idea it was they were testing, and what they expected to happen.

Effective experiments rely on a wide range of knowledge, understanding and skill. Most fundamental, perhaps, is the ability to decide what evidence is needed to uphold or reject a hypothesis: can the experiment really be a good test of the idea? Then the experimenter needs the ability to identify all the variables which need to be controlled (1.10) and the ingenuity to invent ways of controlling them, as well as the practical skill to think up a valid, workable experimental procedure and carry it out. This apparently complex process is possible at primary level only because, like other science skills, experimentation in a well managed science programme is an extension of children's natural exploratory and investigative play: a more refined, reasoned and disciplined version of what they do spontaneously. Children do not need to be taught the capacity to be scientific because they have it already. They need to be taught how to become more scientific.

MIC LIBRARY

WITHDRAWN FROM STOCK

1.10 'FAIR TESTING' AND THE CONTROL OF VARIABLES

Although the idea of a single scientific method cannot be upheld, the scientific community expects that hypotheses will be tested thoroughly and fairly before they are published in research papers or books. Children can and should begin at primary level to develop both an understanding of the principles behind this kind of testing and the practical ability to carry it out. The practical arrangement of a toy car experiment is used to illustrate this.

Identifying variables. The first stage in scientific testing is to identify clearly what the focus of investigative interest is. This may not be simple. For example, if children are investigating how far a toy car will move when pushed by releasing a stretched rubber band, there are many factors which could be changed and which would affect the outcome if they were. Every factor that we can observe and/or measure is called a variable. In the toy car investigation, the variables include: the kind or number of elastic bands used, how thick and how long they are, what quality of rubber they are made of, how far they are stretched, how the toy car is released, how large a load it carries and the surface it runs on. Our first step is to list as many of these variables in the situation as possible.

The independent variable. After we have identified the variables, we decide which of them is relevant to the hypothesis we want to test. This may require children to state their hypothesis and predictions in a much more precise way than they had done up to that time. For example, if the hypothesis is that 'Using two elastic bands makes the toy car go further than one', then the focus of interest is the number of bands used. This is the variable which the tester is going to change in order to see what happens, and it is known as the independent variable. It is part of the hypothesis which guesses what is the **cause**, and the guessed **effect** is how far the toy car moves.

The dependent variable. The next stage of the testing procedure is to identify what outcome is to be observed or measured in order to find out the effect of changing the independent variable. This is called the dependent variable, and in our example it would be the distance travelled by the toy car. The dependent variable is the guessed **effect** of the cause–effect relationship expressed or implied in the hypothesis.

Control variables. Once the independent and dependent variables have been identified, the next stage of the testing procedure is to identify all other variables which could affect the outcome. For the test to be fair, these must be controlled, which

1035255683

means that they must be kept the same throughout the test procedure. These are known as control variables and in our example these are all those originally noted, except the number of bands used. If these variables are not controlled, the test cannot produce a valid result. For example, if the number of bands was varied, but the amount by which they were stretched was not kept exactly the same each time, it would be impossible to say which of the two variables had produced any differences observed, so the hypothesis would not have been fairly tested.

Summarizing a fair test procedure. This can be made easier by following a simple sequence of questions:

1. What should be changed in the test? (Identify the independent variable.)
2. What should be observed to see the effect of changing the independent variable? (Identify the dependent variable.)
3. What should be kept the same to make sure the test is fair? (Identify the control variables.)
4. How will the results be used to decide if the hypothesis can be upheld? (Work out what would be concluded by the different outcomes.)

Although children often like to rush into carrying out tests, they gradually need to learn that it is good scientific practice to adopt a disciplined approach and make sure that these questions have been clearly thought about before the practical work begins. If not, a great deal of time may be wasted on what turns out to be an invalid or badly devised test procedure.

Despite our best efforts, however, sometimes children need to have a frustrating or disappointing experience of presenting their evidence to the class, and facing the criticism that it does not test the hypothesis in a way that persuades others is really fair. In our example, it may be necessary for the children to realize that they cannot say for sure that two elastic bands make the toy car go further, because they did not take enough care to stretch them to exactly the same extent, before they fully realize the importance of following this method. Until this point, they may have been using the idea of fair testing in a ritualistic, uncomprehending way, because 'the teacher told us to do it like this' or because of a vague sense of social fairness: 'we keep them all the same, just to be fair'.

We want them to be able to claim that they **know that** two elastic bands make a toy car go further than one, having used their **know how**: they have tested their idea rigorously and they have evidence that the effect (of the toy car going further) was not due to a different cause (a different amount of stretching).

1.11 THE ROLE OF SCIENTIFIC CONCEPTS AND LANGUAGE IN SCIENCE EDUCATION

1.11.1 Language

In science, as in any other human activity, the need to communicate clearly and efficiently has led to the development of a specialized language, which can become a jargon if it is used insensitively or out of context. When scientific language is used correctly, a term such as 'gravity' is like the tip of the proverbial iceberg: a convenient verbal shorthand for a complex set of concepts which the speaker shares with the remainder of the group, and which contribute both to understanding and the ability to use scientific ideas to investigate further.

A problem with using specialized language in primary science occurs when mere use of a technical term is taken, either by the teacher or by the children, as evidence of understanding. When trying to describe or explain what has been observed, both children and adults may assume that the correct use of a word in an appropriate context is all that is required. Instead of being the tip of an iceberg of shared understanding, the word has become a thin layer of ice over a void of ignorance.

For example, if I hold up a ball, then release it so that it falls, and ask what happened, even quite young children are likely to answer 'Gravity pulled it down!' and sit back, convinced that this pleases the teacher because it answers all possible scientific questions about what they have just seen. But this raises two professional questions for the teacher. First, am I sure the child really does understand the full implications of what has happened and what s/he just said? Second, if I accept this reply, will it short-circuit all the observation, reasoning, discussion and growth of understanding to which even a simple event can give rise? Here is a way of coping with this teaching problem.

1.11.2 The 'describe–explain' strategy

The premature use of scientific language is unproductive, even when it is appropriate to the context, because it leads away from focusing on the experience which is of paramount importance if children are to develop their knowledge and understanding. A very simple strategy which can overcome this problem is to make as sharp a separation as possible between describing what has been observed and explaining why it happened or came to be that way: **first describe carefully, then explain.**

In the example of the dropped ball, a description might be: 'While it was being held, the ball was not moving. When it was released, it started to fall. It fell straight down and seemed to get faster as it fell, until it hit the floor. It bounced four times, getting lower each time, then rolled across the floor and stopped. After that it didn't move any more.' What is noticeable about this detailed description is that it does not involve any specialized scientific language or concepts, and this is true of most events, situations and changes that children at primary level will observe and investigate.

In most situations, a teacher can discourage a premature explanation of what children have observed until they have thoroughly described it, with all relevant details noted. Until this has been done, it is often not possible to assess exactly what needs to be explained. In the case of the falling ball, the teacher can focus on two separate sets of events: what happened before the ball hit the floor, and what happened afterwards. We observe that before the ball hit the floor, it began by not moving and then moved when it was released. We can describe the way it was moving as something that changed. Then we can explain that forces which were out of balance were acting on it (11.5) (see Figure 11.9d). Our description of the ball as seeming to carry on moving faster, can then be explained by saying that there was a force which was making it fall and it must have been acting on the ball all the time it was falling. At this point, the nature and identity of the force can be explored by asking a directed sequence of questions, such as:

'In what direction did the force act?' (Straight downwards, i.e. vertically.)
'Does the force always seem to act that way?' (Yes.)
'Is it acting all the time?' (It seems to.)
'Do you know a name for this force which tends to make things fall, always acts straight down and acts all the time?' (Gravity!)

Unlike description, scientific explanation does require the use of special concepts and language (in this case, forces out of balance, see 11.3), but technical terms should be used only after the explanation has been developed, to communicate what has been found out. Technical terms are important, because as scientists we need to communicate effectively, but their use can be deceptive if the user does not fully understand what they signify.

1.11.3 The role of scientific concepts

The 'describe–explain' strategy is useful because it not only helps to prevent short-circuiting of investigation by premature use of scientific language, but also it shows clearly the role of concepts in science and science education. At primary level and in most everyday situations, scientific concepts are not needed to describe the world. Their role is in identifying causes and developing scientific explanations for what has been observed, in helping people to make sense of their experience in scientific terms and to make accurate predictions. Separating description and explanation can make it much easier for teachers and children to understand both the nature of scientific concepts and the proper use of the specialized language to which they have given rise.

Note that the 'describe–explain' strategy does use a somewhat artificial distinction. Particularly as children grow older, descriptions may require specialized language if they are not to become over-long and wordy, and explanations often lead back to fresh observations and the attempt to make a better description. If the children reach this stage, however, it is unlikely that the premature use of scientific language will be a problem: it is far more likely that the investigation itself will have assumed its proper role as the driving force behind the children's activity.

Refer to the CD-ROM for summaries of Progression in learning SCIENTIFIC ENQUIRY.

REFERENCES

Department for Children, Schools and Families (DCSF) (2003) *Excellence and Enjoyment.*

Skinner, B.F. (1964) *New Scientist,* May 21.

Smith, Frank (1978) *Reading.* Cambridge: Cambridge University Press.

Wastnedge, E.R. (1968) 'Nuffield Junior Science in Primary Schools', *School Science Review,* 61(217): 639–47.

PART 2

LIFE PROCESSES AND LIVING THINGS

The National Curriculum Attainment Target 2 (Sc2) includes teaching the scientific knowledge developed by biologists about humans, animals, plants, variation, classification and the environment.

Chapter 2 is about the first part of Sc2: some fundamental ideas about what life is (Sc2.1). Teachers may plan a curriculum which follows these Attainment Targets in the same sequence as they are presented in the National Curriculum, and therefore start their teaching with life processes and living things. However, a teacher who recognizes these as rather abstract and general ideas, may teach them later and/or through topics arising from other parts of Sc2, to make the ideas more meaningful to young children. This alternative approach is explained in section 1.4.

Chapters 3, 4 and 5 are about the other Attainment Targets of the National Curriculum: Chapter 3 is about Sc2.2 – humans and other animals; Chapter 4 is about Sc2.3 – green plants; Chapter 5 is about Sc2.4 – how living things vary and can be classified; and Sc2.5 – living things in their environment.

Refer to the CD-ROM for A QUICK GUIDE to Sc2.

Refer to the CD-ROM for Progression in learning SCIENTIFIC ENQUIRY (Sc1) through LIFE PROCESSES AND LIVING THINGS (Sc2) levels 1 to 6.

2 LIFE PROCESSES

2.1 THE CONCEPT OF 'LIVING'

At some point in their learning, we want children's understanding of living things to include some deep thinking about what it means to be alive. Teachers may introduce the idea by setting a classification task to sort things which are alive, from those which are dead (i.e. were once, but are no longer alive), and those which are non-living (i.e. never were alive). The problem with this approach, especially for young children, is that many living things such as plants do not obviously seem to be doing things that show that they are alive. Many children (and some adults) do not regard plants as being alive, or they think that plants are somehow less alive than animals. Although this idea may seem to match our everyday experience, scientists understand the concept of 'living' differently.

We may remember learning in secondary science, that living things are often characterized by a set of life processes: **nutrition** (feeding), **respiration** (breathing and energy transfer), **response** to changes in the environment, **movement**, **excretion** (removal of waste), **growth** and **reproduction**, that are common to all living things. This is a useful checklist. But here again there are problems with using it carelessly in teaching science to young children. If we ask young children to use this list as a set of criteria to distinguish living from non-living things, then we will have to acknowledge that not all living things do all the activities. Worker bees, for example, do not reproduce and some living things, such as dormant trees, bulbs and seeds, do not seem to be active at all. Primary-age children need a different approach to understanding the idea of living. If we expect children to learn scientific **ideas** which do not match the **evidence** of their own experience, they are likely to doubt what we teach them in Sc1: that scientists' ideas have to be consistent with their evidence. As a starting point for a fresh approach, try thinking about what we mean by 'living'.

An alternative understanding of 'living'

Imagine a motor car in a field, surrounded by a fence, left for a hundred years. How would it have changed by the end of that time? The steel bodywork would probably have rusted away completely, with the rust washed away into the soil, and little would be left of the remainder apart from lead from the battery, plus any other metals resistant to corrosion, as well as items of plastics and glass. Now imagine a young oak tree, fenced round and left in the same way. In a hundred years it would be fully grown, the habitat for hundreds if not thousands of animals, and probably surrounded by young oak trees.

This simple thought-experiment sums up what is distinctive about living things: the way they change over time. If left to themselves, non-living things sooner or later break down and become simpler, the materials which make them up spread out and become dispersed in the environment. Living things, on the other hand, if not interfered with, eaten or afflicted unduly with disease, change on their own, spontaneously, in almost exactly the opposite way. They grow larger, more complex and usually make more living things like themselves. They do this by taking in material from their environment and incorporating it into their own bodies. Non-living materials can of course be built into complex things such as motor cars, but these changes are not spontaneous: they are brought about by humans working on the materials, not by the things on their own. Living things have the power of spontaneously growing larger, more complex and more numerous which makes them so distinctive. The fact that once they are dead they decay, often very quickly, shows that the only special property they have, is that of being alive. Very few non-living things can grow or reproduce, and those which can (crystals, for example), do so only in very special conditions, and even then they neither grow more complex nor carry out any of the other activities we associate with living things.

This way of thinking about **living** helps us to see richness and complexity in the idea of life, as well as inspiring a sense of awe and wonder. Our challenge is: how can we teach this to children?

Let's start with easier examples of 'living' and gradually give children more (and more difficult) examples of 'living' over a long period of time, to enable them to accumulate the experience through which the more abstract and generalized knowledge described above can be learned. Most animals are obviously alive, so maybe this would be a good place to start exploring what life means. Later, to learn that seeds, dormant bulbs and other plants are also alive, children will need to give them the conditions needed for growth (4.3), to observe them over a period of time and to keep careful records of their appearance by drawing or photography, and find out whether and in what ways, they change. If the plants are growing bigger and more complex, and especially if they are reproducing more individuals like themselves, they must be alive, just as animals are. Having established the basic idea that all living things are distinguished by the ways in which they change without interference from outside, *then* we can teach about life processes to deepen their knowledge.

2.2 AN OUTLINE OF THE PROCESSES OF LIVING THINGS

Nutrition is the process by which living things obtain and, if necessary, modify the materials they need to sustain life, grow and reproduce. There are two fundamentally different patterns of nutrition. Plants (and some microbes) can take in simple chemicals from the environment and use energy such as light from the Sun, to build up complex, high-energy food chemicals (photosynthesis, 4.4). All other living things, such as animals and decomposers (5.8), have to obtain their food chemicals ready-made by feeding on plants or other living things (5.7). This usually involves digesting the food (3.3) into simpler chemicals which the body can absorb. Food chemicals are used both as a source of energy (respiration, see below and 3.6) and as the raw material for building up and replacing tissues in growth, reproduction and maintenance of the body (3.11).

Respiration is the process within cells by which living things break down some kinds of food chemicals in their bodies and use them as a source of energy. To do this, most (though not all) living things need a supply of oxygen and a means of removing the waste gas: carbon dioxide. The process of gas exchange, by which oxygen is made to enter the body and carbon dioxide to leave it, is called breathing. Larger animals have special organs to make this process very rapid and efficient such as the lungs of humans and other mammals (3.6) and the gills of fish. Respiration, of which breathing is a necessary part, is a complex chemical breakdown process in which energy from food (chemical-potential energy, 9.2.8) is made available for all life processes, including the movement of muscle (3.5) and the building up of new and replacement tissues (3.11). Respiration is sometimes said to be like a process of burning, with food as the fuel but this is misleading. Burning (8.3.2) is a high-temperature process in which fuel and oxygen are combined chemically very rapidly, so that the burning material and the environment are strongly heated. In contrast to this, respiration is a low-temperature process in which food is broken down and energy transferred in a series of controlled steps, so there is much less heating and the energy can be transferred in ways which the body can use.

Response to stimuli is necessary to living things because they exist in an environment which is constantly changing and often threatens their survival. They are much more likely to survive if they can detect and respond to changes which could affect them. The overall response of an animal or plant is called its behaviour (3.10 and 4.3). Larger animals have specialized sense organs to detect changes (3.10) and many of their responses are very fast: for example, a frog catches a fly in less than a hundredth of a second. Most plants do not have specialized sense organs and most of their responses are slower, made by growing in different ways (4.1 and 4.3).

Movement is often the most obvious response made by both animals and plants to changes in their environment. Because animals need to find food, most are able to move about actively. This also makes it possible for them to avoid other animals which could kill and eat them and also to seek out favourable conditions, such as shelter, refuge or a social group. Some animals do not move around in this way, but remain fixed and capture their food as it passes: sea anemones and barnacles are examples. Plants, because they make their own food, do not move around as animals do, and (apart from some floating waterplants) need a fixed root system for anchorage and taking in water (4.2). With the exception of 'exploding' seedpods, fast plant movement is very rare. Most examples of plant movement which children can observe result from patterns of growth, such as seedlings bending towards light, the opening of flowers and the twining of tendrils.

Excretion All chemical processes in living things produce waste materials which must be removed. The process by which this is done is called excretion. Both plants and animals produce carbon dioxide as a waste product of respiration (see above) and release it into the atmosphere. Plants in light produce oxygen as a waste product of photosynthesis (4.4) which maintains the gas balance in the atmosphere (5.8). Because animals eat other living things, they usually have a surplus of some food chemicals which cannot be stored and must be broken down and excreted from the body (3.3). Plants, on the other hand, produce only the food chemicals they need and so have much less of a waste disposal problem.

Growth is the name for overall increase in size of a living thing. Growth of living things, viewed over their whole life-span, doesn't mean simply becoming bigger (as a growing crystal does), but becoming more complex, able to do more and behave in a greater variety of ways: compare a newly hatched tadpole with an adult frog, or a seedling with a mature tree, for example. Growth involves building up new living material and requires both food chemicals obtained through nutrition and energy from respiration. Most large animals have a normal size range and a growth period when young, after which their size does not increase. After this growth period, animals do in fact keep growing, but in another way: their body tissues 'wear out' and have to be replaced. Plants, in contrast, usually keep growing for most of their lives, either continuing to get bigger, as trees do (4.3), or multiplying by non-sexual reproduction, as bluebells and other bulbs do (4.5).

Reproduction can be thought of as a special kind of growth, which tends to increase the size of the population rather than the size of the individual. Living things are vulnerable. Most of them have a limited life-span and there is always the possibility that they will be eaten, or killed in some other way. Without repro-duction, there would be no younger animals or plants in the habitat to replace those which die, so reproduction is the process which perpetuates life on Earth. If it fails, as sooner or later it does for most kinds of animal and plant, the result is extinction (5.5). In many plants, some kinds of (asexual) reproduction are simply an extension of the way they grow (4.5), but both plants and animals have devel-oped a more specialized, sexual mode of reproduction. Sexual reproduction essentially involves the formation of special sex cells, often but not always in dif-ferent parents, and their joining together, in the process of fertilization. Children usually learn about the main examples (mammals and flowering plants) in which a female cell which does not move (the egg-cell) is fertilized by a much smaller male cell (sperm or pollen-grain) which moves towards and eventually joins with it. From the fertilized egg-cell, the new individual (foetus in animals, seed in flow-ering plants) develops. Both kinds of sex cells contain information in the form of DNA, which controls much of the new individual's growth and development. Variation in inherited DNA, however, ensures that although sexually reproduced offspring resemble their parents, they are never exactly like them.

3 HUMANS AND OTHER ANIMALS

INTRODUCTION

The title of this chapter implies that the group of living things that we call animals includes a sub-group called humans. Humans are a kind of animal. All this is using scientists' terms. However, teachers need to listen to young children's usage of these words and be prepared to hear an amusingly different meaning. Children may think that animals are in an entirely different group of living things from humans, so that humans are not animals. This may come from hearing adults say things like 'Stop doing that – don't be an animal!' about some 'bad behaviour' or from seeing a notice saying 'No animals allowed' which means that adults are allowed but non-human animals are not. Go to section 5.1 for more knowledge about the classification of animals.

3.1 BASIC HUMAN ANATOMY

Learning about the structure of the main parts of the human body is a helpful starting point from which to learn about how the body functions and how it may be cared for. A logical start is the skeleton as the framework and then to learn about the muscles and other organs which are attached to it and both supported and protected by it.

Children's ideas need to develop using information from books, charts and CD-ROMs, but at primary level this needs to be linked closely to children's direct experience and knowledge of their own bodies. Begin by focusing on the names of the main external body parts, and link to learning in English and physical education. Learning about internal anatomy can then begin with an investigation of body 'landmarks'. These are points at which the skeleton can be felt beneath the skin. Children should link the landmarks they can feel on their own bodies with drawings or, preferably, models of the human skeleton. This should enable them to gain a much more accurate sense of body structure than is possible otherwise. Also, it is consistent with the Sc1 based teaching approach: that scientific ideas are linked in children's thinking with evidence, which as far as possible is gained directly from first-hand experience.

Activity 3.1.1 helps identify body landmarks.

Help children to find the main body landmarks

Head: the top of the head or cranium (young children must feel this gently); eyebrow ridges, cheek-bone and eye socket; lower jaw, its joint and the angle below the ear.
Arm and hand: shoulder and elbow joints (feel movement); lower arm (twist and feel that there are two parallel bones); wrist, knuckle joints.
Neck: collar bones between the hollow at the base of the neck and the shoulder on either side.
Chest: ribs; breast-bone; base of breast-bone and bottom of rib-cage.
Spine: bend forward, feel bones (vertebrae) below neck and in the small of the back.
Hip region: the upper edges of the hip-bone (pelvis) from the side of the body round towards the back.
Leg: top of thigh-bone and joint with hip; knee-cap; shin-bone; ankle and heel bones; joints of toes.

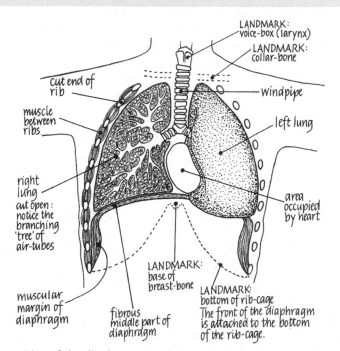

Figure 3.1 *The position of the diaphragm in relation to body landmarks and the main organs of the chest region, seen from the front*

Activity 3.1.2 relates body landmarks to major internal organs.

Major internal organs of the body   The central organs of response and control in the body are the brain, which fills the upper part of the skull (cranium) completely, and the spinal cord, which runs from the brain, down through a tube formed by a large hole in each of the bones of the spine (vertebrae). The remaining major organs (apart from muscles, see 3.5) are all in the main part of the body, or trunk. To understand their basic layout it is useful to think of the trunk as being divided into two regions, the chest region (thorax) and the belly region (abdomen). The organ which separates the two regions is the diaphragm, a dome-shaped sheet of fibre-tissue (tendon) and muscle, which is attached to the lower edge of the rib-cage (Fig. 3.1). Once the shape and position of the diaphragm are understood in relation to the skeleton, learning about the other major organs is much easier.

The top of the diaphragm is about level with the bottom of the breast-bone. Above this is the chest or thorax, which is filled with the two lungs, together with the main air-pipes which serve them (3.6), and the heart (3.8), with its large blood-carrying tubes. The heart lies slightly to the left of centre at the level of the fifth rib, counting downwards. To gain an idea of where and how big it is, clench the left fist and place it on the chest so that the inside of the wrist is over the left nipple. The fist itself then shows, approximately, the size, shape and position of the heart.

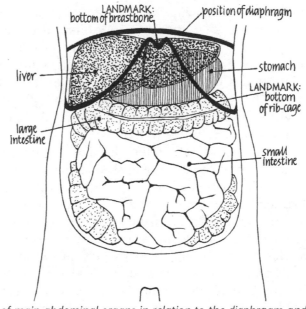

Figure 3.2 *Position of main abdominal organs in relation to the diaphragm and rib-cage, seen from the front. The liver is directly under the diaphragm and partly protected by the front of the rib-cage. It lies partly over and in front of the stomach*

Below the diaphragm is the abdomen. The position and size of the main abdominal organs (stomach, liver, small and large intestines) are shown in Figure 3.2. The stomach and liver lie just below the diaphragm and are partly protected by the lower part of the rib-cage. The stomach is much higher in the body than is commonly imagined. Its size and position can be shown approximately by placing the left hand flat over the front of the body, with the thumb folded into the notch at the bottom of the breast-bone. The kidneys are just inside the body-wall at the back, on either side of the spine. Their position can be felt by finding the gap on either side of the spine between the upper edge of the hip-bone and the bottom of the rib-cage.

3.2   NUTRITION: TEETH AND DENTAL CARE

Apart from water and salt, our food consists of complex, high-energy chemicals (3.4). Very little of the food we eat is in a form which can be used by the body. Nearly all of it has to be broken down into simpler chemicals, a process known as digestion. To carry out this process we have a long tube through our bodies called the gut (alimentary canal). Food is taken into the gut through the mouth, and waste (faeces) is expelled from the anus (3.3).

Digestion begins with chewing, which is carried out by the teeth and jaws. This breaks up the food, mixes it with saliva and softens it so that it is easier to swallow and to digest (3.3). Teeth grow from, and are anchored in the bones of, the upper and lower jaws. Each tooth is a bony structure, with a nerve and blood supply at its centre and a covering of smooth, white dental enamel, the hardest material in the body. The main bony part of the tooth, the dentine, is fairly hard and very tough (ivory is dentine), and it supports the enamel, which is much harder (7.1.2) but also more brittle (7.1.7).

Humans have two sets of teeth in their lifetime. The first set (milk or deciduous teeth) are formed in early childhood and shed as the second, permanent, set grow under them and push them out. Care of permanent teeth is particularly important because, unlike bones and most other body parts, tooth enamel cannot be repaired or renewed if it is chipped, cracked or damaged chemically. Damage to the enamel makes it possible for microbes to attack and decay the softer dentine underneath. If the decay reaches the nerve and blood supply in the centre of the tooth, pain (toothache) will be felt, which if untreated may lead to a serious infection (abscess) in the root of the tooth and the bone of the jaw. There are two main causes of damage to enamel and subsequent decay: abuse of the teeth and poor dental hygiene. Even when food is chewed safely and thoroughly, teeth will still be at risk if they are not cleaned. Chewed food of any kind is usually more or less sticky and often fibrous. Even thorough brushing may fail to remove particles of food which lodge between the teeth and which will be very quickly inhabited by microbes already living in the mouth.

One by-product of food decay is acid which attacks tooth enamel chemically, roughening and pitting its surface, so making it easier for bacteria to form a layer (plaque) and attack it still further. Acid production is encouraged by consuming too much sugar, particularly in the form of sweets, some soft drinks and ice lollies, which coat the teeth with a thin film of sticky syrup. This quickly becomes acidic as microbes feed on it. The main way of preventing tooth decay and gum disease is regular, thorough brushing with toothpaste, which contains a very fine abrasive capable of removing bacterial films and so preventing the build-up of plaque. Coupled with the use of floss or interdental brushes, it greatly reduces the frequency of tooth decay in most children and adults. More controversial is the use of fluoride in drinking water or tablets, though it is now added to most toothpastes.

Activity 3.2.1 gives ideas for investigating dental plaque and the effect of brushing teeth.

The number and form of the teeth which an animal has, can give a lot of information about the kinds of food it eats and therefore about its relationship with other living things. Because humans have a varied diet, our teeth are not very specialized. The front ones (incisors and canines) are good for chewing or pulling pieces from a larger lump of food, while the broad back teeth (premolars and molars) are well-adapted for crushing and macerating food to a pulp. Many other animals have much more specialized teeth related to their diet (5.6).

3.3   NUTRITION: DIGESTION

Swallowing   Food in the mouth, which has been softened and moistened by chewing and saliva, is formed into a ball by the tongue and moved to the back of the mouth. There it triggers a reflex action (3.10) which results in swallowing. There are two tubes running down through the neck. In front is the windpipe (trachea) leading to the lungs (3.6), and behind it the gullet (oesophagus), leading to the stomach. To feel where the gullet runs, swallow a mouthful of warm (not hot) water. In swallowing, a flap (epiglottis) closes over the top of the windpipe so that food or liquid does not normally enter it, but goes further back and down the gullet. If liquid or solid material does enter the windpipe accidentally, it triggers a choking reflex, consisting of violent coughing which continues until the material has been ejected. The gullet is a muscular tube, which moves the food pellet down to the stomach. As the food reaches the lower end of the gullet, the upper end of the stomach opens to let it in.

Activity 3.3.1 is about how to investigate what happens when food is chewed.

The stomach The stomach is a muscular bag, closed at both ends by a ring of muscle, whose function is to collect food and begin its digestion. It does this by adding water with chemicals in solution and churning the mixture into a semi-liquid pulp. The liquid added to the food contains quite strong hydrochloric acid, which kills nearly all the microbes eaten with the food. It creates highly acidic conditions favourable for the working of the digesting chemicals, also present in the stomach juice (enzymes, see below). When the food has been broken down sufficiently, the ring of muscle at the lower end of the stomach opens to allow it, a little at a time, into the next part of the gut.

Activity 3.3.2 investigates where food goes when it is swallowed.

The ideas contained in the remaining parts of this section on nutrition cannot easily be taught using direct evidence, so good sources of indirect experience need to be provided by the teacher.

Peristalsis The whole of the gut is a muscular tube, which mixes the semi-liquid food inside it and moves it along by waves of squeezing action, rather like squeezing toothpaste to one end of the tube. This mixing and moving activity is called peristalsis. Although the churning action of the stomach is quite a violent example of peristalsis, we do not normally feel it at all. If some bad, poisonous or indigestible food is swallowed, however, the normal action of the stomach goes into reverse, we feel the churning of its muscles and we are sick. Vomiting is a very important defence by the body against poisons (excess alcohol, for example) and infection by microbes.

Digestive enzyme Chewing and pulping of food in the mouth and stomach is only the preliminary phase of digestion. The actual breakdown of foods into a form the body can use is a chemical process, carried out, like all chemical changes (8.3) in the body, by special chemicals called enzymes. Enzymes similar to the ones we use to digest food are used in 'biological' washing powders, to digest food and stains so that they dissolve in the water and are washed away. This is exactly what happens in the digestion of food. Enzymes made by the body are mixed with the liquid food, so that the complex food chemicals are broken down into simpler ones which will dissolve in water. In this form they can be taken into the body and transported around the body by the blood (3.7).

Absorption and transport   When the partly digested food leaves the stomach, it enters the first part of the intestine (the duodenum), then the small intestine, where digestion is continued and completed. The small intestine has a remarkable structure. Its lining has millions of small projections which look like the pile of a carpet, with tiny blood-vessels (capillaries, see 3.8) running through them. All together these have a very large surface through which digested food from the gut contents can be absorbed. All the digested food is transported by the blood to the liver, which is like a complex chemical factory. It receives the digested food, processes some of it further and distributes it to the rest of the body as it is needed for growth or respiration.

Defaecation   When all the useful digested food has been taken out of the gut contents, what remains is moved by peristalsis to the large intestine. Before the waste is removed from the body, most of the water which had been added to the food in the stomach is now absorbed by the intestine, to be available for re-use by the body. Normal reabsorption of water makes the waste food in the gut into a solid mass (faeces) which is finally ejected through the ring of muscle (anus) at the lower end of the gut, a process known as defaecation. One reason why fibre is an important part of a healthy diet (3.4) is that it helps peristalsis to work efficiently, so food and faeces are moved through the gut quickly and we don't become constipated. In contrast to this, harmful microbes in the intestine may mean that the body needs to get rid of the waste food very quickly, which results in diarrhoea. Very severe diarrhoea, caused by diseases such as dysentery and cholera, results in uncontrolled dehydration of the body, which may be fatal. Such diseases, caused by contamination of drinking water, were very common in Britain before the middle of the nineteenth century and are still a major problem in the developing world today.

3.4 NUTRITION: FOOD AND DIET

The overall range of food which an animal eats is its diet. A correctly balanced diet for any animal is the range of foods which will enable it to stay healthy in the long term. For humans, a balanced diet includes a variety of foods, together with the vitamins they contain, water and minerals. There are three main groups of foods: carbohydrates, fats and proteins.

This is another area of science where the ideas cannot easily be taught using direct evidence, so good sources of indirect experience need to be provided by the teacher.

Carbohydrates   are chemicals which the body either uses as a source of energy or converts to fat for storage. The two main carbohydrates eaten and digested by humans are sugars and starch. The sugar *glucose* is the only common ingredient of our food which can be absorbed directly and very quickly by the stomach without digestion. Other sugars, and starch, are changed to glucose by digestion and then absorbed. Glucose is also the main material used as an energy source in respiration (3.6) and the body is constantly supplied with it by the blood (3.7). The only carbohydrate stored by the body is a small amount in the liver. If more sugar and starch are eaten than the body needs, the surplus is stored as fat. In times of food shortage this may be life-saving, but when food is plentiful it can lead to obesity. There is no way that the body can dispose of an excess of carbohydrate other than by respiring it (during exercise, for example) or storing it.

Obesity Obesity is becoming a major problem among children and adults in both Britain and the USA. Discussion of the complex social and biological factors which have contributed to this situation are beyond the scope of this book, but most children are likely to benefit from being helped and encouraged to eat a balanced diet (see below), eat in moderation and take more physical exercise (3.9). Science education can play a significant part in this process by promoting children's understanding of their own bodies and their response to food and exercise.

Fats, which may be in a solid or liquid, oily form, are a very efficient way of storing high-energy food, both for animals and plants. Fat taken in as food can, after digestion, be used as an energy source in respiration (3.6), and fat stored in a person's own body is used in the same way if other energy sources such as carbohydrate are insufficient for their needs. As with carbohydrate, excess fat in the diet cannot be removed from the body and has either to be respired or stored in fatty tissue.

Proteins Carbohydrates and fats are, in animals, only useful as sources of energy. Proteins have a more varied role. When digested, they produce a range of up to 20 chemicals called amino-acids. These are used by the body as the raw material for making or replacing living tissue. This means that adequate supplies of protein are essential, not only for growth in childhood, but for continued health throughout life. The protein supply also has to be fairly constant, because surplus amino-acids cannot be stored and they have to be removed from the body. This is done by the liver, and produces chemicals which can be respired or stored as fat, and a waste product (urea) which is removed from the blood by the kidneys (3.7) and expelled from the body in the urine.

Vitamins   are complex chemicals which the body needs in small quantities but cannot make for itself. They are not foods in the ordinary sense of the term, but are more like a chemical tool-kit which enables the body to carry out complex chemical changes. Detailed information on vitamins and foods which contain them can be obtained from health promotion agencies. If a particular vitamin is missing from a person's diet, they will suffer from a distinctive illness called a deficiency disease because one or more essential body processes cannot be carried out. For example, sailors on long voyages in historic times often had no fresh fruit or vegetables for long periods, so there was no vitamin C in their diet and they suffered from the deficiency disease known as scurvy. To overcome this, the British Navy issued rations of lemon or lime juice to its sailors, which led to the American nickname for the British: 'limeys'. A balanced and varied diet (see below) usually supplies all the vitamins a person needs, but people on restricted diets may need to take vitamin supplements to remain healthy.

Water Humans share with all land-dwelling animals the problem of conserving water in their bodies. Living tissue is made up largely of water, and to humans and most living things even a moderate loss of water is fatal, so unless water supplies are plentiful, dehydration is a constant danger. The human body is fairly efficient at conserving water: we have an almost waterproof skin, quite good water recovery from waste food in the gut, and kidneys which can concentrate chemical wastes in the urine. But in spite of this, each of us wakes up in the morning about 1kg lighter than when we went to bed, because of water loss from the lungs during breathing and slow evaporation (6.2.2) from the skin. Even without vigorous exercise and sweating, humans need to drink water daily if they are to remain healthy and active. Twenty-four hours without water usually results in acute thirst, and after more than a few days, can be fatal. The water in lakes, ponds and rivers contains many kinds of microbe, a few of which can cause serious or fatal diseases in humans, such as cholera and dysentery (3.3). This danger is greatly increased if water is contaminated, for example by inadequate sewage disposal. Water also dissolves many chemicals, some of which are poisonous. Examples include fertilizers and industrial chemicals, which are serious pollutants if allowed to contaminate natural water supplies. Water purification is therefore one of our most important technologies, since our whole lifestyle and civilization depend on an abundant supply of purified drinking-water. Indeed, an abundant supply of clean water is likely to be the biggest single contributory factor in the improvement of health in any society, far outweighing the whole of medicine in its overall beneficial effects.

Minerals in the diet are different from minerals in the earth (7.4). As part of our food, a 'mineral' is a simple chemical we need to stay healthy. The main examples children may need to know about are salt, iron and calcium. Salt (sodium chloride) is found in solution in the blood and all other body fluids. If salt is lacking in the diet the body can conserve it to some extent, but some is always lost in sweat and urine, so at least a small intake is necessary. During vigorous exercise, salt loss in sweat increases and there may be a need to take salt in order to prevent cramp (severe, uncontrolled muscle contraction). Excess salt in the diet is removed from the body by the kidneys, but in the long term can cause medical problems such as high blood pressure. Two other very important minerals are chemicals containing iron, needed for making the haemoglobin in red blood cells (3.7), and others containing calcium, which is essential for the hardening and strengthening of bones and teeth (3.5). Normally both are obtained in sufficient quantities as part of food, but if they are lacking in a particular diet, or if large quantities are needed (calcium in pregnant women, for example), mineral supplements may be required to maintain health.

Dietary fibre Although this is not seen as a food for humans since they cannot digest it, dietary fibre or *roughage* is an essential part of a balanced diet. Dietary fibre is made of cellulose, the main structural material of plants (4.2), and the main sources of it in the human diet are vegetables, fruit, whole-grain cereals and bread. Without it, the gut cannot move food and undigested waste efficiently (3.3) so waste stays longer in the large intestine and constipation sets in. This is not merely uncomfortable: it has been shown to contribute, in the long term, to cancer of the large intestine. Animals which feed mainly on plants (herbivores, 5.7) can digest cellulose, which is for them the main source of carbohydrate.

Balanced diet Detailed advice on diet and healthy eating related to local conditions and foods is readily available from health promotion agencies. Humans, like other mixed-diet animals (omnivores, 5.7), can digest, use and stay healthy on the basis of eating a very wide variety of foods. Some modern methods of processing, however, make foods which taste good but which are lacking in some of the ingredients necessary for health, such as vitamins or dietary fibre, or which have too much of otherwise good things, such as sugar, fat and salt. In Britain, prepared foods should now have an analysis of their food and fibre content on their labels, which are informative when learning about diet and healthy eating. Unless they and their families are already diet conscious, children can be encouraged to eat less sugar, fat (especially animal fat), salt and highly processed foods generally, and to eat more high-fibre and raw, unprocessed foods. Sugar, fat and salt need special attention because they are often concealed in the diet. Sugar is used in a very wide variety of processed foods (look at a can of baked beans, for example) and even lean beef (red muscle) is 40 per cent fat, whereas chicken meat and white fish are very low in fat.

3.5 SKELETON, JOINTS, MUSCLES AND MOVEMENT

Movement in animals is brought about by a specialized type of tissue called muscle (see below). On its own, muscle would not enable an animal to move about: the force exerted by the muscle has to be applied in some way. Animals have a wide variety of methods of applying muscles for movement, but the one with which children will be most familiar is the jointed skeleton. Two great groups of animals have developed jointed skeletons: the arthropods, including crabs, woodlice and all the insects, whose skeletons are on the outside; and the vertebrates or backboned animals, whose skeletons are inside their bodies (see 5.1).

Bone Humans are mammals and, like birds, reptiles, amphibians and fish (except sharks and rays), they have skeletons made of bone. As a material, bone is very strong in relation to its size, fairly hard, and tough (7.1.2–7.1.7). Thinner bones such as ribs are slightly flexible; thicker ones such as the long bones of the arm and leg are more or less rigid. Bone is a living tissue. It is formed when a soft, tough tissue, rather like the gristle in meat, is hardened by the addition of minerals, mainly calcium phosphate, which are taken in as part of the diet (3.4). Bone forms in the foetus during pregnancy (3.11), and the skeleton continues to grow until adulthood. At birth, the top of the skull has not hardened because the brain inside is not fully grown, so there is a soft area on a baby's head (the fontanelle) which must be treated gently and with great care.

The **skeleton** is the complete system of bones joined together. It has four main functions:

- protection of some vulnerable organs (brain, spinal cord, lungs, heart and liver);
- forming a framework which supports the main organs of the body;
- making a lever system on which muscles pull to enable the body to move about;
- making red blood cells in the soft tissue (marrow) inside ribs and pelvis.

The skeleton allows movement because most of the joints which connect the bones can be moved.

Activity 3.5.1 investigates the human skeleton.

Joints in the skeleton are of three main kinds. The joints between the bones which make up the main part of the skull (cranium) and between the spine and the pelvis normally allow no movement at all. The second kind of joint is found in the spine, whose bones (vertebrae) are joined by thick discs of tough, flexible tissue. Each joint allows only a small amount of movement, but together they allow the whole spine to be flexible and at the same time very strong. Most of the other joints in the skeleton are of the third kind, which allows fast movement: examples are the joints of the shoulder, elbow, wrist, fingers, hip, knee and ankle, and the joint between the jaw and the main part of the skull. The bones are held together, so that the joints are prevented from falling apart, by very strong elastic strips of tissue called ligaments. The skeleton as a whole forms a complex set of lever systems, with the bones as the levers and the joints as the pivots (11.7). The forces required to move the levers are exerted by muscles which are attached to the bones and pull on them.

Muscles and tendons   All movement in the body is brought about by muscles. Our muscles are very like the lean red meat which is the muscle of cattle or other animals. Muscle has a very distinctive property. If a nerve message reaches it from the brain or spinal cord, it will contract, becoming shorter, wider and more firm to the touch, and exerting a pulling force on whatever it is attached to. Muscles can move in only one way: they can only pull; they cannot push. In order to make the bones of the skeleton move, the muscles must be firmly attached to them. The attachment is by way of very tough, strong cords called tendons. Tendons are easily felt and seen, for example by sitting on a chair, putting one hand under the seat beside you and pulling upwards with the elbow bent. A tendon can then be felt, like a hard, rigid cord, on the inside of the elbow. When the arm is resting on the table the tendon can still be felt, but it feels softer and is more flexible because it is not under tension. Tendons at the back of the knee (hamstrings) and ankle (Achilles' tendon) can be felt and seen when half squatting.

    Children can learn about the action of muscles on the skeleton, including an understanding that muscles can only pull, not push. This means that any to-and-fro movement of a joint, such as bending the elbow and straightening it again, must involve at least two muscles. In fact, muscles operate joints in pairs. This can be shown by investigating the muscles of the upper arm.

Let one arm hang loosely. Feel the muscle (biceps) in the front of the upper arm: it is relaxed and quite soft. Now sit in front of a heavy table or desk, put your hand, palm up, under the edge and pull up as if to lift it. Feel the biceps muscle again: it is tense and much firmer because it is 'working' and pulling on the bones of the lower arm. To feel how the muscle changes shape when it contracts, let the arm hang loosely again and, holding the biceps muscle with the other hand, pull up your forearm as far as it will go, until your hand nearly touches your shoulder. When the elbow is fully bent, the muscle is much wider (and shorter) than when the arm is straight.

    The muscle which moves the lower arm the other way and straightens the elbow (called the triceps) is at the back of the upper arm. It can be felt by standing near a wall and pushing against it with the flat of your hand and the elbow half bent. The triceps is hard and tense, but the biceps is soft and relaxed because it isn't pulling. Although the triceps muscle cannot push, it enables the hand and arm to exert a pushing force because it pulls on the outside of the elbow joint. This action can be felt by holding the back of the elbow while straightening the arm.

Muscle pairs can also be felt when bending and straightening the knee (muscles in the thigh) and ankle (muscles in the calf of the leg). Pairs of muscles which move a joint are called antagonistic pairs, not because they work against each other, but because they make the joint move in opposite directions.

Activity 3.5.2 has more ideas for investigating movement.

Activity 3.5.3 helps to find tendons.

Activity 3.5.4 investigates muscles and their action.

3.6 BREATHING AND RESPIRATION

Humans and other animals require a constant supply of oxygen in order to remain alive. The oxygen is used in respiration, the process by which energy in food is transferred for activities such as growth and movement. Breathing is the part of the respiration process in which oxygen is taken into the body. At the same time as oxygen is taken from the air, the waste gas carbon dioxide has to be removed from the body, so breathing is not just an intake of one gas, but an exchange of two. Some animals such as earthworms can breathe through their skins, which are permanently damp and slimy, but most land animals have dry, waterproof skins and rely for gas exchange on specialized internal organs called lungs. A few animals such as frogs use both skin and lungs for breathing.

This is another area of science where the ideas cannot easily be taught using direct evidence, so good sources of indirect experience need to be provided by the teacher.

Lungs Humans and other mammals have two lungs, which are complex air-sacs in the chest (3.1). In the living animal the lungs are always filled with air and so have a spongy structure. They are supplied with air by the windpipe (trachea), which runs down in front of the neck from the throat. The windpipe is reinforced by rings of tough, flexible tissue so that it remains open even when we are asleep. In the chest, the windpipe divides into two tubes, one serving each lung. Inside the lungs, the main air-tubes branch repeatedly, forming a tree-like structure with thousands of branches. At the end of each branch is a cluster of tiny air-sacs, from which oxygen is absorbed into the blood (3.7).

Breathing   In order to maintain the oxygen supply to the body, the air in the lungs must be constantly replaced. This is done by pumping stale air out and sucking fresh air in; the set of actions we call breathing. The lungs cannot fill and empty themselves because they are unable to move or change shape. The pumping action is achieved by changing the shape of the chest, which is done in two ways, both of which can be investigated by children and result in air being sucked into the lungs and pushed out. The first method can be experienced by sitting upright and using the muscles between the ribs to pull the rib-cage upwards and outwards. This makes the chest and lungs larger, so air is sucked in down the windpipe. When the muscles are allowed to relax, the rib-cage falls again and air is pushed out. The second type of breathing can be experienced by lying on your back on the floor. The weight of the body then pushes the rib-cage up, so it is difficult to pull it up further in order to breathe. In this situation, breathing is carried out by using the diaphragm (3.1). When breathing in, the diaphragm pulls down and flattens, making the chest larger and sucking air into the lungs. At the same time, the liver, stomach and intestines are pushed further down, so the abdomen is pushed out and becomes rounder. When breathing out, the diaphragm relaxes and muscles at the front of the abdomen pull in and flatten, making the organs inside push the diaphragm up again so that the chest becomes smaller and air is pushed out of the lungs.

*Activity 3.6 illustrates a way of modelling the **second method** of breathing.*

Normal breathing, when a person is at rest, uses both of these breathing actions, but diaphragm breathing is the more important of the two. Because rib-cage breathing can take in and pump out large quantities of air very quickly, it is particularly important during vigorous exercise such as running (3.9). Diaphragm breathing is more important when the rib-cage cannot be lifted easily, for example when a person is lying down or asleep, and for singers who need a lot of breath control.

Gas exchange   The lungs of an adult human contain up to about 5 litres of air. In normal breathing when the person is at rest, only about a tenth of this is changed with each breath, but this so-called tidal volume increases during exercise (3.9). Each of the thousands of tiny air-sacs in each lung is supplied with a network of very small blood-vessels (capillaries, 3.7), through which the blood is constantly circulating. Oxygen from the air passes through the thin lining of the lung, is taken up by the red blood cells (3.7) and transported to the heart to be pumped round the rest of the body. In normal breathing, about a quarter of the oxygen in the air is taken into the blood. At the same time, carbon dioxide produced by respiration (see below) is released from the blood into the air within the lung, water evaporates from the moist lung lining and the air is heated by the blood. As a result of all these changes, air breathed out is warmer, more humid (6.2.2), and has less oxygen and more carbon dioxide than air breathed in.

Respiration is the process of chemical changes which uses oxygen to break down food (in humans, usually the sugar glucose) in order to transfer energy (9.2.8) for movement, growth and other living processes. Respiration is carried out in every part of the body, so every part needs a blood supply to deliver oxygen and remove carbon dioxide. It is a complex, low-temperature process, quite different from burning, which can be summarized as:

$$\text{glucose} + \text{oxygen} \rightarrow \text{carbon dioxide} + \text{water}$$

3.7 BLOOD

Blood is the red fluid which is circulated to all parts of the body and which acts as its main means of transport. Blood consists of a pale yellow watery fluid, the plasma, in which are suspended a variety of living cells, each of which has specialized functions. The main functions of the blood are: transporting oxygen by the red blood cells; responding to injury and infection by the white blood cells; and transporting digested food and waste products by the plasma. By becoming heated in some parts of the body and cooled in others, the blood also plays an important part in maintaining body temperature (3.9).

Activity 3.6.3 explores body temperature.

Here is another area of science where the ideas cannot easily be taught using direct evidence, so good sources of indirect experience need to be provided by the teacher.

Red cells, which give the blood its characteristic colour, are formed in the soft tissue (marrow) of the ribs and hip-bone. Each red cell in humans is active for only about four months, so very large numbers of new ones are formed, and old ones destroyed, every day. The cells are red because they are filled with the iron-containing pigment haemoglobin. If not enough iron is present in the diet (3.4), insufficient red cells will be formed and the person will suffer from a form of anaemia. Haemoglobin has the property that it takes up and carries large amounts of oxygen from the lungs, but can release it again in the tissues of the body where it is needed for respiration (3.6). The red cells are also partly responsible for carrying carbon dioxide produced by respiration from the body tissues to the lungs so that it can be breathed out.

White blood cells,   like red cells, are formed in bone marrow, but they are much less numerous. There are many different kinds, which together form a very important part of the body's defences (the immune system) against microbes and viruses. Some cells can chemically recognize and attack microbes; others make special chemicals capable of killing microbes or rendering them harmless. Another kind congregate in an injured area and clean up dead or damaged tissue so that healing can take place more easily.

Blood plasma   is the liquid part of the blood, which contains a very large variety of chemicals in solution. It transports digested foods to all parts of the body. They are extracted from the blood by the various body parts which need them for life processes such as respiration and growth. Plasma also carries waste products in solution, including some of the carbon dioxide produced by respiration. It also carries urea, the waste product from the breakdown of excess protein (3.4) in the liver. The urea is carried to the kidneys, where it is removed from the blood before being excreted from the body in urine. Blood plasma, together with tiny bodies in it called platelets, is also responsible for clotting, which is the main defence against bleeding from wounds to the skin. When blood is exposed to air, a complex series of chemical changes occurs, which results in the plasma becoming solid and sticky. The platelets stick to the solid mass, so that bleeding is stopped and a protective layer is formed, beneath which healing and repair can proceed.

3.8   THE HEART AND CIRCULATION OF THE BLOOD

Blood acts as a transport system by being moved round the body. This is done by the heart, which is a muscular pump situated in the chest just above the diaphragm, to which it is attached, and slightly to the left of centre (Fig. 3.1). The heart is in fact a double pump, whose two halves work together. One half receives blood from the body and pumps it to the lungs; the other receives blood returning from the lungs and pumps it round the body. This ensures that all the blood regularly goes to the lungs to have its oxygen supply renewed and carbon dioxide removed.

The action of the heart   Each half of the heart consists of two chambers which pump blood (Fig. 3.3). The upper chamber (atrium) on each side has thin walls and acts mainly as a blood reservoir. The lower chambers (ventricles) have thick, muscular walls with a unique spiral structure. Each ventricle has an inlet and an outlet valve to prevent blood flowing backwards, i.e. in the wrong direction. At the start of a heartbeat the muscles of the ventricle relax and blood flows through the inlet valve from the atrium into the ventricle on each side. Then the muscles of the ventricles contract, so that blood is pumped out of both ventricles at once. The spiral structure of the muscles means that blood is not simply squeezed out of the ventricles but is almost wrung out of them, giving a very efficient pumping action. This action closes the inlet valve between the atrium and the ventricle on each side, so that blood cannot flow back into the atria, but opens the outlet valves leading to the large blood-vessels (arteries, see below) which carry blood from the right side of the heart to the lungs and from the left side to the body.

Activity 3.8.1 is about how to listen to the action of the heart.

Arteries   Blood circulates round the body in a strictly one-way system, through living pipes or blood-vessels. Every time the heart pumps there is a surge of blood through the system, and the large blood-vessels carrying blood from the heart have thick, elastic walls. These blood-vessels are called arteries, and most of them lie deep inside the body where they are protected from injury. This is important because blood flow in a large artery is so fast that if the wall is cut or punctured it is very difficult to stop the bleeding and this may be fatal.

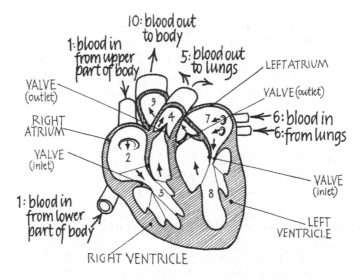

Figure 3.3 *The heart cut open to show its chambers and valves. Cut surfaces are shaded. The sequence of numbers and arrows shows the path of blood from the body to the heart (right side) and out to the lungs (1–5); then back to the heart (left side) and out again to the body (6–10)*

Capillaries   As arteries reach different parts of the body, they branch many times, each time leading to smaller and thinner-walled blood-vessels. These lead, in all parts of the body, to fine networks of tiny, very thin-walled blood-vessels called capillaries. Looking carefully at the white of the eye with a magnifying glass, it is possible to see some of the small arteries and the way they branch in the transparent outer layer, but capillaries are much smaller still and they are visible only with a microscope.

Activity 3.8.5 helps to observe capillaries.

> **An analogy of arteries and capillaries** is that they are rather like a road transport system. The big arteries are like motorways: they allow very fast passage of traffic, but there are only a few places where one can get onto or off them, so delivery and collection of goods is impossible while travelling on them. Capillaries are like small roads in a city or the country: traffic moves much more slowly, but it is possible to collect and deliver goods easily. The blood in capillaries flows slowly. In most parts of the body it delivers oxygen and digested food and collects waste for disposal. The lungs also have a very dense network of capillaries, but there the exchange works the other way: the blood delivers waste in the form of carbon dioxide and collects oxygen.

Veins   After passing through capillary networks and exchanging material with tissues of the body, the blood flows back to the heart through blood-vessels called veins. Veins have a slower blood flow than arteries, with little or no pressure surge, so they have thinner walls and valves to prevent blood flowing backwards. Many of them run close under the skin and can be seen through it, for example on hands and arms. Because their walls are thin, the deep red blood inside veins makes them appear as bluish lines, darker than the skin on either side.

Activity 3.8.4 helps to observe veins.

Pulse   Each heartbeat produces a surge of blood in the arteries. At a few points on the body, arteries run close enough to the skin for these surges to be felt. This is the pulse, which can be used to find out how many times the heart is beating each minute.

> **There are two places at which children should be able to feel their pulse.** Children can be helped to find the pulse in the wrist (radial pulse). Guide them to hold out one hand, palm upwards. Stretch the fingers and feel the two tendons running up the wrist to the hand. Let the hand relax and feel for the pulse with index and middle fingers, in the hollow just to the outside of the tendons, below the base of the thumb. Once they have found a radial pulse, a good way of showing it is to

mount a drinking-straw upright on a drawing pin (thumbtack) using a blob of Blu-tac and place the head of the pin on the pulse-point, keeping the hand very still. The pulse will move the skin and make the straw rock to and fro in time with it.

Finding the neck or carotid pulse is done by lifting the chin and finding the angle in the lower edge of the jaw-bone. Find the pulse in a hollow about 3 cm below and slightly forward of the jaw angle, and use only a very gentle pressure to feel it. Once it can be found reliably, the carotid pulse is usually easier to feel and count in children than the radial.

Activity 3.8.2 and Activity 3.8.3 are about how to investigate the pulse.

3.9 EXERCISE AND ITS EFFECTS

Observing the effects of exercise on the body is one of the most useful ways in which children can begin to investigate how their bodies work and respond to changing conditions. It is useful to have a range of exercises. A good basic one is the step-up. Step-ups are done by stepping up with both feet onto a platform at about the height of a chair on which the child would normally sit. A chair can be used for step-ups, but should always be held firmly by an adult. A complete step-up is four movements (each foot up, then down) and should be done in a measured time: four seconds is convenient, giving 15 step-ups a minute. Step-ups give a standard unit of exercise which can act as a control (1.10) with which other forms can be compared. Measurements and observations of the changes brought about by exercise should include: pulse rate; breathing rate (breaths per minute) and observations on the use of ribs and diaphragm (3.1); observations on skin condition (flushing, sweating, see below). The effects of a standard exercise, say 30 step-ups in two minutes, can then be compared with other exercises, such as 60 step-ups, sprinting 50 m and playing a fast-moving game for five minutes.

Safety note: at no time should children or adults attempt to measure the volume of air breathed, either in total or with each breath. Measurements of this kind, especially with young children, should be made only under medical supervision. If any children participating in an investigation show signs of distress, they should stop exercising immediately and rest under observation by a responsible adult.

The main short-term changes likely to be observed after exercise are: increase in the pulse rate; increase in the breathing rate; change in breathing action with more use of the rib-cage; flushing of the skin; sweating.

Exercise and heart rate   During exercise the body is moved much more in each minute than when at rest, so the work-rate of the muscles which move the body increases, which requires them to transfer energy at a faster rate (9.1). Energy transfer in living tissue is brought about by respiration, which requires oxygen, so the demand for oxygen also increases. Oxygen is delivered to the muscles by the blood. Increased oxygen demand requires the heart to increase the blood supply to the muscles, which it does by beating faster.

Activity 3.9.1 investigates exercise and the action of the heart.

Exercise and breathing   An increased rate of respiration in muscles increases not only the demand for oxygen, but also the rate at which the waste gas carbon dioxide is produced. Increased carbon dioxide in the blood is detected by the brain, which stimulates the muscles responsible for breathing (3.6) to work more rapidly and vigorously, so increasing the breathing rate and volume of air taken in with each breath.

Activity 3.9.2 investigates exercise and breathing.

Exercise, heating and cooling   The increased activity of the muscles causes them to become heated (9.1.2). This causes them to heat the blood flowing through them, which if not controlled would lead to over-heating of the body and possibly to brain damage. The increase in blood temperature is detected by the brain, which controls the blood flow to different parts of the body. More blood is diverted to flow through the skin, which becomes hot and flushed as a result. The hot skin heats the air around it, so both it and the blood are cooled. At the same time, the sweat glands in the skin produce a thin film of perspiration on the skin, which evaporates (6.2.2), so cooling the skin and the blood still further.

Activity 3.9.3 investigates exercise, skin and body temperature.

Longer-term effects of exercise   In the longer term, consistent moderate exercise has many beneficial effects on both children and adults. The ability to continue exerting oneself (stamina) and levels of performance increase, while the action of the heart, breathing and circulation all become more efficient. Moderate exercise, coupled with a balanced diet, can also make a major contribution to reducing obesity or preventing it altogether (3.4).

3.10   SENSES, RESPONSE AND CONTROL

One of the most distinctive features of living things is the way they respond to changes so that their chances of survival are usually increased. Many responses of animals are to changes in their own bodies. One important set of these, which children can investigate, are the changes in breathing, pulse rate and the body's cooling system brought about by exercise (3.9). Other responses are to changes in the environment. Humans, like other animals, use specialized sense organs to detect changes and to gather information about their surroundings.

There are five sense modes:

- **Vision**: the eye forms images from light entering it.
- **Hearing**: the ear responds to sound.
- **Smell**: the lining inside the top of the nose detects chemical vapours and gases breathed in.
- **Taste**: the tongue (usually together with the sense of smell) detects substances in solution in the mouth.
- **Touch**: a range of sensory organs, both in the skin and in most parts of the body, respond to touch, pressure and temperature change.

In all cases, what the sense organs do is to generate a very complex set of messages in the form of nerve impulses (see below). These travel through nerves to the brain. Through investigation and learning, much of which is carried on during play in early childhood, humans learn to recognize and remember thousands of items of information about things as diverse as the faces of familiar people, the sound of different musical instruments, the scent of roses, the taste of strawberries and the difference in the textures of silk and sandpaper.

Children can best learn about senses by focusing partly on the sense organs themselves but mainly on learning to identify and distinguish a wide range of experience in all the sense modes, together with the relevant vocabulary. They can do colour matching, discrimination and naming; identifying the sources of different sounds (musical and other); matching smells and flavours (eyes shut) with their sources (eyes open); identifying and describing the forms and textures of objects felt but not seen. Of all human senses, sight is the most important for most people, and for children it is the sense which they can investigate, and with which they investigate, more than any other, so we focus on it here, with some additional notes on the other senses.

Vision   The eye focuses light entering it (13.9.4) into an image on the sensitive lining at the back of the eyeball (Fig. 3.4). The image is upside-down, and seeing the right way up (i.e. so that sight and touch match up) is learned in very early childhood. Focusing the light and forming an image means bending the light rays by refraction (13.9). Most of this is done by the curved front of the eye. The lens, whose shape can be changed, is only for fine adjustment. This is why people whose eye lens has become opaque (cataract) and been removed can still see with very thick-lensed spectacles or a plastic replacement lens in the eye.

The coloured part of the eye (iris) surrounds a black hole (pupil), through which light enters the eyeball behind. Our ability to see clearly in a wide range of light conditions depends partly on the response of the iris. In bright light the iris expands, making the pupil smaller and preventing too much light entering the eye. In dim light the iris contracts outwards, enlarging the pupil and allowing more light in. Children can easily see these changes by observing each others' eyes, but they should never shine a light into an eye, either their own or anyone else's. It is thought that the detailed pattern of colour in each person's iris is unique to them, and in the future this may be widely used as a means of identification.

Activity 3.10.1 is about how eyes respond to changing levels of light.

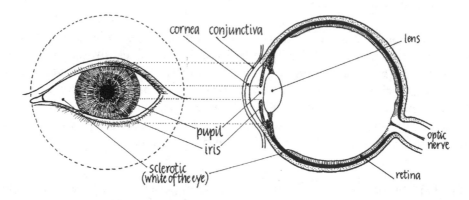

Figure 3.4 *The eye as we see it, related to a section of the eyeball. The cornea and conjunctiva together form the clear, curved front of the eyeball. Notice how little of the eye is normally exposed: this helps to protect it*

The layer at the back of the eye (retina) contains two kinds of light-sensitive cells: rods, which respond to light and dark; and cones, which respond to colour (13.11). When light falls on these cells it causes a complex series of energy transfers (9.1), which result in electrical signals to the brain. Cones do not respond strongly unless the light is quite bright, so in poor light conditions we see mainly in shades of grey with very little colour. Colour-blindness, which often runs in families (i.e. is hereditary), occurs when some or all of the cone-cells do not respond normally to particular colours of light.

We see clearly only a very small part of the scene in front of us, on which our gaze is fixed. This can be investigated by enlarging some text on a photocopier and trying to read a line without moving the eyes at all: only a few letters can be seen clearly enough to read them. The picture we have of our whole field of vision is built up by the brain, which directs very rapid scanning movements of the eyes. These can be seen by giving a person a large and interesting picture to look at, then watching their eyes move as they explore it visually and learn about it.

Activity 3.10.2 investigates how much we can see clearly.

Mammals and birds which feed by hunting (predators, 5.7) have eyes at the front of the head. This enables them, by looking at the same object with both eyes at once, to judge how far away it is; an obvious advantage when chasing or pouncing on prey. This is binocular vision, which can easily be investigated by trying to decide whether similar objects are the same distance away, or which is slightly nearer, with both eyes open and then with one eye shut. Comparing success rates usually shows clearly the dependence of judging distance on binocular vision.

Activity 3.10.3 investigates judging distances.

Hearing   Apart from the external ear or pinna, the ear is wholly internal and so cannot be observed, but there are nevertheless some simple observations which children can carry out which will help them understand their hearing better. The pinna acts as a funnel, directing sound waves (13.1) into the tunnel leading to the eardrum, but normally humans can hear sounds from all round them. In contrast, many animals use and move their external ears much more than humans do, in order to increase sensitivity and locate the source of a sound. This can be experienced by making an ear-trumpet from a cone of thin card with a small opening at the narrow end. Placed carefully in the ear, this makes it possible to hear sounds further away than normal, but hearing then becomes much more directional so the area from which sounds can be heard is smaller.

Activity 3.10.4 investigates ear trumpets.

The sensitivity of different people's hearing can be compared by holding the source of a quiet sound, such as a ticking watch, at different distances from the ear in a very quiet room and finding how far away it can be heard. Judging where a sound is coming from can also be investigated, first with both ears open and then with one muffled. As with vision, both ears have to receive sound (binaural hearing) for the direction of the source to be judged accurately. Both investigations offer excellent opportunities for devising 'fair testing' procedures (1.10) and for finding how widely different people's perceptions vary.

Activity 3.10.5 investigates judging direction of sounds.

Smell and taste are linked. Apart from four basic tastes (sweet, sour, salt and bitter), the detection of flavour requires the nose membranes to be active as well as the tongue. This can easily be shown by sucking a peppermint. With the nostrils pinched it merely tastes sweet, and the peppermint flavour is detected only when air can flow up from the mouth and out through the nose. Mapping the areas on the tongue which respond to the four basic tastes is often described as a simple investigation, but without quite elaborate experimental design and precautions (for example, blind trials and washing the mouth after every tasting) the results are almost certainly bogus.

Activity 3.10.6 investigates tastes and flavours.

Touch is in fact three senses, each with its sensory organs in the skin and tongue: pain, temperature, contact and pressure.

Pain is detected by nerve-endings near the skin surface which register pain if the skin is injured.

Temperature sensitivity in the skin is a response to changes in temperature (see 9.3.2) rather than to degrees of hot and cold. This can be shown by the classic demonstration of dipping one hand (not just one finger) into hot water and the other in cold for two minutes, then moving both to tepid water and observing the sensation registered by each.

Activity 3.10.7 investigates temperature sense.

Contact sensors are near the surface of the skin, but their distribution over the body is very uneven. There are far more of them in each square centimetre of the skin on the fingertips than any other part of the body except the tongue and lips, so the skin is correspondingly more sensitive.

This can be shown by pushing pins into either end of a bottle cork, one at one end and three, about 5 mm apart in a triangle, at the other. Touching the skin on different parts of the body with the single pin or three at once, and finding whether the subject can tell the difference, demonstrates variations in sensitivity. It is also useful to compare the lower lip with the cheek and the tongue, and to extend the investigation by using different numbers and patterns of pins.

Activity 3.10.8 investigates sensitivity to touch.

Pressure sensors are much deeper in the skin, and provide information on how hard the skin is pressed against a solid object. This is very useful when using the hands to manipulate tools and materials by squeezing, pulling, bending and twisting them (11.1).

Kinaesthetic sense is our awareness of exactly where our body parts are in relation to each other. For example, even with their eyes shut, most children know very accurately where their hands are in relation to their heads. This awareness is made possible by stretch receptors in muscles which tell us not only how far limbs are extended and in what direction, but also how hard our muscles are pulling (3.5). Gymnasts and dancers, in particular, develop this kinaesthetic awareness to a very high degree.

The brain and nervous system is the main way in which the various parts of the body communicate with each other. The central parts of the nervous system are the brain in the skull and the spinal cord in the backbone, from which nerves branch out to every part of the body. They carry information both to and from the brain, in the form of tiny electric currents, which are conducted chemically, in quite a different way from metallic conductors (10.2). The brain receives and coordinates a very large amount of information from all parts of the body and sends nerve impulses back which control all the main body activities.

The activities of which we are usually most aware are those which we can control **consciously**, such as walking, picking up an apple or smiling. This kind of activity is called **voluntary** action, because we can choose when and whether we do it. In contrast, a great many activities on which our lives depend go on without our having any conscious control over them or, in many cases, even being aware of them. These are called **involuntary** actions and examples include peristalsis in the gut (3.3) and the pumping of blood by the heart (3.8). The regulation of breathing involves both kinds of activity: although we have some voluntary control over it (holding the breath, for example), an involuntary control takes over when we are asleep or under stress from severe exertion.

A third kind of control is most often associated with emergencies, when very fast response is needed to prevent or minimize injury. When the hand is accidentally in contact with a sharp or very hot object, for example, it is jerked away before pain is felt. This is a **reflex action**, and is very fast because an 'emergency' message goes to the central nervous system and a return signal is sent back immediately, in this case to the arm muscles. Only later, when signals reach the main part of the brain, is pain felt. Other examples of reflex actions include the coughing reflex when a solid or liquid enters the windpipe (3.6), and blinking when something moves very fast near the eye. Because the whole point of most reflexes is to prevent damage, this kind of action is something to know about rather than experiment with.

3.11 GROWTH AND REPRODUCTION

The more obvious kind of growth is growth in size, which involves the building up of new living tissue from materials provided by digested food (3.3) and delivered by the blood (3.7). Energy transfer from respiration (3.6) is also needed because more complex structures are being built up from simple chemicals. The main food needed for growth is protein, so if the diet of children is deficient in protein, their growth is likely to be retarded. They are also likely to have other health problems because their resistance to disease is low.

As children grow in size they are also growing in a less obvious way: tissue replacement. This continues throughout life. Most living tissues, especially if they are very active, need constant replacement and repair if they are to continue working properly, and this goes on all the time in most parts of the body, even in children. Once adulthood has been reached, growth by replacement and repair continues, even though increase in size slows down and stops. This explains why adults as well as children continue to need protein in their diet. If adequate supplies of protein are not available, tissue replacement is either reduced or stopped altogether, so tissues such as muscle waste away, and an undernourished adult becomes weak and emaciated. Growth is controlled by a range of chemicals called hormones made by the body, under control from the brain. From birth to adulthood the balance of hormones changes, so that there is not only overall growth but also specialized development such as the changes at puberty which lead to sexual maturity.

This is another area of science where the ideas cannot easily be taught using direct evidence, so good sources of indirect experience need to be provided by the teacher.

Development and maintenance of a human foetus In humans, the fertilized egg becomes embedded in the lining of the womb (uterus). There it develops into two main parts: the baby (foetus) and a special structure (placenta) to maintain it, which grows into the wall of the uterus. The foetus and placenta are joined by the umbilical cord. Blood from the foetus circulates through the cord to the placenta and back again; blood from the mother circulates through the lining of the uterus. A two-way exchange is set up, by which the foetus is supplied with digested food and oxygen from the mother's blood, while its waste products, including carbon dioxide, are transferred to the mother's blood for removal. The foetus, surrounded by a sac of watery fluid which helps to protect it, is totally dependent on the mother.

Birth   The wall of the uterus is mostly muscle, which becomes thicker and stronger as well as larger, as the foetus develops. The baby is born by being pushed out of the uterus when the very powerful muscles contract and force it down the birth canal (vagina). As the baby is born, a lot of changes happen very quickly. Blood supply to the placenta is cut off and the circulation of blood to the baby's lungs takes over. The baby takes a first, very large, breath to fill its lungs with air, and cries loudly. This is a reflex action which helps to expand its lungs fully and get its breathing muscles working. The umbilical cord is cut and tied to prevent infection and any leakage of blood. The cord has no nerve supply, so neither the mother nor the baby is hurt by this. Later, the placenta detaches itself from the lining of the uterus and is expelled from the birth canal as the afterbirth. Some days later, the end of the cord left on the baby withers and drops off, forming the scar tissue called the umbilicus or tummy-button.

Parental care   Baby mammals vary very much from one species to another, in how far they have developed at birth and what they can do. The young of plant-eating herd animals such as cattle, deer, sheep and horses can stand and move with the herd within a very short time. In complete contrast, the young of flesh-eaters and other animals which have secure refuges (dogs, cats and rabbits, for example) are blind and completely helpless at birth and for some weeks afterwards. All mammals, however, care for their young to a very high degree. Mammals are the only animals which feed their young with milk, a suspension (8.1.2) of fats in water which also contains proteins and other foods in solution. Its mother's milk is, under normal circumstances, the best food for any young mammal because it is not only a perfectly balanced diet, but also helps to complete development of the baby's resistance to disease (immune system).

Most mammals and birds do not merely feed their young, but also teach them skills they need for survival, such as how to find food and how to fit into a social group. It is interesting and revealing to compare patterns of reproduction and parental care in different animals. A frog, for example, lays several hundred small eggs but does not care for them at all. A blackbird lays between three and six much larger eggs and not only incubates them, but feeds the chicks after hatching, teaches them to fly and helps them to begin looking for their own food. A human mother usually has one baby at a time, which is very large in comparison with her own size, and which, in favourable circumstances, is cared for within a social group (typically, the family) for many years.

This pattern is clear: at one end of the scale, animals have many small young with no parental care, relying on big numbers and chance for some to survive. At the other extreme, only one large offspring is produced at a time, is fed, cared for and taught for many years in order to give it the best possible chance of survival.

Humans are right at one extreme of this pattern of reproduction, and understanding this can contribute to personal and social education. Human babies, though not blind at birth, are helpless, and their development in all cultures is longer and more complex than that of any other animal. It is most likely to be successful when the baby is born into a social group whose members care for and help each other. This is why, even from a biological perspective, families or other stable social groups within which children grow up are not a luxury or an optional extra: they are an essential part of our survival strategy as a species.

3.12 TOBACCO, ALCOHOL, DRUGS AND THEIR ABUSE

The effects of these substances on the human body and on personal health are well known by scientists. The Science National Curriculum at Key Stage 2 requires the teaching of some of this knowledge. However, education in this area is complex and sensitive. Teachers should be provided with up-to-date training or guidance, be well informed by health promotion agencies and the police and they should use the teaching approach agreed by the school community. This is likely to integrate the teaching of relevant scientific knowledge with the school health education and personal and social education programmes which have regard for each child's age, stage and maturity.

The following notes are intended only as a guide to the main scientific concepts which are needed by teachers for a basic understanding of how these harmful substances affect the body and behaviour.

Background knowledge Tobacco, alcohol and other drugs are substances which have marked effects on the way the body works, a person's behaviour, or both. Tobacco and alcohol are exceptional in that their consumption by adults is still legal, whereas that of other 'soft' and 'hard' drugs is illegal unless they are used, as some are, under medical supervision. All these substances are potentially harmful, but vary very much in their effects. A minority, of which alcohol is one, do not seem harmful in small quantities unless taken under the wrong circumstances, for example before driving a car. They are, however, harmful in excess. The majority are always dangerous, either because they can have unpredictable and lethal side-effects or because, like tobacco, they damage the body and impair health when taken in any quantity. The main reasons why these substances are grouped together, and regarded as potentially or actually dangerous, is that anyone taking them regularly will develop a tolerance of them and may become dependent on them, with consequences for their health and personal life which may range from the unpleasant to the disastrous.

Tolerance   When tobacco smoke, alcohol or a drug is taken for the first time, it produces an effect on the way the body works, or on behaviour, or both. This may be pleasant, but more often is unpleasant: first doses of most of these substances produce nausea and quite often induce vomiting. If the substance is taken repeatedly, however, the body adjusts to it and a tolerance to it is built up. One effect of tolerance is that the effects of the substance are reduced: a greater dose has to be taken in order to produce the same effect as before. This is easily observable in people who drink alcohol or smoke tobacco in an attempt to relieve tension or anxiety: if not consciously checked, their consumption increases. One reason why tobacco, alcohol and drugs are regarded as being dangerous is the characteristic of tolerance and therefore increased consumption.

Dependence   develops as a result of tolerance, when a person cannot work or behave in what they regard as a normal way without repeated doses of the substance. Dependence is shown by a person's behaviour or physical state when the substance is not taken at all, or is taken in smaller quantities than their habitual dose. If their behaviour is affected, for example by anxiety, bad temper or depression, they are said to have an emotional or psychological dependence. If their physical state is affected so they have withdrawal symptoms such as pain, vomiting, or uncontrolled shaking, they have a physical dependence, which is also called addiction.

Although there are differences between emotional and physical dependence, they are closely related. Experimenting with any potentially harmful substances is very dangerous (and illegal), but individuals most at risk are those who are vulnerable in other ways. Severe physical and emotional dependences, and substance abuse generally, are closely linked to social and psychological factors such as boredom, anxiety, despair, lack of a feeling of personal worth and the desire to become or to be seen as one of a high-status social group.

Tobacco and smoking   Because smoking is not illegal, though decreasingly socially acceptable, it is not necessarily regarded as an example of substance abuse, but it should be. Tobacco smoke, whether inhaled directly or from someone else's cigarette, is harmful in any quantity. Tobacco smoke is a complex mixture, but the substance in it which has the most effect on the body is nicotine. The nicotine content of smoke is variable, and is measured by collecting the sticky residue (tar) from smoke, so cigarettes are classified in health warnings according to their tar content: the higher the tar, the more harmful the cigarette. In the short term, cigarette smoke causes the air passages of the lung to pull inwards and become smaller, so breathing becomes more difficult. At the same time it reduces the amount of oxygen the blood can carry. It also prevents the lining of the lung from clearing itself naturally of dust and other irritants, and causes it to make more of the liquid (mucus) on its lining. The long-term effects of smoking may take years to develop, but are usually severe and often fatal. The main effects are emphysema, chronic bronchitis, coronary heart disease and lung cancer, which results from chemicals in tobacco smoke causing genetic mutation of normal cells into cancerous ones. Pregnant women who smoke also risk damaging their babies.

Emphysema is the breakdown of the fine air-sacs in the lungs which are responsible for the absorption of oxygen. These are weakened by the smoke, then further damaged and burst by violent coughing brought about by bronchitis (see below). The result is that lungs take in a smaller fraction of the oxygen than normal, so the sufferer becomes out of breath after only a small exertion.

Bronchitis Because the air-tubes (bronchi) in the lung are irritated by smoke, they make more of the slimy fluid (mucus) which normally covers them. At the same time they are prevented from working to clear themselves as they normally do. The result is that the smoker has to try to clear the lungs by coughing. This irritates the air-tubes still further, causing bronchitis and greatly increasing the likelihood of infection (pneumonia). It may also contribute to the development of emphysema (see above). Over 95 per cent of people suffering from chronic (i.e. constant) bronchitis are smokers.

Coronary heart disease Smoking increases the tendency for arteries (3.8) to become blocked with fatty deposits. This can lead to obstruction of blood flow in any part of the body and 95 per cent of people with diseases of their leg arteries are smokers. If the heart's own blood supply is blocked, the result is a heart attack. About 25 per cent of all deaths from heart attacks are thought to be as a result of smoking.

Lung cancer Cancer is caused when cells mutate and the normal control over the rate of growth of a tissue is destroyed. If this is untreated the tissue grows uncontrollably, usually forming lumps of cancerous tissue (tumours) which make it impossible for that part of the body to work properly. Some kinds of cancer can be caused by chemicals (carcinogens), and tobacco smoke contains at least 60 different ones. Tumours develop in the air-passages of the lung, so making part of the lung useless. About 90 per cent of lung cancer is caused by smoking, and even inhaling other people's smoke (passive smoking) is harmful. A person who smokes any cigarettes is 8 times more likely to die of lung cancer than a non-smoker; if 20 cigarettes are smoked every day the risk is 13 times greater.

Smoking and pregnancy   Smoking reduces the capacity of the blood to carry oxygen. Probably as a result of this, babies born to women who smoke during pregnancy are on average smaller than those of non-smoking mothers, and more of them die in the first year of life. Smoking during pregnancy also carries a higher risk of stillbirth or miscarriage.

Advice on smoking   For both children and adults, basic advice on smoking is simple: if you haven't started smoking, don't; if you have, give up now. If you can't stop on your own, seek help. The idea that smoking when young damages a person for life and that they might as well carry on is entirely false. If a person who smokes 20 cigarettes a day stops smoking entirely, after 10 years the risk of disease will have reduced to almost the same level as a non-smoker of the same age.

4 PLANTS

4.1 PLANTS AS LIVING THINGS: OBSERVING AND RECORDING CHANGE

Many children and some adults have difficulty in believing that plants are alive because they show no obvious activity: they don't appear to 'do anything'. This belief is unlikely to be changed quickly or easily. We are being scientific when we believe ideas that are consistent with evidence. However, scientists who claim to be knowledgeable about plants say that they are alive. This clash between everyday experience and scientific ideas happens in learning science quite often. Scientific ideas can be perceived as **counter-intuitive**: not obviously consistent with everyday experience. In this situation, we would be unscientific if we did not try to understand the scientists' evidence for their belief and also to test the idea for ourselves if we can. Teachers who find that their children do not think of plants as alive, can encourage them to investigate plants, wherever possible, in such a way that their ability to grow, respond and reproduce (2.2) is emphasized. This always means observing how plants change over time, which requires patience and good record keeping. Teachers may find that even when the idea becomes more familiar and accepted, children may still persist in thinking that although plants are alive, they are somehow less alive than animals are.

Section 4 is about how to cultivate plants in the classroom and plan the resources for teaching about green plants.

Young children can observe plant activity, focusing on noticing and recording changes in size and shape in plants as they grow and respond to stimuli. Records can include drawing, photography and making measurements, which are more reliable if a leaf or stem is marked harmlessly, for example with a small dot of white correcting fluid, to provide a reference-point. Children can make simple records in a table of such measurements as a plant's height, the number of leaves and the length of stem between leaves. Changes in the shape of growing leaves can be recorded and, if necessary, their area measured, by drawing round them carefully on squared paper. A decorative alternative is to spray a water-soluble dye such as 'Brusho' onto paper with a leaf pressed gently to it. Dye can then be washed off the leaf, which should continue to grow normally, while the 'shadow' of the leaf on the paper provides a permanent record of its shape.

From their active growing points (4.3), many plants produce sequences of very similar leaves or flowers, arranged at intervals down the stem. Because the youngest parts are nearest the tip, shoots and flower-spikes of this kind form what is in effect a time-sequence, showing the way in which the parts develop. Once the principle of growth and change over time is well established, these can be used very effectively to observe development, particularly that of flowers and fruits (4.5).

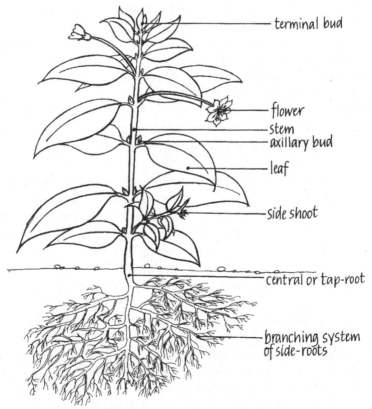

Figure 4.1 *The main parts of a flowering plant. The part of the plant above ground is the shoot system; the part below ground is the root system. The side-shoot and flowers have developed from axillary buds*

○ *Activity 4.1.1 is about how to measure stem and leaf growth.*

4.2 BASIC STRUCTURE AND FUNCTION IN FLOWERING PLANTS

The basic structure of flowering plants (other kinds of plant are briefly discussed in 5.2) can be understood in terms of a central axis, with specialized parts growing from it. Figure 4.1 is a drawing of a generalized flowering plant. No actual plant is exactly like this, but the drawing can usefully be thought of as a basic construction plan on which many variations are possible. It can be useful as a reference-point when trying to understand the forms of particular plants and identify their parts. In most plants that children will observe, but not all, the part above ground is the shoot system and the part below ground is the root system.

○ *Activity 4.2.1 investigates shoot systems and Activity 4.2.2 investigates root systems.*

Stem   In a shoot system the central axis is the stem. This supports the leaves so that they can exchange gases with the air and absorb light energy in order to make food (4.4), and the flowers in positions where they are likely to be pollinated (4.5). Stems also transport water and mineral nutrients (4.3) from the root system (see below) to the leaves and flowers. In many plants the stems are upright or branching, but in others they creep along the ground and may take root, so allowing the plant to colonize new areas of ground and reproduce itself (4.5).

Support, water supply and transport   In order to support leaves and flowers effectively, upright or branching stems need a remarkable combination of mechanical properties (Chapter 7). They must be stiff enough to support the weight of the shoot system as a whole, but flexible enough to bend and so avoid damage when the wind blows or animals push past them. They need to be elastic so that they will spring up again after they have been bent over, and very tough, so that if they are damaged they do not break off short and there is a possibility that they could repair themselves and carry on growing. In woody plants, the stems live for many years and grow in thickness, becoming harder, increasingly strong and very tough, as in the trunks and branches of trees.

All stems gain strength and toughness from their fibre-tissues, which also lend the same qualities to materials made from them, such as paper, card and some kinds of string. However, in both leaves and younger stems, water has a very important part to play in supporting the plant. Soft plant tissues are full of watery sap, which makes them quite stiff but also springy and elastic in bending (7.1.4–7.1.5). This stiffness not only keeps the plant upright but also keeps leaves held out so that they can intercept sunlight for photosynthesis (4.4). The importance of water can be seen if the plant loses too much by evaporation. Leaves and young stems wilt and droop down, and if the plant cannot obtain water within a short time, it may die.

Stems transport water upwards from the root system to the leaves and flowers, together with nutrient chemicals (4.3). Water evaporates from the shoot system and more water with nutrients in solution, is pulled up through a specialized tissue (xylem) to replace it. In trees and other woody plants, the xylem of older stems is the wood. Transport of food is more complex. It is carried out by a specialized tissue (phloem), which in trees forms part of the bark. In a tree during the growing season, food is transported down from the leaves for use or storage, but also upwards to growing shoots, flowers and developing fruits. In trees in spring, large amounts of stored food are moved up through the bark again, to provide materials and energy for the growth of new leaves (see also 4.4).

Leaf   The leaf is part of the shoot system. Leaves develop on the sides of stems, by which they are supported and supplied with water. Leaves can usually be distinguished because each has a bud (axillary bud) in the angle between its base and the stem (Fig. 4.1). The overall flat, thin form of most leaves is an adaptation (5.5) for their main function of making food by photosynthesis (4.4). Their form allows them to take in light energy and exchange gases with the air very efficiently. At the same time, all parts of the leaf have to be supplied with water and need a transport system to carry away the foods they have made to other parts of the plant. This is provided by the midrib and veins of a leaf which form a branching network system, easily seen with a hand-lens in a leaf held up to the light. The midrib and veins, like the stem, also have tough fibre tissues which help them to support and strengthen the thin leaf blade without making it too stiff. As a result, leaves are flexible: they can bend and move easily in air currents without damage, unless the wind is very severe.

Deciduous and evergreen trees   In many parts of the world, plants have a problem in obtaining enough water during part of the year, usually in the dry or cold season. Large plants such as trees solve this problem in two ways. Deciduous trees and shrubs shed all their leaves for part of the year, so that each leaf lives only for six to nine months. Evergreens, in contrast, have leaves which live for longer than a year but which are protected from drying up in a variety of ways. Some (for example holly, ivy and rhododendron) have a thick, glossy wax coating, while others are needle-like (pine and other conifers) or like tiny scales (heather). They do shed leaves, but because each one lives for longer than a year, they are not usually shed all at once.

Flowers   Flowers are special shoots whose function is sexual reproduction (4.5). Their various parts can be seen most easily in simple, open flowers such as the buttercup and tulip (Fig. 4.2 a, b). In the buttercup flower, the outermost parts (sepals) form a protective jacket round the flower-bud as it develops. The tulip has no sepals, but its petals are thicker and tougher, so they protect the inner parts of the flower in a similar way. Flowers pollinated by insects (4.5) need to attract them. To do this their petals may have bright colours, scent and make a sugary liquid (nectar).

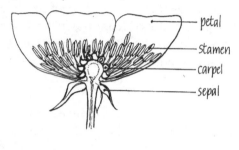

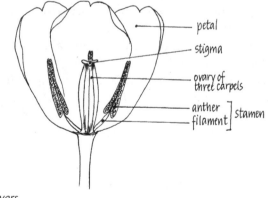

Figure 4.2 *Parts of flowers*

Inside the petals are the reproductive parts of the flower. The male parts (stamens) each consist of a stalk (filament) carrying a small sac (anther) which makes the male sex-cells (pollen). The filament holds the anther in such a way that an insect visiting the flower is likely to brush against some pollen and carry it away to another flower. The central part of the flower is the female part (ovary) in which the seeds will develop if pollination is successful (4.5). The ovary may be made up of many small, separate parts (carpels), as in the buttercup, or the carpels may be joined together to form a single structure, as in the tulip. The ovary, or each separate part of it, has a special receptive area (stigma) which receives pollen and so it is often sticky. The sticky stigma of a tulip flower is particularly large and easy to see. In many flowers the stigma is held on a stalk (style) in such a position that an insect visiting the flower is likely to brush against it, before it reaches the stamens, and leave pollen from another flower on it. The bluebell is one flower which shows this clearly.

Activity 4.2.3 is about how to investigate flowers.

Buds and bulbs   A bud is a shoot whose stem has not grown in length and whose leaves have not expanded, so they are tightly packed together. A Brussels sprout is an example of a large bud which is also edible. Most buds found at the bases of leaves are much smaller than this, but once they start to grow they will form shoot systems. A good way to see buds develop is to take cuttings and root them in water or compost. Suitable plants include willow twigs in late winter, pelargoniums ('geraniums') in late summer, and varieties of Tradescantia at almost any time.

In some plants, buds grow very large and make a specialized kind of shoot. One kind, which children can easily plant and see growing, are the bulbs of hyacinths, daffodils, tulips and onions. These are specialized underground shoots which are greatly enlarged buds. The fleshy scales are the leaves, which store food and water. They are joined to the stem, which is the 'plate' at the base of the bulb, from the bottom edge of which the roots also grow. Each year, new leaves grow from the centre. Their tops are the green leaves we usually see; their bases are the juicy storage leaves which make up the bulk of the bulb. When these grow old and die they form the brown papery 'skin' which helps to protect the bulb. The corms of crocuses are rather similar, except that the bulk of the corm is a short, stout stem.

Root system   The root system of plants is usually underground, because its main functions are to exploit the soil in order to meet the plant's needs. Most plants have a root system which anchors it in the soil, providing the shoot system with stability and support; absorbing water and mineral nutrients from the soil (4.3); and transporting these to the base of the shoot system. Some roots also store large amounts of food, transported to them from the leaves by the stem.

Roots have as many different forms, as shoots have. Some plants have a large central tap-root in which food is stored: carrots and parsnips are examples. Others have a central root when young, which branches out as the plant develops to exploit increasingly large volumes of soil, in order to meet the needs of the expanding shoot system. On a small scale, this kind of root system can be seen in bean plants, which are easily grown in the classroom (4.3), while on a larger scale this is the system developed by most trees. Some other plants such as grasses never have a central root at all, but develop a highly branched system of slender, fibrous roots.

Many plants have roots which develop directly from stems. This is what gardeners hope will happen when they take cuttings, but it also happens naturally when plants such as strawberries and creeping buttercup send out runners to colonize new areas (4.5). Ivy is a plant which climbs by means of roots, which grow out of its stem into cracks in walls or tree-bark. These aerial roots do not absorb any water: their only function is support. Roots also grow directly from stems when a bulb (see above) grows roots from its base.

Some plants have 'roots' which are not roots at all. Iris and Solomon's seal, for example, have a stout, slowly creeping stock which looks like a root, but is actually a stem (rhizome) because it has buds from which green shoots and flowers develop. It also has roots growing from it which anchor the whole plant and take up water in the usual way. Ginger is a rhizome, used in cooking.

Roots as anchorage   In order to anchor plants effectively in windy conditions, roots, like stems, have to be tough and flexible, but their main strength needs to be in withstanding pulling rather than bending forces (7.1.3). When plants such as trees grow for many years and develop large shoot systems, their root systems are usually about equal in size. In an oak tree, for example, the roots do not usually go as deep as the shoots are high, but spread a good deal further, giving the tree a broad, stable base. Like the trunk and branches, the roots of trees grow in thickness, becoming woody, strong and extremely tough to support the great weight of the plant above ground.

Absorption: root-hairs   Apart from support, the main function of roots is the taking up of water and mineral nutrients (4.3) from the soil. To do this effectively, the outer layer of a growing root develops, just behind its tip, what looks like a covering of white fur. This is made up of root-hairs: very slender outgrowths which can push between soil particles as they grow, providing a huge area through which water can be absorbed.

Children can observe root-hairs by cutting small slits in a thin sheet of plastic foam, putting a cress seed in each, soaking the foam in water and hanging it inside a jar with the lid on. As the seeds germinate and their roots grow out, they will form root-hairs in the humid air, so children can see them easily.

In most plants, root-hairs are short-lived. They grow only on new, extending roots and last only a few weeks. The advantage of this for the plant is that the soil it is exploiting for water and nutrients is continually changing, so a good supply can be maintained.

4.3 PLANT GROWTH

A major difference between the growth of plants and that of animals, which children can easily observe, is that whereas animals grow all over, the roots and shoots of plants grow in particular places. The most obvious growth is at shoot tips, where new leaves or flowers are forming, expanding and being moved apart as the stem grows longer, and observation of seedlings (see below) will show that roots grow at their tips in a similar way.

Long-lived woody plants (trees and shrubs) have stems and roots which become thicker all over, but here again all the growth comes from a special layer (cambium), just inside the bark. This produces wood to the inside and bark to the outside. Because wood is not produced in winter it grows in layers (annual rings) with a more or less distinct line between one season's growth and the next. Bark can easily be stripped from most woody twigs in spring and summer, because the cambium is active, soft and easily pulled apart. As tree trunks grow in thickness, the expanding wood stretches the outer layers of the bark so that they split, forming furrows or peeling off in pieces.

Activity 4.3.1 investigates patterns of plant growth.

Seeds and germination   Seeds are the product of sexual reproduction in flowering plants and conifers (4.5). The seed is an undeveloped plant (embryo), with a store of food, in a protective coat. Many plants are grown for their edible seeds. In a cereal grain, for example, the food-store is mostly carbohydrate (starch), the embryo is a source of protein and the protective seed-coat provides us with dietary fibre (3.4). Most seeds are fairly hard, dry and apparently inactive: they are alive, but dormant (2.2). In order to become active, the seed has to be in conditions which are favourable for growth. Some seeds need special conditions to break their dormancy, but for most, the three conditions needed are: a supply of water, a supply of air and a suitable temperature.

The early phase of a seed's growth is known as **germination**. The best seeds for children to observe are large ones, such as broad beans. These can be grown in jars lined with absorbent paper and then filled with sand. Seeds pushed down between the paper and jar are held firmly, and watering can be carried out easily by keeping the sand damp. Root and shoot growth will proceed in a more natural way if the jar is shaded with black paper.

It is difficult for children to obtain direct evidence that air is needed for germination, but gaining evidence that water is needed is simple: if the seeds remain dry, they never germinate. The importance of temperature can be investigated by placing soaked seeds in a refrigerator, with a control batch in the classroom. The seeds in the cold will not germinate until they are brought into warmer conditions. It should also be noted that, although light is needed for healthy plant growth, it is not needed for germination of most seeds, which will readily begin their growth in the dark.

Activity 4.3.2 is about how to observe germination.

The first phase of germination is water uptake. Beans can be measured, weighed and drawn before and after having been soaked in water for 24 hours, to show the large quantity of water they absorb. Water enables the embryo to become active and start digesting the food reserves of the seed so that these can be used for growth and respiration. The first sign of growth is usually the splitting of the seed-coat as the root (radicle) begins to emerge. In most seeds the root grows out before the shoot, to provide anchorage and absorb water. When the root emerges from a bean, children will be able to see whether they have planted the seed the right way up, i.e. so that its root points down as it emerges. If not, the root will respond by turning as it grows until it points down; an example of a response in plants (see below).

The shoot, which usually emerges some days after the root, responds in the opposite way: if upside-down, it will turn as it grows to point up. The emerging shoot is bent over, so that as it pushes up through the soil the delicate leaves in the bud at its tip will not be damaged. As it emerges into the light the shoot-tip unbends and the leaves start to expand. As the shoot of the seedling grows, the root system will also be expanding, branching out so that it can absorb more water and nutrients to support the rapid growth of the whole plant.

Many seeds have their food-store in two very thick structures which are actually leaves, even though they do not look like leaves. In some, such as the broad bean, these seed-leaves (cotyledons) stay in the ground during germination, but in others such as the sunflower they emerge as the first green leaves of the shoot: thick, rounded and quite unlike the leaves which develop later.

Conditions for healthy plant growth   The conditions under which plants will continue to grow well are similar to those needed for germination, but with two additional requirements. Because seeds have a food-store they can germinate and begin to grow with no more than a supply of water and air. To sustain growth in the long term, the plant has to be able to make food by photosynthesis, and for this light is needed as an energy source (4.4). In addition, a supply of mineral nutrients is needed for the plant to use the food it makes for growth, in particular for making proteins. Mineral nutrients are simple chemicals which plants normally take in with water, through their roots from the soil.

Children can gain evidence of the **need for nutrients** by comparing the growth of plants in silver sand, which supplies no nutrients, with the growth of very similar plants in soil. Suitable plants are seedlings of cereals such as wheat or oats, all planted in similar pots. Another kind of evidence can be gained by comparing some which are given pure water only, with little or no nutrient supply, with others which are watered with liquid houseplant fertilizer, used in accordance with the maker's instructions. After a few weeks the difference in growth and appearance shows clearly the role which nutrients play in healthy growth.

Children can gain evidence of the **need for light** for healthy plant growth. If seedlings are germinated in the dark they grow more rapidly than normal but become thin, spindly and have only a yellow colour in their leaves rather than the normal green. A more successful way to show this, however, is to start growing bulbs in the dark, then bring some into the light as they begin to sprout. Daffodils can be used in winter; onions during the rest of the year. Those left in darkness show the same rapid growth and yellow colour as the seedlings, but when brought into the light they recover better, developing the normal green colour of chlorophyll (4.4).

Some plants which live in dry regions of the world can survive for a long time without water, but in order to remain alive and grow, most plants need a constant supply. If they are deprived of water their shoots wilt and become floppy. If water is supplied at once, wilted plants will usually recover, but eventually a point is reached where they cannot recover and they die.

Activity 4.3.3 investigates conditions needed for germination.

Growth and response   Observing plants germinate and develop shows clearly that they are just as active as animals are, but live at a slower pace: the changes take longer. The same is true of their responses. Plants respond in many ways to changes in their environment, and some of their responses are easier to observe than those of animals, but because they take hours or days rather than seconds or minutes, they are often overlooked. The responses children can observe most easily are those to light and gravity, which can clearly be related to the plants' survival.

Children can gain evidence that shoots need to be in light, to support the idea that they have the best chance of making food by photosynthesis if they grow both upwards and towards any light source.

Help children gain evidence of a plant's response to gravity by placing a potted plant on its side and observe it growing more on its lower side so that in a few days it turns upwards, even in the dark. Seedlings make a similar response, but even more quickly. If put in light from one side, almost any plant will detect the direction of the light and respond by growing more on the shaded side. This causes the shoot to bend towards the light, and seedlings show particularly rapid responses of this kind: it is usual to see obvious bending within 24 hours.

Roots need to grow downwards to anchor the plant, and they do this by a response to gravity which is exactly the reverse of that shown by shoots: the root of a seedling bean placed horizontally grows more on its upper side, so that it turns to grow downwards. Most roots do not respond to light. Children can see the responses of roots and shoots by deliberately planting beans upside down, i.e. with the seedling root pointing upwards, and recording the sequence of growth.

Activity 4.3.4 investigates the effects of environmental conditions on plant growth.
Activity 4.3.6 investigates the response of shoots to light.
Activity 4.3.7 investigates the response of shoots to gravity.
Activity 4.3.8 investigates the response of roots to gravity.

4.4 PHOTOSYNTHESIS

Unlike animals, plants do not have to take in high-energy foods, because they make their own. The process by which they do this is called photosynthesis. It is difficult to carry out useful investigations of photosynthesis at primary level, though children can sample and enjoy some of its products, but some understanding of it is important because it is the basis of all food-chains (5.7) and it maintains the gas balance in the atmosphere (5.8). It can therefore be seen as a process on which almost all life on Earth depends.

The energy source for photosynthesis is light, normally light from the Sun. In most plants by far the greatest amount of photosynthesis takes place in the leaves. Because the leaves are flat and thin, they allow the plant to have a very large area exposed to daylight, so that even if the light is not very bright the leaves have a large energy source available. Some of the light energy falling on the leaf is absorbed by the green pigment chlorophyll. Like other green-coloured substances, chlorophyll absorbs red and blue light and reflects the green (13.11.2). When an ordinary material absorbs light energy, it is simply heated as a result

(9.2.4). What is unusual about chlorophyll is that most of the light energy it absorbs can be transferred as chemical-potential energy (9.2.8) in a complex series of chemical changes. These result in the formation of high-energy food chemicals, such as grape-sugar (glucose) and cane-sugar (sucrose).

Activity 4.4.1 investigates plants as food makers.

This is another area of science where the ideas cannot easily be taught using direct evidence, so good sources of indirect experience need to be provided by the teacher.

The raw materials for photosynthesis are water absorbed by the roots from the soil and transported to the leaves by the stem, and carbon dioxide gas, taken in directly by the leaves from the air around them. The waste product is oxygen, which escapes from the leaf into the air. This exchange of gases, like the absorption of light energy, is made much more efficient by the flat, thin form of the leaves. Photosynthesis can be summarized chemically thus:

$$\text{carbon dioxide} + \text{water} \rightarrow \text{sugars} + \text{oxygen}$$

Plants and the gas balance   The above summary of photosynthesis shows that in the light plants take in carbon dioxide, which is breathed out by animals and produced by the burning of fuels (8.3.2, 9.2.8), and exchange it for oxygen, which animals need for respiration and without which they would die. Life on Earth depends on the balance between the two gases (6.1), and photosynthesis is the only way in which it can be maintained.

Plants, like animals, use food as a source of energy for their living processes such as growth and reproduction. Like animals, they transfer energy by breaking down food by respiration, which requires oxygen. In bright light this process is hard to detect because the plant is making food by photosynthesis much faster than it is being used in respiration. In the dark, a plant respires and exchanges gases with the air, like an animal does, taking in oxygen and giving out carbon dioxide. Over a 24-hour period, however, the plant will take in more carbon dioxide than it gives out, and will give out more oxygen than it takes in, and end up with a surplus of food which can be used for growth or storage.

Transport, growth and storage of food in plants Food made by photosynthesis is transported away from the leaves by the stem and distributed to all parts of the plant. Some of this food is used in shoots and roots for growth and the rest of it is stored. Like animals, plants need proteins to make new living tissue and grow, but unlike animals they can make proteins for themselves using sugars from photosynthesis and mineral nutrients from the soil. As part of their growth, plants also use food made by photosynthesis in quite a different way. Unlike animals such as humans, plants have no specialized skeleton to give them support. As they grow, the living tissues of plants develop built-in support from a tough, strong, fibre-forming chemical called cellulose, made from sugars. In soft tissues like leaves this support remains flexible, but in thick stems and roots which have to support a great weight of shoot it becomes hard and very tough: the material we call wood. Plant fibres such as cotton, which is almost pure cellulose, are also the products of growth using the foods made by photosynthesis as the raw material. Humans cannot use cellulose for food because they cannot digest it, though other, plant-eating animals can. It is, however, an important part of the human diet as dietary fibre (3.4).

Plants do not usually use all the food they make for growth: large amounts are often stored, and are an essential food source for humans and many animals. In this way, plants form the basis of food-chains (5.7, 5.8). As well as soft tissues which we can use for food, many plants store food in their wood and bark, not only in stems but in roots as well. Children can usefully observe and eat a range of raw plant foods. One of the commonest stored foods is starch, a carbohydrate, which we obtain mostly from potatoes (swollen underground stems) and cereal grains (seeds). Sugar-cane and sugar-beet store so much sugar that it can be extracted as the sugar we use, but carrots store enough sugar to taste quite sweet. Many plants store fats in the form of oil, particularly in seeds such as sunflower, peanuts and Brazil nuts. Sweet, fleshy fruits such as plums, oranges and strawberries are rather different, because their food-stores are not for the plant's use, but to attract animals which distribute their seeds (4.5).

Activity 4.3.5 investigates plants and water.
Activity 4.4.2 investigates plant products as energy stores.

4.5 PLANT REPRODUCTION

Humans and nearly all animals which children will observe can make more of their own kind in only one way: sexual reproduction. Plants reproduce sexually, but many also have other ways of increasing their numbers, more directly related to the ways in which they grow. The life-cycle of any living thing can be seen as a sequence of events or stages, centred on its reproduction. The life-cycle of plants, including both sexual and asexual stages, is summarized in Figure 4.3.

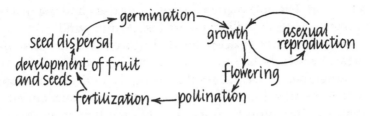

Figure 4.3 *Life-cycle of plants*

Asexual reproduction   Any kind of reproduction which does not involve fertilization (see below) is asexual, i.e. non-sexual. Many plants with which children are likely to be familiar multiply in this way. The most obvious examples are plants which grow outwards rather than upwards, rooting as they spread: creeping buttercup, strawberry and bramble are examples. As their shoots touch the soil they form roots at the tips, and buds grow at the rooting points to form independent plants. Many more plants spread by way of creeping underground shoots, which grow outwards and then send green shoots up into the air. Bindweed, stinging nettles, couch grass (twitch) and many other troublesome weeds are plants of this kind. Still other plants do not spread rapidly, but form dense colonies, for example daisies on a lawn and expanding clumps of daffodils or bluebells.

The ability of plants to reproduce asexually is exploited by gardeners in propagating good varieties of plants by cuttings (a form of cloning). These are most often pieces of shoot which are cut from the parent plant and placed in conditions which encourage root growth: usually warmth and a humid atmosphere. In some plants the shoot does not branch, so leaf-cuttings are used instead, as in African violets and begonias.

Activity 4.5.1 investigates plants' asexual reproduction.

Sexual reproduction in plants   As in animals, sexual reproduction in plants involves the fertilization of a female egg-cell by a male sex-cell, which in plants is formed by the pollen grain. In plants, sexual reproduction involves four distinct phases: pollination, fertilization, the development of seeds and fruits, and seed dispersal. The plant's life-cycle begins again with germination of the seed (4.3).

Activity 4.5.2 investigates plants' sexual reproduction.

Pollination   To be able to fertilize the egg-cell, the pollen grain has first to be moved from the anther which makes it, to the receptive stigma on the ovary (4.2).

This is pollination. The pollen grain cannot move itself and so must be carried. The two commonest agents of pollination are insects and wind.

Insects are attracted to insect-pollinated flowers because they make a sugary liquid (nectar) on which the insects can feed. The nectar is often 'advertized' by brightly coloured petals, scent, or both. The pollen of these flowers is fairly heavy and sticky. The detailed form of flowers varies a great deal, but all of them make it likely that a visiting insect, on its way into the flower to feed on nectar, will brush against the stigma. If the insect is carrying pollen, the stigma is likely to pick some up from its body. The anthers are also positioned so that insects are likely to collide with them, covering themselves with pollen. Bees, which are important as flower pollinators, actually collect pollen and use it as a high-protein food in rearing their larvae.

Wind-pollinated flowers are quite different from insect-pollinated ones. Grass flowers are a good example: they are small, not brightly coloured and have neither scent nor nectar. Instead of the anthers and stigma being inside the flower, they hang outside to catch any air-current that is moving. The pollen is very light, dry and dust-like, so it is easily blown off the anthers and carried on the wind. When breathed in by some people, pollen of this kind causes hay fever. The stigma of a grass flower is feathery, so it filters the passing air currents and has a better chance of catching a pollen grain of the right kind. Other wind-pollinated flowers children may find are the catkins (male flowers) of birch, alder and hazel; but those of willow ('pussy-willows') are pollinated by insects.

Activity 4.5.3 investigates pollination.

Fertilization   After pollination, the pollen-grain grows a very slender tube, visible only with a microscope, from the stigma into the ovary. The female egg-cells are in the tiny, undeveloped seeds (ovules) which can be seen by cutting open the ovary of a flower such as a bluebell. The pollen-grain makes a special sex-cell which is moved down the tube into the ovule and joins with the egg-cell it contains. This is fertilization, and if the egg-cell is not fertilized, the seed will not develop.

Seeds and fruits   After fertilization, many changes occur in the flower, often quite rapidly. The petals and stamens wither and fall off and the ovary begins to grow bigger. The fertilized ovules in the ovary grow to form the seeds, each seed being an embryo plant, with a food-store, in a tough protective coat (4.3). During development the seeds are protected by the ovary, sometimes called the seed-case. The sequence of changes can easily be seen in plants which have simple spikes of flowers, such as bluebell, snapdragon and willow herb.

The ovary or seed-case, with the seeds inside it, is the fruit. In many plants the seed-case develops in such a way that it helps to spread the seeds away from the parent plant once they are ripe (see below). Observing how fruits are related to the way that their seeds are dispersed is an excellent way to introduce the concept of adaptation (5.5, 5.6).

Activity 4.5.4 investigates the development of fruit and seeds.

Seed dispersal   If all the seeds produced by a plant simply fell to the ground and germinated, there would be overcrowding, few would survive and the plant would spread slowly, if at all. This means that reproduction is more likely to be successful and ensure the survival of that kind of plant if the seeds are dispersed. There are many ways in which this can happen, each of which involves a special development of the seed-case. The three main groups of seed dispersal are:

- *Dispersal by animals*: sweet, fleshy fruits (cherries, blackberries) are eaten by animals; the seeds remain undigested and are passed out with their faeces. Hooked fruits (goosegrass) catch on the fur of mammals and are carried away before they drop off or are removed.
- *Dispersal by wind*: some fruits (dandelion, thistle) develop parachutes and others (sycamore, lime) a wing, so that when they fall the wind will carry them for some distance before they reach the ground. The fruits of poppies and campions are like pepper-pots: the small, light seeds are shaken out and scattered as the slender stems are moved by the wind.
- *Self-dispersal*: some plants develop seed-cases which shrink as they dry, setting up large tension and twisting forces. When the fruit finally snaps, the seeds are thrown or flicked out over a wide area. Examples include gorse, broom, vetch, violet and cranesbill.

Activity 4.5.5 investigates the dispersal of fruit and seeds.

5 VARIATION, CLASSIFICATION, ADAPTATION AND THE ENVIRONMENT

INTRODUCTION

There are two reasons for developing an ability to recognize animals and plants found locally and those learned about through reading, TV programmes or the internet. First, it enables children to communicate effectively about living things which interest or concern them. Second, the ability to name even the broad group to which an animal or plant belongs makes it possible to access information about it, identify it more accurately and learn about it in more depth. This is particularly important when investigating the ways in which plants and animals are adapted to their ways of life (5.6) and the role which they play in their habitats (5.7), because detailed information can often be obtained only through long-term observation which children cannot carry out for themselves.

5.1 A VARIETY OF ANIMALS

In the summary of information given here, animals which children are likely to find in local habitats are listed, while those which they may know about from reading, TV, the internet, visits or holidays are given in square brackets. Related animals are listed on the same line, so each line represents a distinct group. The summary is followed by a brief description of each major group.

Animals are divided into two great groups: those which have backbones (vertebrates) and those which do not (invertebrates). Invertebrates are much more varied, so it is easiest to distinguish them by a process of elimination. If an animal is not a fish, amphibian, reptile, bird or mammal, it is an invertebrate.

Section 5.1 provides advice about how to observe a variety of animals.

5.1.1 Invertebrates

There are 25 major groups; children are likely to gain direct experience of only **three**. Keys to these are given in section 5.4.

Molluscs: slugs, snails [octopus, squid]
This group includes octopus and squid, but children will usually observe slugs and snails. These have slimy skins, no legs and move on a muscular 'foot'. Each animal has both male and female sex organs (i.e. is hermaphrodite). They mate and lay eggs. They have simple eyes on stalks; most feed on living and dead plants, which they rasp with a toothed tongue. All slugs live on land; different snails live on land, in fresh water and in the sea.

Annelids: earthworms, leeches
Annelids are worms with no legs, slimy skins and round bodies divided into segments. Children may observe earthworms and leeches. Leeches live in fresh water by sucking blood from large animals or preying on small ones. They have a sucker on their hind end to anchor them while feeding, and can swim by passing waves along the body. Earthworms live on land, feeding on dead leaves which they grind up with soil in their gut. They are very important in soil formation and fertility (7.4). They are hermaphrodite, but mate and lay eggs.

Arthropods:
- *crustaceans*: woodlice [crabs, lobsters, shrimps]
- *arachnids*: spiders [scorpions]
- *chilopods*: centipedes
- *insects*: dragonflies, damselflies, grasshoppers [locusts], earwigs, houseflies, bluebottles, craneflies, aphids, bugs, ants, bees, wasps, butterflies, moths and beetles

Arthropods, the 'jointed foot' animals, are a very large and diverse group, which includes far more kinds of animal than any other. All, at least when adult, have jointed legs and a skeleton which is on the outside of the body. They grow by shedding this periodically and growing a new one. They have separate sexes and lay eggs. Children are likely to encounter **four** of the 13 major classes of arthropods.

1. **Crustaceans** include crabs, shrimps and lobsters, but the most familiar ones are woodlice, which are the only land-dwelling members of the group. Woodlice have oval bodies distinctly divided into segments, with a pair of legs to each, and short feelers (antennae). They feed on decaying plant material. The female

retains the eggs in a special pouch until they have hatched. Woodlouse behaviour may be studied as an example of adaptation (5.6).

2. **Arachnids** include spiders as well as scorpions. Spiders have bodies divided into two distinct parts. The front part (cephalothorax) includes the head and bears four pairs of legs. It is most often separated by a narrow waist from the abdomen behind. Nearly all spiders prey on other animals, but none eats solid food: they inject their prey with digestive juices and suck in the resulting liquid. Many spiders trap their prey in webs which have a beautiful pattern, but the ability to make these is not learned: it is an example of inborn (instinctive) behaviour.

3. **Chilopods** are the centipedes. They have long, narrow, segmented bodies with one pair of legs to each segment, and long antennae. They are fast-moving predators which live in the soil or under stones, and have poison fangs on the underside of the head.

4. **Insects** are a very large and diverse group. All have, at least when adult, a body divided into three parts (head, thorax and abdomen) with three pairs of legs on the thorax. Most also have two pairs of wings on the thorax, but flies have only one pair and worker ants have none, while in earwigs, bugs and beetles the forewings are thicker and harder, forming a case for the thin hind-wings. Insects have two main ways of developing. Dragonflies, damselflies, grasshoppers, earwigs and bugs hatch from eggs as nymphs, which have six legs and are obviously insects, though they may not reach anything like the adult form until their final moult. The other kinds of insect hatch into more or less worm-like grubs (larvae) which may be difficult to identify as insects at all. At the end of their growth the larvae enter an apparently dormant phase inside a special case (pupa). During this time they undergo profound changes (metamorphosis) to develop the form of the adult insect (imago).

5.1.2 Vertebrates

These are animals with backbones and skeletons inside their bodies, including a protective brain-case (cranium). In all except the soft-skeleton fishes, the skeleton is made of bone. There are **five** major groups; children are likely to encounter or learn about all of them. Keys to these are given in section 5.4.

Fish:
• *soft skeleton*: [sharks]
• *bony skeleton*: stickleback, minnow, bullhead [ornamental and tropical fish]

All live entirely in water and breathe by pumping water over gills at either side of the head. All lay eggs, but in some these are retained in the body of a parent until they hatch: guppies are an example. Sticklebacks are remarkable for nest-building and the care of eggs and newly-hatched fry by the male.

Amphibians: newts, frogs, toads

Newts, frogs and toads live on land for most of the year, but all lose water easily by evaporation, so have to stay in damp places and hunt mainly at night. They breathe air with simple lungs but can also breathe through their skins. They breed in fresh water, laying eggs which are fertilized externally and protected by a coat of jelly. These hatch into a juvenile phase (tadpole) which breathes with gills until its lungs develop. Newts can be distinguished from lizards because lizards have a scaly skin which is quite dry.

Reptiles: [turtles, tortoises] [lizards, snakes] [crocodiles]

Reptiles have dry, scaly skins which resist water loss, and breathe air with lungs. They breed on land, fertilization is internal and nearly all lay soft-shelled eggs which hatch into young resembling the adults in form. Children are not likely to encounter native snakes and lizards during fieldwork, but extinct reptiles (dinosaurs) are always of interest.

Birds: ducks, geese, hawks [falcons, eagles], domestic fowl, turkeys, partridge, pheasant, pigeons [parrots, budgerigars], owls, [gulls], [kingfishers], woodpeckers, perching birds (includes all common garden and town birds not listed above)

Birds have feathers, breathe air with complex lungs and maintain a high, constant body temperature (are 'warm-blooded'). Fertilization is internal and they lay hard-shelled eggs which are protected and incubated until hatching. Parental care is highly developed, involving feeding and usually teaching of skills and behaviour as well. Most birds can fly and many migrate long distances to exploit seasonal food supplies.

Mammals:
- *egg-laying*: [platypus, spiny ant-eater]
- *pouched*: [kangaroos]
- *placental*: hedgehog, mole, bats, whales, porpoises, [dolphins], hare, rabbit. Carnivores including dog, cat, fox, weasel, [wolf, bear], [seals], [elephants]. Single-hoofed mammals including horse, [rhinoceros]. Cloven-hoofed mammals including pig, cow, sheep, deer, [camels, giraffe]. Rodents including mouse, rat, hamster, guinea-pig, gerbil. Primates including [apes], human beings.

Mammals are warm-blooded animals whose females feed their young with milk. By far the biggest group of mammals are those which sustain the foetus in the uterus with a placenta (3.11). All have water-resistant skin; in most this is covered with fur which helps to maintain their high body temperature. Apart from the whales and their relatives, all mammals breed on land, and all show a very high degree of parental care.

5.2 A VARIETY OF PLANTS

Section 5.2 provides advice about how to observe a variety of plants.

Plants are no more difficult to place correctly in their major groups than animals are; but the overwhelming majority of plants that children will encounter are members of **one** group: the flowering plants. Dividing these into smaller groups (the equivalent of distinguishing ducks and falcons among birds, or rodents and carnivores among mammals) is much more difficult, and for most purposes unnecessary at primary level, so this is not attempted here.

Plants   There are four major groups; children are likely to encounter all of them. Keys to these are given in section 5.4.

Algae: blanket-weed in ponds, bright green coloration on trees and walls, [seaweeds]

Bryophytes: mosses, liverworts

Pteridophytes: ferns, horsetails

Spermatophytes: seed plants
• *conifers*: pines, spruces, firs, cedars, cypresses, [juniper], yew
• *flowering plants*: monocotyledons, dicotyledons (Includes all familiar large plants, except those listed above).

5.3 A VARIETY OF OTHER LIVING THINGS

Section 5.3 advises about how to observe a variety of other living things.

Although the living things children are likely to be most aware of are animals and plants, there are others which influence our lives profoundly in a variety of ways, and which belong to neither group. Children may need to learn about three of them: bacteria, fungi and lichens.

Bacteria   are microscopic organisms which have a much simpler structure than the cells which make up animals and plants. Bacteria are very small: typically a few thousandths of a millimetre long, and exist everywhere in the environment, even in our bodies, in enormous numbers. A few can make their own food using light or chemicals as their energy source, but most obtain their food by digesting dead or, more rarely, living material. The result of digesting dead material is decay, and the role of most bacteria is as decomposers (5.8), recycling material in the environment. When bacteria attack living material, either plant or animal, they cause disease. Other kinds of disease can arise when bacteria decaying food excrete poisonous waste which is then eaten by an animal. This danger is a major reason why food hygiene is important. It is worth emphasizing to children that very few of the many kinds of bacteria in the environment cause diseases in humans, but those that do can be very serious, so personal hygiene is also important.

Examples of bacterial activity which children may encounter include the spoilage of food already referred to. Decayed food usually has an offensive smell caused by the products of bacterial digestion: avoiding it is an instinctive (inborn, unlearned) defensive behaviour. They should also learn about the formation of bacterial plaque on teeth, and tooth decay (3.2); and may investigate the making of yogurt from milk (8.3.1), which uses different bacteria from those which make milk go sour.

Fungi are sometimes incorrectly described as plants. They are a separate, distinct and very large group of organisms, most of which feed by digesting (decaying) dead remains of plants and animals. With the bacteria, they are the main decomposers of the ecosystem (5.8). The body of most fungi is threadlike, spreading throughout whatever food they are digesting. The large 'fungi' which are frequently seen in autumn, such as mushrooms and toadstools, are simply the reproductive bodies of a much larger organism. Some of these are edible, but others which look quite like them are deadly poisonous and kill people every year. Children should be warned against eating any fungi not identified as edible by a competent adult. Some fungi attack plants, causing diseases such as blights and mildews, and a few cause diseases of animals.

When fungi digest food, they produce a range of chemicals as a result. Some of these are poisonous and offensive, but controlled decay by fungi gives many cheeses their distinctive flavours and textures. The most widely used fungus, however, is also one of the most unusual: yeast. Wild yeasts live in sugary liquids such as nectar and fruit juice. When their air supply is shut off they do not die, but respire by converting the sugar to alcohol, which is the basis of brewing and winemaking. Yeast grows very fast in a warm environment and gives out carbon dioxide gas as it respires. This is the basis of its use in dough to leaven it, making the bread lighter, easier to chew and digest and improving its flavour (8.3.1).

Activity 5.3.1 considers how to observe food-decaying microbes.

Lichens   are not a single organism but a close association (symbiosis) between a fungus and a green alga (5.2). The alga can live without the protection of the fungus, but the fungus cannot live without the food made by the alga. Lichens are very diverse and are found in all parts of the world, partly because some of them can withstand extremes of heat, cold and drought. They have no roots, and are very important as the first colonizers of bare rock, which in many areas begins the process of soil formation (7.4). Most are slow-growing, and because they absorb water through their upper surface, are very sensitive to pollution in air and rainwater. As a result, they can be used as indicators of how clean the air is and how pollution levels are changing.

5.4 CLASSIFICATION

The National Curriculum for Science requires pupils, in Sc2.4, to learn to identify living things using keys and assign them to groups. Thus classification can be thought of, alongside observation, questioning and hypothesizing, as an important component of being scientific. So it is worth remembering this general, investigative meaning of classification: a purposeful ability to sort any set or collection of things into groups based on observation and thinking about similarities and differences. Scientists often use this skill in learning, just as young children do and have developed many ways of putting living things into groups, with a range of purposes, one of which is to make keys for identification.

Classification using keys

Keys are devices used to classify or identify unknown members of a population. To classify things is to put them into groups which have something in common, such as stars, mountains or cathedrals, whereas to identify something is to distinguish it as a particular kind of thing within its class, or even as a unique individual. For example, my body classifies me as a male human, but my fingerprints identify me as an individual.

Anything can be classified and identified by making and using keys. Examples could include cars, foods, football teams and buildings; but here attention will be confined to plants and animals. Many books on plants, animals and other organisms concentrate on identification and most of these use keys. Because accurate naming is needed to gain access to information on particular kinds of living things, learning to use keys is a useful and important skill.

Two types of key   All keys work by requiring the user to make a structured sequence of observations and to take decisions on the basis of these. There are two main ways in which they can be constructed. The simpler but less useful of these is the decision-tree, which is based on questions. At each stage, questions are posed which require a simple yes or no answer, and the layout is in the form of a diagram, so that the route through the key is easy to follow. Examples of decision-trees are given in Figures 5.1, 5.2 and 5.3.

The more complex form is the statement-key. At each stage the user has two (occasionally more) statements from which to choose, each of which leads either to an identification or to the number of the next section to be consulted. This is more complex, but also more accurate than the decision-tree, because more information is both available to and required from the user at each stage. The statement-key to invertebrate groups given below has exactly the same structure as the decision-tree in Figure 5.1, so that the two can be compared.

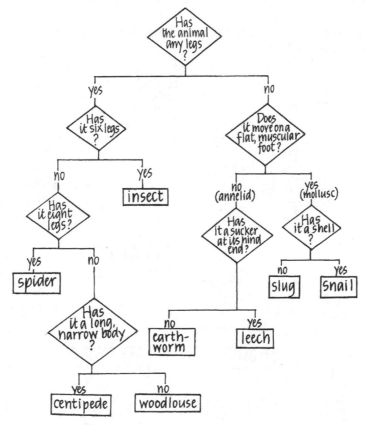

Figure 5.1 *Key to groups of invertebrates*

Key to major groups of invertebrate animals

1. Has legs	2
Has no legs	5
2. Has six legs	insect
Has more than six legs	3
3. Has eight legs	spider
Has more than eight legs	4
4. Body more or less oval, feelers short	woodlouse
Body long and narrow, feelers long	centipede
5. Moves on a flat muscular foot; eyes on stalks	6 (mollusc)
Body wormlike; does not move on flat under-surface	7 (annelid)
6. Has spiral shell into which animal can retreat	snail
Has no shell, or only a tiny one	slug
7. Sucker at hind end; lives in water	leech
No sucker; lives in soil	earthworm

A corresponding pair of decision-tree and statement-key are given for vertebrate animals in Figure 5.2.

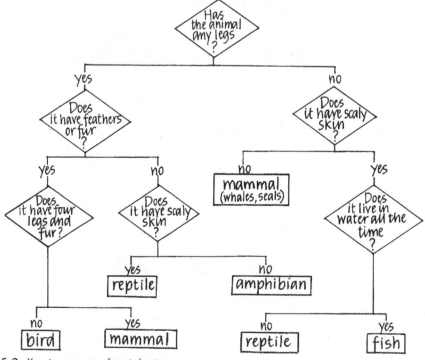

Figure 5.2 *Key to groups of vertebrates*

Key to groups of vertebrate animals

1. Has no legs   2
   Has legs   4
2. Has scaly skin   3
   Has no scales (large marine animals)   mammal (whales and seals)
3. Lives all the time in water; breathes by pumping
   water over gills   fish
   Lives on land (occasionally swims)   reptile (snake)
4. Has body covering of feathers or fur   5
   Has smooth, warty, slimy or scaly skin   6
5. Has four legs and fur (hair) on body   mammal
   Has two legs, two wings and feathers   bird
6. Has smooth, warty or slimy skin   amphibian
   Has scaly, dry skin (some also have a shell)   reptile (lizards, crocodiles,
                                                   tortoises, turtles)

Key to major groups of plants

1. Plant body not divided into different parts.   2
   Plant body divided into at least two different parts
   (stems, roots, leaves)   4
2. Grows under water   alga
   Grows on soil, tree-bark or walls   3
3. Plant microscopic, forming green layer on trees and walls   alga (Pleurococcus)
   Plant body ribbon-like and branching, 5–15 mm wide, often
   curly at edges   liverwort
4. Plant has green leaves   5
   Leaves present only as tiny brown scales   horsetail
5. Never has flowers, cones or catkins   6
   Has flowers, cones or catkins   7 (seed plant)
6. At least some leaves 2 cm long, usually much longer   fern
   All leaves less than 2 cm long, low tufted or creeping plants moss
7. Plant woody (tree or shrub)   8
   Plant not woody   flowering plant
8. Leaves needle- or scale-like; may have catkins or cones,
   but no flowers   conifer
   Leaves broad or, if needle- or scale-like, with obvious flowers flowering plant

   The limitations of the decision-tree become more apparent as accurate separation of groups becomes more difficult; for example, when an attempt is made to classify all the plants children might find. One such attempt is given in Figure 5.3. It would work for most plants, but a few such as duckweed and some heathers could be misplaced using it. The extra observation called for by the statement-key given below makes it more reliable, though it is more difficult to use.

The keys given here are intended as illustrative examples, which may also be useful in classifying animals and plants into broad groups. When beginning to use keys, children should be given examples of the decision-tree type which are restricted in scope, concentrating on a small set of related variables such as the size and shape of leaves in a given range of commonly grown trees and shrubs, or the characteristics of wild flowers found around the school. To begin with, the selected plants or animals should be few in number and very easily distinguished. Progress can then be made by including an increased number of organisms which require more detailed observations in order to distinguish them. Only when children have developed the basic skills of using simple keys should they attempt broader classifications, such as the ones given here, or the use of statement-keys.

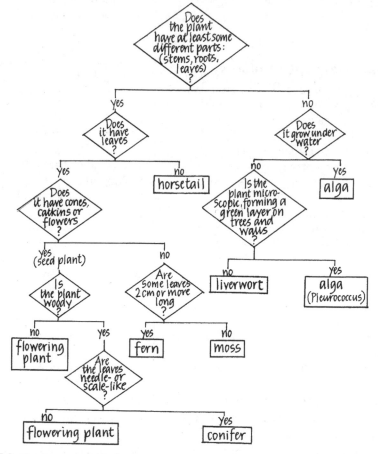

Figure 5.3 *Key to groups of plants*

5.5 ADAPTATION

Opportunities, problems and variety. A simple investigation of the plants and animals in an area can easily show that there are many places where a great variety of living things can be found. In order to survive, any living thing has to exploit **opportunities** in its environment to meet its needs, while solving the **problems** and withstanding the stresses placed on it. Most plants need soil for anchorage and as a source of water and nutrients, light and air to make their own food and, in some cases, animals to carry their pollen and distribute their seeds. Their main problems are likely to be lack of water and light, being eaten by animals, or disease. An animal needs food, water and, in most cases, shelter provided by a hiding-place, the security of a social group, or both. Its main problems are likely to be hunger, thirst, exposure, being preyed on and disease.

The **variety** of living things in any part of the world is a reflection of the range of opportunities offered by the environment and the problems it poses. In some parts of the Earth's surface such as the driest deserts and the middle of the Antarctic continent, the opportunities offered are so limited and the problems so severe that almost nothing lives there. Over most of the planet, however, both the opportunities and the problems are very varied and the variety of life is correspondingly wide. The same thing can be seen in miniature in many urban environments. In a tarmac playground surrounded by high walls the opportunities for living things to become established are few and their problems usually severe, so the variety of life is small, though often greater than many people imagine. In a wildlife garden next door, opportunities abound and problems are less acute, so a much greater variety of living things becomes established.

Adaptation Life is a balancing act: if a living thing (organism) can exploit enough opportunities and solve enough problems, it lives and reproduces. If not, individuals or the whole population die out. A variety of organisms can live in most habitats because each tends to exploit different opportunities and solve different problems in order to survive. To do this effectively, organisms are specialized in their body structure, in their behaviour, or both. This specialization is called adaptation.

Adaptation is any feature of the body or behaviour of an organism which fits it for its environment and helps it to survive. Examples are all around us, but often they are difficult to understand because not enough is known about the opportunities and problems of the living things we observe. The concept needs to be established by looking at some very clear and simple examples.

Introductory investigations

Children can learn about adaptation by thinking about and discussing characteristics shown by the beaks and feet of birds. Pictorial and written information about their structure and lifestyles is readily available and their adaptations are clearly and obviously related to their feeding and movement. Children may also be able to follow-up some of their learning by first-hand observation if a bird-table is set up. The main examples are:

- *insect eaters*: robin, tits, wren, hedge-sparrow;
- *mixed diet*: blackbird, song-thrush, starling;
- *small seed-eaters*: finches (sparrow, chaffinch, greenfinch).
  All the above are perching birds (passerines) with specialized beaks but unspecialized feet.
  All the following have both beak and foot adaptations:
- *predators*: owls, hawks;
- *tree-climbers*: tree-creeper, woodpecker;
- *fishing swimmers*: gulls;
- *mud-sieving swimmer-divers*: ducks;
- *waders*: curlew, redshank.

Having used birds as an example to introduce the concept of adaptation, it can be further explored by way of case-studies made at first hand. Examples are suggested in section 5.6.

Activity 5.6.1 investigates adaptations of the skulls of mammals.
Activity 5.6.2 investigates adaptations of fruits and seeds to wind dispersal.
Activity 5.6.3 investigates adaptation and the environment.

5.6 CASE-STUDIES IN ADAPTATION

How children observe and learn about adaptation at first hand is likely to depend on the resources available. This is an example of an area where the topic approach (1.4) is particularly useful. Brief notes are included here on three possible case-studies, which show the connection between observation and explanation needed in work of this kind.

Case-study 1

Skulls of mammals. The skull of any mammal gives more information about its life-style than any other part of its skeleton. This is because the major parts of its feeding mechanism (jaws and teeth) are in its head, and so are most of the major sensory organs. It is usually most productive to concentrate attention on the jaws and teeth, and on the position of the eyes as shown by the eye-sockets. Suitable skulls may usually be borrowed from museum loans services, and the most useful fall into two main groups:

- *hunting predators*: dog, cat, fox
- *plant-eaters*: cow, sheep, deer, horse, rabbit, squirrel, rat.

It is not necessary to have a wide range of specimens to make this study worthwhile: only two skulls of contrasting types, such as those of a dog or cat and a sheep or rabbit, are needed to observe the main adaptations.

Hunting predators have both eyes facing forwards. This is most clearly shown in the cat which, like humans, has a complete ring of bone round its eye-sockets. Forward-facing eyes enable the hunter to use binocular vision (3.10) to judge the distance of its prey accurately.

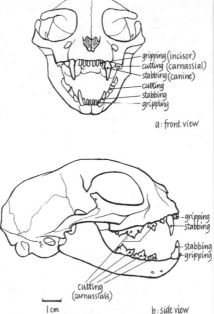

Figure 5.4 *Skull of a carnivore (domestic cat). Notice that larger carnivores such as dogs also have large crushing molars behind the cutting teeth*

The jaws and teeth of hunters have many adaptations (Fig. 5.4). The jaw is specialized in two ways: it has a hinge-joint which does not allow much sideways movement, and the lower jaw (mandible) is narrower than the upper. When the jaw is closed, some lower teeth (canines, carnassials, see below) pass inside the upper ones to stab and slice. The teeth are of four main kinds, which from front to back are:

- *incisors:* rounded and fairly blunt; meet and grip for holding and tearing apart;
- *canines:* long, curved and pointed; pass and stab to kill the prey;
- *carnassial teeth:* sharp and saw-like; pass and cut to slice up flesh (skin is usually pulled and torn off);
- *molars:* blunt and knobbly; meet and crush for breaking up small bones; in some small carnivores such as cats (Fig. 5.4) these are very small or absent.

(Continued)

(Continued)

The teeth are adapted for holding and killing prey, tearing it apart and cutting pieces off before swallowing them. The food is not chewed much, but this does not impair digestion because protein and fat are relatively easy to break down in the gut.

Plant-eaters have skulls which are more varied in structure than those of hunters, but all have adaptations in common (Fig. 5.5). The eyes are at either side of the head. This gives all-round vision and therefore a better chance of seeing a predator or other danger. As a result, plant-eaters have only a narrow field of binocular vision, but because they do not hunt, they have less need to judge distance accurately.

The jaws of plant-eaters are more loosely hinged than those of hunters, so as well as being moved up and down they can be rotated to give a grinding action. The lower jaw is only a little narrower than the upper, so the teeth meet rather than passing one another. All the plant-eaters have a wide gap between their front (biting) teeth and their cheek (grinding) teeth. This enables them to feed continuously, grinding up one mouthful of vegetation while biting off the next.

The front, biting teeth of plant-eaters are varied and different animals show three main adaptations: the horse has upper and lower teeth, which meet and cut as it bites. Sheep, cows and deer have only lower teeth in front, which they use to hold plants against the gum of their toothless upper jaw, pulling them off with a move-

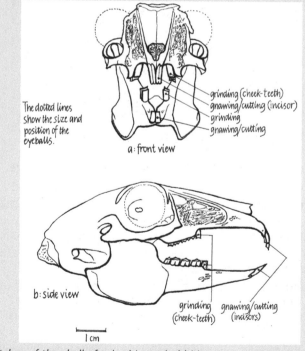

Figure 5.5 *Sketches of the skull of a herbivore (rabbit)*

ment of the head. Rabbits, rats and squirrels have paired, chisel-like teeth, with which they nibble and gnaw (Fig. 5.5).

The cheek-teeth of plant-eaters are broad, with sharp ridges on top. These animals digest plant fibre for carbohydrate (3.4), but because this is difficult to digest it has to be ground up first. The cheek-teeth are specialized for this, but are themselves ground away in the process, so unlike the teeth of hunters (and humans) they keep on growing throughout the animal's life.

The approach used here, of focusing attention on particular structures then seeking to explain what has been observed, can be used equally well to study adaptations in other animal groups and habitats. Possible examples include swimming, breathing and feeding in aquatic insects. It is also the basis for what is known of the adaptations of extinct animals such as dinosaurs.

Case-study 2

Behaviour of woodlice. Woodlice are one of the commonest invertebrate animals and the only land-dwelling crustaceans (5.1). They feed mainly on decaying plant material, usually in dim light conditions at dawn and dusk. They are always in some danger of death from water loss, so they have a strong preference for humid, damp conditions. They do not, however, like wet conditions and can easily drown if their living-places are flooded. Woodlice can easily be kept for a few days in a small tank with a layer of damp, decaying leaves in the bottom. Pieces of apple or carrot can be put in for food, though whether these are ever eaten is doubtful, as they aren't usually decayed enough.

The adaptation of woodlice which children can investigate is their behaviour, which has obvious survival value. If 20 woodlice are put onto a layer of damp, decaying leaves in bright light, they will quickly move down into the leaves and disappear. Asking children why they do this is a very effective way to generate a range of explanatory hypotheses (1.7). The most obviously testable hypotheses are likely to be those which relate to the adapted behaviour: they move as they do because they don't like strong light (or do like dark) and don't like dry conditions (or do like damp ones).

The easiest way to test these explanations is by using very simple choice chambers, which can be made from plastic Petri dishes. If light–dark preference is being tested, half the lid of each dish should be painted black and conditions should be kept humid, for example by putting a layer of damp paper towel in the bottom of the dish. Ten woodlice are put into the dish, which is kept in bright light, and a record kept of how many can be seen at one-minute intervals. Usually they will show a strong preference for dim light. When testing for moisture preference, a plain dish should be used, with half the bottom covered with damp paper and half with dry. The light should be kept dim by putting a black card over the top. To observe the animals, lift the card slowly, count the number in each half and then replace it. Usually a strong preference for damp conditions is shown. The survival value of both observed behaviours can then be discussed and decisions made as to whether the original hypotheses have been upheld.

Case-study 3

Adaptations of weeds. Weeds are opportunists: they exploit environments which other plants have not colonized. There are many reasons for their success: sometimes the environment is unfavourable for other plants, and in other cases disturbance has created a new environment which other plants have not yet exploited. One example of each is discussed here.

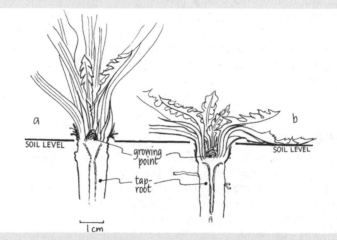

Figure 5.6 *Rosette weeds: dandelions cut vertically: (a) growing in short, unmown grass under a hedge, (b) growing in regularly mown grass*

Rosette weeds are perennial plants adapted to colonizing heavily trampled soil and closely mown lawns. Examples include dandelions, hawkweeds and plantains. Their adaptation is one of structure: they can grow as a flat, round rosette of leaves from a single growing-point, so they suffer only minor damage when other plants would be crushed or cut to pieces (Fig. 5.6). They have very tough roots, so they are hard to pull up, and a main growing-point below ground level, so that even if their leaves are cut off or crushed they can quickly grow again. Interesting studies can often be carried out in early summer into rosette weeds flourishing in areas which are trampled bare in winter, such as goal-mouths and shortcuts between hard paving. Numbers of weeds can be related to intensity of trampling and the relative resistance of grass and weeds to trampling observed. Individuals can be dug up to see how their anatomy helps to ensure re-growth after damage.

Some weeds have adaptations of reproduction rather than structure, which enable them to exploit newly disturbed soil before other plants can become estabished. They usually grow from seeds and have very short life-cycles; germinating, growing, flowering and setting seed in two or three months. Two particularly useful examples are groundsel and bitter-cress. Plants can be dug up and grown outdoors in pots, to be observed as they flower and set seed, which can be collected and sown so that children can see the whole life-cycle. Very rapid seed production is only one of the adaptations: others include effective seed dispersal (by wind for groundsel and 'exploding' capsules for bitter-cress), rapid germination and very fast growth at almost any time of the year. All these adaptations help them to exploit environments which are available only for a short time, such as gardens in winter, the edges of fields and building sites.

Another aspect of plant life in which adaptation can readily be observed is the dispersal of seeds, discussed in outline in section 4.5.

Activity 5.6.2 investigates seed dispersal.

5.7 ECOSYSTEMS: FEEDING RELATIONSHIPS

Animals and plants living in a particular area are adapted (5.5), not only to environmental conditions such as climate and soil, but also to each other. Any part of the Earth may include a variety of areas (habitats), which may be natural or influenced by human activity to varying degrees. Examples which children might investigate include woodland, meadow, pond, stream, rocky seashore, wall, garden and field margin. Each habitat is distinguished not only by the environmental conditions in it, such as light, temperature, rainfall and soil type, but also by the range of living things which inhabit it. One of the greatest contributions of the life sciences during the past century has been the growth of an understanding that the living things in a habitat do not and cannot exist in isolation, but form a community whose members depend on each other. Understanding the interdependence of living things and their habitats is the aim of the ecologist. One way to develop this understanding is to investigate the relationships between members of a particular community. Such relationships are together known as an ecosystem.

Feeding relationships of humans   One of the most basic aspects of any ecosystem, and the one which children can most profitably investigate, is feeding relationships. This involves, for any organism, tracing its food back to its origins. An appropriate starting-point is the food which children themselves consume. Humans are animals which normally have a mixed diet (omnivores), including both plant and animal material. Tracing the animal material in the human diet back to its sources shows that all of it, and therefore all our food, has its origins in plants. Results can be shown graphically, using either pictures or words, for example:

Human ← egg ← hen ← grain ← plant

From the first, the fundamental point can be made that, in one way or another, we depend upon plants for all our food. This can then be linked to the concept of plants as living things which produce their own food by photosynthesis (4.4), using light from the Sun as their energy source (9.2.4).

The ideas contained in this section cannot easily be taught using direct evidence, so good sources of indirect experience need to be provided by the teacher.

Feeding relationships within ecosystems   Humans depend for their food on plants, but does the same principle apply more widely, to other animals in any habitat we might investigate? To find out, it is necessary to know the range of living things which inhabit an area, and use this to gain access to information about their diet, as well as observing them at first hand wherever possible. If children are successfully to do this at first hand, teachers need to select a small number of local, accessible habitats, research these in detail and use a topic approach (1.4) to their studies.

Activities 5.7.1 and 5.7.2 give more ideas on investigating feeding relationships.

Food-webs, producers and consumers   Because observation of habitats may be difficult and their populations may change or fluctuate, it is often useful, in addition, to use second-hand information to learn about feeding relationships. As an example, a set of information on feeding relationships among larger animals in a garden is given in Table 5.1. This can be used in a variety of ways. One of the most productive is to make a set of labels for each animal or group, and plot feeding relationships by laying these out on large sheets of paper, to which they can later be glued if the chart needs to be made permanent. Plotting all the information in Table 5.1 on a single chart will show how complex feeding relationships within a habitat are likely to be, but is not otherwise very useful. It is more productive to find out where the food of a single animal comes from. As an example, the feeding relationships of a robin are shown in Figure 5.7.

A set of feeding relationships shown in this way is known as a food-web. Plotting the food-webs of different animals using the information provided shows that all their food, like that of humans, can be traced back to plants. Photosynthesis is the only source of food in almost every ecosystem, so plants are known as producers. Animals, because they rely on this food but do not produce any of their own, are known as consumers. The various roles which different animals play within the ecosystem are reflected in the way in which they appear at different levels in food-webs. Those which feed on plants (herbivores) are near the bottom, while those which eat other animals (carnivores) are higher up, further away in terms of feeding from the production which maintains the whole system. Right at the top are predatory carnivores which are not themselves preyed on. They are often called top-carnivores, and the main one in the garden ecosystem is the tawny owl.

Food-chains and pyramids   Other important ideas about feeding relationships can be developed by concentrating on a single strand in a food-web. For example, one such strand in the food-web of the robin is:

robin ← insect larvae ← leaves ← plants

Table 5.1 Feeding relationships among larger animals in a garden ecosystem

Animal and group	Eats	Is eaten by
Birds:		
Tawny owl	mice, voles, sparrows, shrews, (? tits), snails, slugs, worms	
Blackbird	caterpillars, earthworms, fruit and seeds, soil-dwelling larvae	
Song-thrush	earthworms, snails, soil-dwelling larvae, caterpillars, fruit and seeds	
Finches (sparrow, chaffinch)	seeds, some caterpillars	tawny owl
Tits (blue and great)	aphids, caterpillars, some fruit and seeds	?tawny owl
Robin	caterpillars, earthworms, soil-dwelling larvae, fruits and seeds	
Mammals:		
Wood-mouse	snails, young plants, buds, fruits and seeds	tawny owl
Short-tailed vole	grass and other plant shoots	tawny owl
Common shrew	earthworms, woodlice, caterpillars	tawny owl
Hedgehog	earthworms, woodlice, caterpillars, snails, slugs, fallen fruit	
Soil dwellers:		
Earthworms	dead leaves	blackbird, song-thrush, tawny owl, robin, shrew, hedgehog
Soil-dwelling larvae	roots of plants	blackbird, song-thrush, robin
Woodlice	almost any dead and decaying plant material	hedgehog, shrew
Plant pests:		
Slugs	living and dead plant material	tawny owl, hedgehog
Snails	living and dead plant material	tawny owl, song-thrush, wood-mouse, hedgehog
Aphids	plant sap (by sucking)	tits
Caterpillars (insect larvae)	plant shoots of all kinds	blackbird, song-thrush, robin, tits, finches, shrews, hedgehog

This is known as a food-chain. Food-chains are useful because they can help us see more clearly how plants and animals are related in the ecosystem. One way to do this is to look at the actual amounts of material involved in a food-chain. For example, great tits feed themselves and their young mainly on insect larvae, which eat plants, so their food chain is:

$$\text{great tit} \leftarrow \text{larvae} \leftarrow \text{plants}$$

Observations have shown that during the three weeks it takes to rear a brood of 8–10 chicks, they and the parents eat between 8,000 and 10,000 larvae. These are taken from trees and other plants whose leaves together must weigh several hundred kilograms, since even a small garden can produce half a tonne (500 kg) of dead leaves a year. Putting in the amounts of material involved, the food-chain looks like this:

$$\text{great tits} \leftarrow \text{larvae} \leftarrow \text{plants}$$
$$10\text{--}12 \qquad 8{,}000\text{--}10{,}000 \qquad \text{at least } 500 \text{ kg}$$

This shows what has been found in all food-chains of this kind: a small number of carnivorous animals prey on a much larger population of herbivores, which in turn feed on a very large amount of plant material. Because of this relationship, food-chains are sometimes called food-pyramids, with the large mass of plant material making up the base of the pyramid.

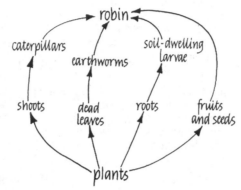

Figure 5.7 *Food-web of a robin*

To develop a realistic idea of the feeding relationships within an ecosystem we need to chart food-webs to see the complexity, and food-pyramids to appreciate the numbers of living things and amounts of material involved. Together they emphasize not only the way in which all living things depend on the food produced by plants and therefore on light energy from the Sun (13.8), but also the way in which populations are naturally controlled. Each step of the food-pyramid must always be much smaller than the one below it, on which it depends. Great tits could never be as numerous as the larvae on which they feed, and a plague of caterpillars could not be sustained for a long period because they would destroy the plants and with them the means of food production. The food-pyramid also helps to explain the disastrous effects of some of the poisonous chemicals which pollute the environment.

5.8 ECOSYSTEMS: DECAY, RECYCLING AND INTERDEPENDENCE

The feeding relationships of animals and plants make up the more obvious and conspicuous part of the ecosystem. The fact that there must be more to discover becomes apparent when we remember that no plant or animal lives for ever. Although living things have been living, dying and depositing waste material on the Earth for millions of years, we are not engulfed by their dead remains or their waste. When a living organism dies, its body undergoes changes similar to those which affect any non-living thing: it breaks down, becomes simpler and is dispersed into the environment (2.2). The only difference is that dead bodies and animal waste do not under normal circumstances undergo slow chemical and physical changes of the kind which result in the rusting of iron (8.3.3) and the weathering of rocks: most of their material is actively attacked and broken down very quickly because it is used as food by other living things: the decomposers.

Decomposers   Some animals in the ecosystem (scavengers) eat the dead bodies of other animals, and others such as earthworms specialize in eating dead plant material, an activity which is of great importance in soil formation (7.4), but most of the breakdown of dead bodies is carried out by micro-organisms, both bacteria and fungi (5.3), which together are known as decomposers.

In the ecosystem, decomposers are consumers because, like animals, they do not make food but rely, either directly or indirectly, on the food made by plants. The action of decomposers is what we call decay, and sometimes produces chemicals which smell offensive to us (5.3), though most naturally decaying material simply smells earthy. Decomposers are found in very large numbers almost everywhere in the environment, particularly in the upper layers of most soils, and their spores float in the air like tiny particles of dust. Dead material is colonized within a very short time, the microbes begin to digest it and usually grow very quickly.

Children can easily observe decay as a process of breakdown by carefully collecting dead leaves from undisturbed soil in garden or woodland and separating them into their different layers (Fig. 5.8). At the top are whole dead leaves; at the bottom a soft, dark brown, earthy material (humus) in which no trace of leaves can be found; and in between are leaves in various stages of decay and disintegration. In the process of decay the plant fibre (cellulose, 4.4) is digested and the products respired by the decomposers, releasing carbon dioxide gas to the air and water to the soil. The decay of proteins is complex, but ends with the release of simple chemicals into the soil, which plants take up and use as mineral nutrients (4.3).

Activity 5.8.1 gives more information on this investigation.

Decay as recycling   The essential role of decay in the ecosystem can now be seen clearly. It is natural recycling; the process by which material built into the bodies of living things by their growth processes is released again into the environment after their death, as carbon dioxide in the air and mineral nutrients in the soil. In this way the materials are made available to plants, to be taken up by them and re-used for photosynthesis and growth, so sustaining both them and all the consumers (animals and decomposers) in the habitat. Decay is often regarded by children and adults with distaste. It should rather be viewed as a process which is as essential in its way to the continuation of life on Earth as photosynthesis is.

Without photosynthesis no food could be produced, but without decay the materials which plants need for photosynthesis and growth would be permanently locked away in dead bodies, unavailable for further use.

Interdependence   At primary level, children can learn in at least three different ways that all living things are dependent on each other.

First, investigating feeding relationships by charting food-webs, chains and pyramids shows how animals as consumers depend on plants as producers. Second, finding out how decay occurs shows that both animals and plants depend on decomposers to recycle material, but also that the decomposers depend on the growth of animals and plants for a continued supply of food material. Learning about photosynthesis (4.4) shows a third aspect of interdependence. The respiration of nearly all living things relies on the oxygen produced by plants during photosynthesis, but it also produces carbon dioxide which is one of the raw materials used in that process, so the balance of gases in the atmosphere is conserved.

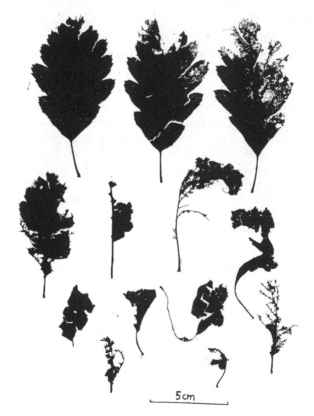

5 cm

Figure 5.8 *Stages in decay of leaves*

PART 3

MATERIALS AND THEIR PROPERTIES

Part 3 is about the Science National Curriculum Attainment Target 3 (Sc3). This Introduction provides an overview of this area of science knowledge. Chapter 6 provides background scientific knowledge for teaching the three parts of Sc3 which are covered by Chapters 7 and 8.

When children are being scientific, learning about materials, their teacher needs to make sure that the ideas and evidence in the classroom are challenged and enriched by scientists' knowledge. This knowledge should be used to help the children to think about their experiences more deeply. Investigating materials by finding out how they respond and change in different ways, and linking their properties to their everyday uses, will enable young children to learn about the properties of materials and their changes.

The key ideas presented in Chapter 6 are: states of matter, understanding and explaining the physical and chemical changes that happen to materials. One of the most powerful ideas in science, the particulate or atomic theory of matter, is presented in a simple form (6.4). All this can be learned before or after reading Chapters 7 and 8, according to the reader's learning style and immediate purposes of reading. A good teacher of science needs to be able to meet the needs of those children who can go deeper into explanations than the majority.

Refer to the CD-ROM for a QUICK GUIDE to Sc3.
Refer to the CD-ROM for Progression in learning SCIENTIFIC ENQUIRY (Sc1) through MATERIALS AND THEIR PROPERTIES (Sc3) levels 1 to 6.

BEFORE WE BEGIN

Scientists use the word **material** differently from its everyday use. Young children are likely to associate the word with cloth, for example, but scientists use the term material to refer to the *stuff* that everything is made of. The more old-fashioned scientific term is **matter**, which can also have its own, different connotations for children. Many teachers see every lesson as a language lesson – to take opportunities to clarify usage of words, as part of clarifying thinking. They are wise to be cautious about how to teach both of these terms to young children and they should be willing to spend time talking about the children's prior understanding.

A second potential difficulty of teaching about materials arises from the decision about where to begin teaching. It is logically attractive to start with what seems to be a basic idea that materials are either solids, liquids or gases and for experienced learners, this could be an appropriate challenge. Furthermore, this concept appears early in the National Curriculum specification for this Attainment Target, and teachers may remember that they learned this apparently fundamental distinction at an early stage of their secondary school science. However, there are two widely held curriculum planning principles for young children: first, that it is good to *start where the children are*, and second, that new direct experience of everyday events and material is the best starting point to stimulate learning. For these reasons, it may be decided to postpone teaching about states of matter until it becomes relevant to later learning, and to start instead with investigations of a wide range of everyday materials. This will enable young children to build up rich and varied experience of materials, their diversity and interesting characteristics, before taking on more theoretical challenges about how those differences are understood.

6 MATTER

6.1 STATES OF MATTER: SOLIDS, LIQUIDS AND GASES

Any object or material can be classified according to whether it is solid, liquid or gas at a particular temperature. Most materials and objects which children encounter in everyday life are fairly obviously in one of these three states of matter. It is essential for children to gather direct evidence through investigating these states and exploring ways of changing one into another, for scientific ideas to be learned. Changes between solids and liquids are easy to observe, but those between liquids and gases can be rather more difficult to investigate and understand.

An object, or the material it consists of, is usually thought of as being solid if it has a shape of its own, which it retains when unsupported by a container.

Activity 8.2.1 investigates modelling a solid.

A liquid, on the other hand, has no shape of its own. If it is in a container it takes up the container's shape, but otherwise it runs out, forming a thin layer on a level surface or collecting in pools on an uneven one.

Activity 8.2.2 investigates modelling a liquid.

It is less easy to develop a firm understanding of the difference between liquids and gases. One way is to think about how a solid, a liquid and a gas behave in a container with a lid on. The solid keeps its shape and the liquid fills the bottom of its container. The gas, like the liquid, has no shape of its own but it fills the container completely and unlike the liquid does not collect at the bottom.

Activity 6.1.1 helps children explore how to distinguish solids from liquids.

Children can investigate the differences between liquids and solids by exploring many examples of solids made up of small particles, such as sand, sugar and salt. They can be encouraged to notice that in large numbers, the particles fill the bottom of a container and if this is tilted they can be poured out, appearing to flow rather as a liquid does. It is important, therefore, not to over-emphasize ease of flow as a property of liquids, since these solids seem to share it. A better approach is to encourage children to look closely at the individual particles with a hand-lens and pencil-point, observing that each grain has its own form and keeps it when pushed or squashed, unlike a drop of liquid. It is also helpful for them to observe that solid particles form a heap when poured out onto a flat surface, which liquids do not. Beginning with coarse particles such as sugar or sand, children can go on to see that finer powders such as flour or baking powder are also solids. It is important to develop the concept of particulate solids before investigating solutions and suspensions (8.1.2).

Activity 6.1.2 helps children explore solids which 'flow'.

Children can gain an understanding that gases are real and have substance, but this needs thought and care. It is not helpful that nearly all gases are invisible and those which are not are highly poisonous! However, with young children especially, a range of experiences such as blowing air to feel a wind and propel things, playing with fans, sails, balloons and windmills can all help to establish this concept. The way in which a gas fills the whole container in which it is confined can be shown by inflating a balloon. The squashed (compressed) air inside stretches the balloon evenly, so it must be pushing out equally in all directions, filling the whole space inside. This can be contrasted to a little water in an air-filled balloon, which collects at the bottom. Another piece of evidence is to point out that if air settled at the bottom of a room, as water does at the bottom of a swimming-pool, one would not be able to breathe up near the ceiling. However, it can be observed that when a light-bulb or tube is changed, whoever climbs up to do it does not need breathing apparatus, so the air in the room must fill it up. Using the word gas with children needs careful thought and planning, to include finding out what their pre-existing ideas are like. They are likely to have heard the word only in the context of the household fuel that makes a cooker or a central heating boiler work, and are unlikely to think of air as a gas.

Activity 6.1.3 helps children explore gases and their properties.

6.2 CHANGES OF STATE

6.2.1 Melting and freezing

Changes of state between solid, liquid and gas are usually associated with heating, cooling and changes in temperature (9.3). An explanation of these changes, though not generally thought of as being part of the primary science curriculum, is given here. Evaporation (6.2.2) and solution (8.1.2) are special cases which should be carefully distinguished from apparently similar changes of state (boiling and melting).

A solid that is changing to a liquid is said to **melt**; a liquid changing to a solid is said to **freeze**. Both changes can easily be observed by allowing an ice-cube to melt and then re-freezing the liquid water. There are, however, two important differences between this example of changing state and others with which children are likely to be familiar. The first is that when ice melts and water freezes there is no intermediate state between solid and liquid. Children will be familiar with, and should also investigate, more gradual changes of state in foods and other chemicals. The second difference is that ice and water change size in a very unusual way when freezing and melting (see below).

Activity 6.2.1 helps children observe melting and freezing of wax.

Gradual changes between liquid and solid   Many foods and other chemicals, especially when heated or cooled slowly, show a gradual change of state between liquid and solid. Chocolate shows a reversible change of this kind very well when heated gently over a water-bath, for example when making chocolate crispies. Less easily reversible, but even more gradual changes, can be seen as ice-cream slowly melts and jelly, cornflour custard and blancmange become cool and set.

Activity 6.2.2 helps children develop their understanding of solids and liquids.

The setting of plaster and concrete is rather different from that of jelly or custard in that it is brought about by chemical changes (8.3) rather than cooling, but both show a similar gradual change of state. Most paints which children use are solid-liquid mixtures (suspensions, 8.1.2) which lose water by evaporation (6.2.2) and gradually solidify as they dry up.

The freezing and melting of water   Liquid water and ice have some very unusual properties. One of these is the change in volume when ice melts or liquid water freezes. Most substances become smaller when cooled and larger when heated (9.3.1), but as water freezes into ice it expands. This can be shown by filling a plastic drinks bottle completely with water, screwing the top on tightly and putting it into a freezer. As the water freezes, the expansion of the ice will split the bottle.

Activity 6.2.3 helps children explore freezing and melting of water.

Although water normally freezes at 0°C, the freezing point is lower if chemicals such as salt have been added to it, so it has to be much colder before the ice-salt mixture will freeze. This explains why crushed rock-salt is used on icy paths. The salt starts to dissolve on the surface of the ice, but the ice is much warmer than the freezing point of the salt solution. The result is that instead of the salt solution freezing, more liquid forms, more salt dissolves and so on. When used on roads, the salt is usually mixed with grit to give vehicle tyres more grip (friction, 11.4) on partly melted snow and ice.

If the temperature continues to fall below 0°C, ice continues to expand. This expansion has had two profoundly important effects on the Earth and living things. The first is that as water seeps into cracks in rocks in the cold regions of the world and freezes, the expanding ice opens up cracks in the rock. The freeze–thaw cycle, which may be repeated every day for much of the year, is a major cause of the breakdown or weathering of rocks and so of soil formation (7.4). The other effect of the expansion of ice is even more important. Because ice expands as it freezes, a kilogram of ice takes up more space than a kilogram of water at 0°C (i.e. the ice has a lower density). The result is that ice floats, so in the cold parts of the world, where lakes, rivers and even the sea freeze over, living things can remain active under the ice, which also insulates them (9.3.6) from extreme cold. If ice sank, lakes, rivers and the sea would freeze from the bottom up and life in cold waters would be much more restricted than it is.

6.2.2 Boiling, condensation and evaporation

Boiling   If water is heated to 100°C and heating is continued, the temperature does not continue to rise, but the water begins to boil. Boiling is the process of a liquid being changed to a gas by heating, and for any liquid it normally takes place at a characteristic temperature: the boiling-point. Unlike evaporation (see below), boiling does not take place only at the surface of a liquid, and gas bubbles can form anywhere. If a saucepan of water is heated, bubbles of gas (steam) usually form on the bottom, but that is only because the heating effect is strongest there. Children may notice that when cold tap-water is heated in a pan or in a plastic kettle with a transparent panel, bubbles form and rise to the top, long before the water boils. These are bubbles of air which was dissolved in the water (8.1.2), but which comes out of solution as the water is heated up.

Children can observe the boiling of water as it provides good opportunities to discuss safety in the kitchen. One way to emphasize this is to point out that boiling water kills and cooks human skin just as it kills and cooks anything else such as potatoes, and does it very quickly. Dissolving chemicals in water causes its boiling-point to rise, so that it is hotter than 100°C when it begins to boil. When a lot of a chemical is added to water, as for example sugar is added when making jam, the boiling liquid is so hot that a special high-temperature thermometer is needed. Boiling syrups and jams are particularly dangerous because they are sticky: a splash on the skin is not only very hot but also does not run off, so it causes much worse scalding than boiling water would do.

When a liquid boils it turns to gas. Water turned to gas by heating is called steam, and is completely colourless and transparent, which means that it is invisible. Only when steam cools down does it form the hot cloud which is usually called 'steam'. This can be shown by looking at water boiling in a pan. The gas above the surface is invisible and only when it rises is it possible to see the 'steam'. What happens is that as the steam rises, it cools to below 100°C and liquid water re-forms (condensation, see below), but in the form of tiny droplets which are so small that they can remain suspended in the air as a mist or cloud. When steam comes into contact with a cold surface, liquid water forms by condensation very quickly. The process of boiling a liquid, collecting the gas, cooling and condensing it is known as distillation, and is often used as a method of extracting and purifying liquids (8.1).

Activity 6.3.1 explores the boiling of water and Activity 6.3.2 explores the condensation of steam.

Children can observe evaporation and condensation and learn that boiling is not the only way of converting a liquid into a gas. They can leave a dish of water exposed to the air, notice that the water seems to disappear gradually, even though it has not been heated to a high temperature, or boiled. It has simply 'dried up' or evaporated. The teacher can say that evaporation occurs when a liquid changes to a gas at its surface and explore liquids which do this much faster than water, for example the surgical spirit used to clean the skin before an injection, which dries up almost instantly. Children can investigate whether evaporation takes place at the surface of a liquid, by comparing equal volumes of water (say 10 ml) and putting one into a shallow dish and the other onto a cloth which is then hung up to dry. The water on the cloth will evaporate much faster than that in the dish because it has been absorbed and 'spread out' (8.1.3), so that it has a much larger surface exposed to the air.

Activity 6.3.3 helps children learn about evaporation.

Water or any other liquid which evaporates, does not actually disappear, but turns into a gas which mixes with the air. This cool gas phase is called a vapour. The gas formed when water evaporates is called water vapour, not steam, because it is not hot. Air is a mixture of many gases, of which water vapour is one, colourless and invisible like the rest. If the air contains a lot of water vapour it is said to be moist or humid. The evaporation of water from the Earth's surface, especially the oceans, and its condensation as clouds and precipitation, are the basis of the water cycle and of much of the weather which we experience (7.5).

Any gas which is cooled sufficiently changes into the liquid state by the process of condensation. If humid air is cooled, the water vapour in it may condense as tiny droplets, rather as steam does, and remain suspended as fog, mist or cloud (7.5.3). If the humid air comes into contact with a cold surface it will condense as liquid water. The air which animals breathe out is warm and very humid. In a room with a lot of people, humidity builds up until water begins to condense on cold surfaces, such as windows in winter, so that these mist over and may have 'condensation' running down them. In cars, condensation from moist air breathed out can impede the driver's vision, so devices such as hot air blowers and electrically heated rear windows are used to re-evaporate the water and give a clear view.

Although evaporation can often continue at low temperatures, it gets faster as the temperature rises. This can be observed by comparing the rate at which puddles dry up on hot and cool days in summer and the effect of a hot air blower on a misted window. The difference comes about because evaporation depends on a transfer of energy (latent heat, 9.2.2) from the liquid to the vapour, so that the liquid tends to become cooler as a result. When the temperature is high, this transfer of energy can take place faster so the rate of evaporation goes up, and if evaporation is very rapid the cooling effect is much more marked. This can be shown by putting a drop of rapidly evaporating but harmless liquid such as surgical spirit onto the skin. It will feel much colder than a drop of water, and colder still if air is blown onto it. The cooling effect of evaporation is important in preventing overheating of the body in many mammals, such as humans (sweating, 3.9) and dogs (panting).

Activity 6.3.4 helps children explore the cooling effect of evaporation.

6.3 EXPLAINING CHANGES

6.3.1 Explaining physical changes

Melting, freezing, boiling, evaporation and condensation are all examples of physical changes. Physical changes may alter the appearance and other physical properties of materials and objects, but the scientific idea is that **the actual substances involved remain the same**. For example, ice, water and steam are all the same substance, water, and changes of state between them do not alter this. A change which does result in the formation of a new kind of substance is a chemical change (see below and 6.3.2) not a physical change.

An important part of the idea of physical change is that however the materials seem to change, they do not change in themselves at all. They are actually the same *stuff*. This *counter-intuitive* idea is not obvious to children. They have a great deal of life experience of bringing about physical changes in a wide range of objects and materials. Their intuitive interpretation of this evidence is likely to be that water and ice have different characteristics because they really are different materials, made of different *stuff*.

There are many physical ways to change materials with which children are familiar, such as mixing, applying forces and heating and cooling. Chapter 8 is about changing materials, not only by these physical methods, but also by chemical ones.

6.3.2 Explaining chemical changes

A change which produces a different kind of material from that which existed before is a chemical change. Children are familiar with many processes which involve chemical changes such as: cooking, rusting of steel, decay and burning. It needs to be clearly understood, however, that at primary level, investigating processes which involve chemical change cannot lead children to an understanding of the nature of chemical change itself.

Teachers should be cautious about simple attempts to distinguish between chemical and physical changes such as reversibility, transfer of energy and the appearance of the products. They are often misleading because it is not the observable characteristics of a change which distinguishes chemical changes from physical ones. Learning to be scientific is not aided by telling children to accept ideas with little evidence. It is often not possible to say, just by looking, whether any particular change is chemical, physical, or involves both. This means that to put a lot of effort into trying to teach the nature of chemical change at primary level is unproductive, because it takes children's learning and inquiry away from their own experience, ideas and evidence. This does not mean, however, that chemical changes should be ignored and their investigation neglected.

The better way is to adopt the topic approach (1.4). Investigate processes and materials familiar to children and select relevant examples of chemical changes. This concentrates on observing what is changed and under what conditions, the changes themselves and the products which result, in the context of the children's own lives, experiences and interests. In Chapter 7, there are three examples of topics. Other chemical changes are discussed more briefly in 7.3, in the context of manufactured materials.

6.4 ATOMS AND MOLECULES

Primary teachers do need to think about the **atomic theory of matter** in a simple way because it enables them to understand more deeply the scientific explanations of physical and chemical change. The atomic or particulate theory of matter is not only one of the most powerful and far-reaching ideas in science: it is one of the most rewarding. A few simple ideas can explain evidence of an extraordinary diversity of everyday events and scientific observations. In its simplest form, the atomic theory is the idea that all material things, whether solids, liquids or gases, are made up of very large numbers of very small **particles** called atoms, which can join together in groups called molecules.

Atoms and molecules are so small that it is difficult to gain a clear idea of their size. If we start with a length of 1 metre, then one thousandth of a metre (10^{-3} m) is a millimetre, which is still within the range of ordinary measurement. One thousandth of a millimetre (10^{-6} m) is called a micrometre and objects of this size, such as many bacteria and microbes, can be seen with powerful microscopes. But to get near to the size of a molecule of sugar, we have to go a thousand times smaller still, to 10^{-9}m, called a nanometre which is one millionth part of a millimetre. As molecules go, those of sugar are quite large, being made up of 45 atoms of three different kinds. Molecules of water, each with only three atoms, are much smaller. Another way to gain some idea of how small atoms are is to imagine things enormously enlarged. One elegant example was given by Andrade and Huxley many years ago: 'If we could magnify a copper wire, of the thickness of a hair, until it was big enough to fill a wide street, the atoms of which it is made would be the size of small specks of dust'.

Another ingenious thought-experiment is attributed to the physicist Lord Kelvin, who devised it about a century ago to show how small molecules are by giving an idea of how many there are in a glass of water. He asks us to imagine a drinking glass of water, whose molecules are labelled so that each one of them can be recognized and counted when mixed with ordinary water. (This would be very difficult, if not impossible, even with modern technology.) In the imaginary experiment, the glass of 'labelled' water is tipped into the sea and left for a very long time (several thousand years) until the labelled molecules are evenly mixed throughout all the oceans of the world. An investigator then goes to the sea and takes from it one glass of water. What are the chances that one or more of the labelled molecules would be taken up? Lord Kelvin calculated that each glassful of water, in all the seas and oceans, would on average contain not one, but a hundred of them!

Two very useful ideas coming from atomic theory are, first, in all materials and at any temperature we normally experience, the particles are not still, but are moving, constantly and very rapidly, and second, that together with this constant movement there are basic differences in the ways molecules are arranged and how close together they are. These ideas are used to explain the characteristics of gases, liquids and solids.

6.4.1 Particles in gases

A gas has no form or structure at all. Particles of air around us move around freely, so they fill any container (such as a room) completely and do not settle at the bottom as a liquid does. They move very fast and collide with each other very frequently. They are spread out, the average distance between them being about 10 times their own size, so a gas can be squashed, pushing its particles closer together. Compressed gas is an example of an elastic material (7.1.5), because when the squashing force is released the gas goes back to its original size.

Heating a gas increases both the speed and violence of the movement of the particles and the distance between them, so it expands and increases its volume. Every litre of hot gas will have fewer molecules in it than a litre of cold gas, so it will weigh less. This explains why heated air rises and hot air balloons can float in the cooler air around them (11.8.4).

6.4.2 Particles in liquids

Cooling a gas to a low enough temperature turns it into a liquid by **condensation** (6.2.2), for example when steam turns into liquid water. The liquid occupies only about one-thousandth of the space that the gas did.

Particles in a liquid are not free to move away from each other, as they are in a gas, so they lie at the bottom of their container, taking its shape. But they can slip past each other, so having no shape of its own, a liquid can flow downwards under its own weight. The particles in a liquid are close to each other, so very large forces are needed to make them move closer still, and therefore liquids cannot normally be squashed or compressed. However, they do change in volume when they are heated and cooled, just as in a gas. Heating makes the particles move more rapidly, so the average distance between them increases slightly and the whole liquid expands. Cooling reverses the process, and these changes are used in liquid thermometers to measure temperature (9.3.2).

6.4.3 Particles in solids

A liquid which is cooled to a low enough temperature will solidify or freeze and form a solid. As the liquid cools, particles move less and less violently and rapidly, and finally join together as the solid forms. In a solid, particles are still moving rapidly by vibrating but they are not free to move past each other so the solid object has a definite shape. The speed of the vibration is affected by temperature, so solids expand on heating and contract on cooling just as liquids and gases do.

Most liquids shrink a little as they solidify, so molecules in a solid are somewhat closer together than those in a liquid (water is peculiar in that it expands as it freezes, 6.2). Solids are normally incompressible, just as liquids are, but in a solid, particles are bonded together to give the definite shape which liquids lack.

7 GROUPING AND CLASSIFYING MATERIALS

INTRODUCTION

Grouping and classifying materials gives children valuable opportunities to continue developing their scientific thinking about sameness, similarity and difference. Science has made an impressive contribution to our understanding so much about a huge range of different materials. Young children gain a sense of this as they observe, measure, sort and classify a wide range of materials. Plenty of investigative experience of many different sorting activities will enable them to gather the evidence and learn some important scientific ideas.

A favourite activity for young children is to sort a collection of interesting things into groups or sets, putting ones that are the same together and talking about what are the similarities and differences. There are several words for what we notice as similar or different, such as: qualities, characteristics or (the term used here) **properties**.

Here is a list of properties that can be attributed to materials and therefore used as criteria to sort and group them.

- Transparent, translucent or opaque   see 13.5.3
- Magnetic properties   see 12.3
- Electrical conductor or insulator   see 10.2
- Thermal conductor or insulator   see 9.3.6
- Mechanical properties which are related to the effects of the
  application of forces: compressibility, hardness, elasticity,
  plasticity, brittleness and toughness.   see 7.1.1–7.1.7

7.1 MATERIAL PROPERTIES AND OBJECT PROPERTIES

At some point, children need to learn the difference between characteristics or properties of the object as an object, and those which arise from the kind of material the object is made of. This is particularly important when grouping materials and objects according to their mechanical properties; that is, how they behave when forces are applied to them.

A **material property** is a property of the stuff or material of which the object is made. It is unaffected by the size and shape of the individual object under investigation. **Object properties** depend not only on the material of which the object is made, but also on its size and shape. The difference between the two kinds of property can be illustrated by considering two objects made of steel: a strip 20 cm long, 2 cm wide and 1 mm thick; and a bar 20 cm long, 2 cm wide and 2 cm thick. Both would be equally difficult to scratch, so their hardness is the same: this is a material property. The bar, however, would need a much larger force to bend it than the strip would. This is a measure of its stiffness, so stiffness is an object property. Table 7.1 provides a summary of the differences between material and object properties.

Table 7.1 Summary of differences between materials and objects

Type of change made	Material property	Object property
Dent or scratch the surface of the object	How easy or difficult it is to dent or scratch: **hardness**	*Not applicable*
Apply a force to try to **deform** the object, either to: • **compress** (squash) • stretch (put it under **tension**) • **twist** or **bend** it.	When the force is no longer applied, the object: • returns to its original shape: **elastic**. • retains the new shape: **plastic**.	If the object cannot be deformed: it is **rigid**: and if it can be deformed it is **flexible**. The resistance to deformation is **stiffness** (specify whether in **compression**, **tension** or **twisting/bending**).
Apply a force to **compress** it into a smaller space	If it gets smaller, it is **compressible** (normally only gases).	*Not applicable*
Apply a force to break or **fracture** the object, either to: • **compress** (squash) • stretch (put it under **tension**) • **twist** or **bend** it.	If the fracture occurs suddenly (tears or cracks spread easily) it is **brittle**, or slowly, it is **tough**.	The size of the force needed to cause the fracture is a measure of the **strength** (specify whether in **compression**, **tension** or **twisting/bending**).

A closer look at forces, materials and objects　When forces act on an object, they may bring about two sorts of change: changes in the way the object is moving (Chapter 11) and changes in its shape. The way in which materials and objects respond when forces are applied to them determines and in many cases limits the uses to which they can be put, and so is of great importance in everyday life. Collectively, the properties which govern how materials and objects respond to forces are known as **mechanical properties**. Investigating and understanding mechanical properties has a reputation for being complex and difficult, but much of the difficulty comes from a confused use of language, particularly in relation to properties such as strength and flexibility. Once the basic mechanical properties are distinguished and understood, and language is being used correctly, most if not all the difficulties can be resolved.

7.1.1 Compressibility

The major differences between solids, liquids and gases are discussed in section 6.1. We can see another important difference when we apply squashing (compression) forces to gases and liquids in closed containers.

> Children can investigate compressibility using a bicycle-pump or a large plastic syringe holding a finger tightly over the hole in the end. When the plunger is pushed in, the air in the barrel is squashed into a smaller space: it is compressed. Compressed gas pushes outwards on the vessel containing it, so if the plunger is released it springs back. Children are likely to have experience of compressing air, through inflating bicycle tyres and balloons.

The property of compressibility means that gas-filled bags and tubes can act as shock absorbers, an effect made use of in car and bicycle tyres, air-beds, inflatable cushions and the air-bags fitted in cars to prevent the driver hitting the steering-wheel in the event of a crash.

We can easily see and understand that when a gas is squashed, its volume decreases, but when we try to squash a solid block of metal or hard plastic there is no detectable change in volume. For all everyday purposes and observations, these solids are incompressible. Because liquids change shape very readily, it may be less obvious that they are just as incompressible as solids are. However, the incompressibility of a liquid is easy to experience.

> If children draw water carefully into a plastic syringe so that there are no air bubbles in it, and place a finger firmly over the end, it is impossible to push the plunger in. Similarly, if a plastic drinks bottle is completely filled with water and the top screwed on, squeezing it has very little effect: it changes shape a little but then cannot be squashed any more. This can be compared with the amount by which the same bottle can be squashed when filled with air. If an elastic container such as a balloon is filled with water and squashed it changes shape, but does not become smaller as it would if filled with air.

Activity 7.2.1 helps children investigate compressibility.

We must be careful to distinguish between compressibility and the changes of shape which some solids undergo when they are squashed. For example, it is possible to squash a plastic eraser out of shape using one's hands, but this does not involve a change in volume: the eraser is still the same size and, like a water-filled balloon, it is incompressible. The same is true of clay and other similar materials.

There are some solids which can be puzzling because they do seem to be compressible. Balsa wood is one example with which children may be familiar, and corks in wine bottles remain tight because they are compressed as they are inserted. The behaviour of these materials when they are squashed can be explained by remembering that although they behave as solids, they are porous (8.1.3), with microscopic cavities in them which are filled with air. When they are squashed, the air in them, like that in a dry sponge, is either compressed or squeezed out so the solid parts move closer together and the volume of the object decreases. The cork, when released, usually recovers its shape, but squashed balsa wood will not spring back fully. This is the difference between an elastic and a plastic material (7.1.5).

7.1.2 Hardness and its estimation

Hardness is a measure of how easy or difficult it is to dent or scratch the surface of a material. It is a material property (7.1) and so does not depend on the size or shape of the object under test. Useful comparisons can be made between a range of common materials by trying to dent or scratch one material with another. In this way, objects such as a lump of modelling clay, a stick of chalk, a piece of wood and a steel nail can be placed in order of hardness. The modelling clay can be dented by all the others so it is the softest. The steel nail can dent all the others but cannot be dented by them, so it is the hardest. The investigation can be extended by trying to find materials which are softer than the modelling clay (e.g. jelly) and harder than the nail (e.g. a hard steel file or a piece of flint). When working with the harder materials children will not be able to produce dents, so the better criterion of scratching one material with another can be introduced.

Since 1820, the hardness of rocks and minerals has been measured by scratching them, according to a standard scale known as **Moh's scale of hardness** with values from 1 (e.g. talc) to 10 (diamond). With the scratching test, these 'standard' materials can be used to find approximate hardness values for groups of common materials such as plastic, metal, wood, brick and stone and, if necessary, to compare a range of specimens from each group.

1	**softest**: talc
2 – 2.5	finger-nail
3	'copper' coin, i.e. an old 1p or 2p coin made of bronze alloy, not coated steel
5.5	steel knife blade, window glass
6 – 7	hard steel file
10	**hardest**: diamond

Some care may be needed to distinguish between scratching and the rubbing off of material. For example, a steel nail will not scratch a flint pebble or a piece of granite, but metal can be rubbed off onto the stone. Seeing this, children may ignore the scratches on the nail and conclude, wrongly, that it is the harder of the two.

Activity 7.3.1 helps children compare and estimate hardness.

7.1.3 Applying forces: compression, tension, twisting and bending

Changes in shape are one of the main ways in which we can tell that forces are acting on an object. Such changes are of two kinds: the object may be pushed or pulled out of shape (distortion or deformation), or it may break (fracture), or both may occur, distortion being followed by fracture.

Children can begin investigating the effects of forces on objects by applying pushes, pulls, twists or bends they can feel with their bodies. Their knowledge and understanding will grow through experience of applying forces to a variety of materials with their hands and simple machines such as scissors (11.7). They should talk about the way in which the forces are being applied – six ways are illustrated by Figure 7.1. Investigating strips of plastic can develop knowledge of different ways of applying forces and the idea that some responses of an object are related to its size and shape as well as to the material of which it is made. Investigations should involve measurement, using arbitrary, non-standard units at first, then standard units. The standard unit of force is the Newton (symbol: N) which is roughly equal to the weight of 100 g, therefore 1 kg presses down, on Earth, with a force of about 10 N (11.1). Forces can be measured using weights or forcemeters. In general, weights are easier to measure with but more difficult to use, whereas forcemeters are easier to use but have scales which children may have difficulty in reading. After starting with rough comparisons based on their senses, children can progress to using non-standard measurements of forces, for example by adding yogurt pots of dry sand. Even older children can usefully start with this but rapidly progress to making more precise measurements using weights and forcemeters.

Activity 7.4.1 helps children explore the effects of applying forces in different ways and Activity 8.5.1 looks more closely at materials in tension and bending.

In the remainder of this section, we focus on the ways in which materials and objects respond to forces applied in three ways: squashing (compression), stretching or pulling (tension) and twisting/bending.

7.1.4 Stiffness and flexibility

An object which shows no change when forces are applied to it would be perfectly rigid. Rigidity is a useful idea for children to link to their experience of many objects such as bricks, thick metal bars and wooden beams as rigid: their shape cannot be changed by any force the children can apply. In reality, even objects which seem to be rigid, such as bars and blocks of steel, do change shape very slightly when quite small forces act on them, but the changes are so small that they are very difficult to measure.

> Children can describe how they change the shape of objects by applying forces to them, using the idea of stiffness. The more the object resists changing shape, the greater the stiffness it shows. Thus a thick steel wire has high stiffness in bending, whereas a thin wire has low stiffness: it is flexible. Stiffness as a property is quite distinct from strength, though the two are often confused, especially when children talk or write about making objects change shape.

Flexibility can be thought of as the property opposed to rigidity and stiffness, but simply to describe an object as 'flexible' can be misleading. **It is important to know how the forces which made it change its shape are applied.** For example, a piece of string is highly flexible (it has very low stiffness) in *bending*, but in *tension* it resists changing shape and will not get longer, so it has high stiffness. It may seem odd to refer to a material such as string as being stiff, but a taut string feels much less flexible and much stiffer than a slack one. Stiffness and flexibility depend on the size and shape of the object as well as on the material of which it is made, so they are both object properties (7.1). For example, a cardboard tube may be very stiff or even rigid when an attempt is made to bend it; but if it is cut down longways with a knife, the cardboard of which it is made is quite flexible. It is the cylindrical shape of the tube which gives it its rigidity.

Activity 7.5.1 helps children to experience stiffness and flexibility and Activity 7.5.2 to experience stiffness and shape.

7.1.5 Elasticity and plasticity

When children apply forces to a flexible object to change its shape, they will notice that when the forces are removed, one of two things may happen. If the object is

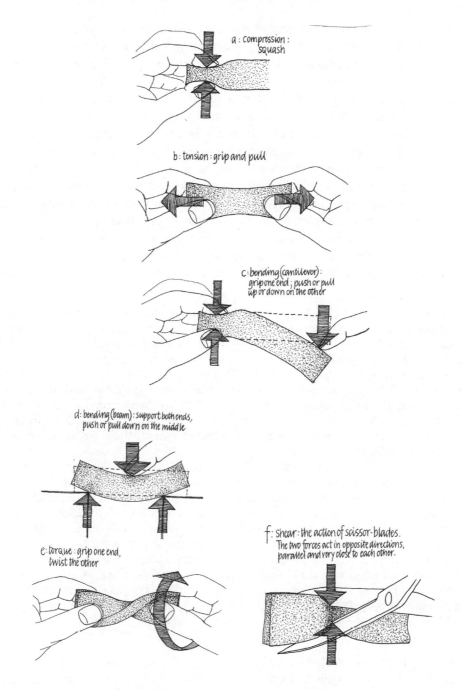

Figure 7.1 *Applying forces in different ways to a strip of plastic foam*

springy and returns to its original shape when released, as a rubber band does, it is elastic, but if the object retains its new shape, as modelling clay does, it is said to be plastic. Elasticity and plasticity are material properties (7.1), but they are not mutually exclusive: most common flexible materials show a combination of the two. When forces are applied to a flexible object, it begins by changing shape elastically and, up to a point, it will carry on changing that way, going back to its original shape when released. This can be observed by repeatedly bending and releasing a piece of thin, stiff card, increasing the force applied and the bending a little each time, and observing what happens when it is released. Up to a point the card regains its original shape, but past a certain point it will not go back all the way: it has changed plastically and part of the bend in it is permanent. Materials such as modelling clay which seem to behave in a completely plastic way have very little elasticity: they start to become permanently distorted almost as soon as a force is applied to them, and they spring back hardly at all when released. Any non-springy flexible object, such as string which is not under tension, shows plastic deformation as its shape is changed.

As pairs of properties, plasticity–elasticity and stiffness–flexibility are independent, but children investigating how real objects behave will usually need to refer to both. For example, children can explore how a rubber block and a thin rubber band are both highly elastic, but the block is much stiffer than the band, because larger forces are needed to change its shape. Observing that cold modelling clay is much stiffer than warm, though both are almost perfectly plastic, can also be used to introduce another important principle: the amount of distortion which any object undergoes depends on how large a force is applied to it. This is another aspect of the principle, very important when investigating forces and movement, that 'the bigger the force, the bigger the change' (11.1).

Children can investigate both elastic and plastic materials. If they measure the length of a rubber band as it is stretched by increasing weights, they will find that the increase in length is a steady one over most of its range, so that if they plot a graph showing length against weight applied, a straight line is likely. If they soften Plasticine slightly by warming it and then making it into spheres, these will show plastic distortion when dropped onto a hard surface. The amount of distortion, shown by the size of the flat circular face produced by the impact, increases as the ball is dropped from an increasing height (11.5.2). This is a particularly suitable investigation for young children because measurement of the distortion is unnecessary: they can make a permanent record of their results by coating the flattened face of the ball with paint and printing it.

Many processes in school and industry exploit a combination of plasticity and elasticity. Making models in card and pop-up books in paper both require sheets of materials to be creased and bent permanently (plastic deformation) while relying on their springiness (elasticity) to retain or make shapes. In making vehicle body panels, sheet steel is permanently pressed into shape using large forces, but still remains somewhat flexible and springy.

Activity 7.6.1 helps children observe elasticity and plasticity.

7.1.6 Strength

'Strong' and 'strength' are words with a complex set of interrelated meanings for both adults and children. Ignoring everyday uses as 'a strong smell' or 'a strong argument', we will think about 'strength' in the context of forces acting on objects. Children are likely to use 'strong' in at least four ways, to express four different ideas:

1. 'He can lift a heavy weight. He must be strong.' (Idea: the ability to exert a large force.)
2. 'She gave the trolley a strong push and it went faster.' (Idea: the large force itself.)
3. 'It's a strong spring. I couldn't squash it very much.' (Idea: the property of withstanding a large force with little change of shape.)
4. 'The thread is thin but very strong. We hung 6 kg on it before it broke.' (Idea: the property of withstanding a large force without breaking.)

Of these four examples, the first two clearly are not concerned with the way objects respond by changing shape when forces are applied to them, and do not use a scientific concept of 'strength'. The third and fourth examples are more problematic. The word 'strong' appears to mean much the same thing in both; but in fact each example represents a distinct scientific idea.

It is the fourth example which uses 'strong' in the accepted scientific sense: as a measure of the forces which an object can withstand before it breaks. The greater the force withstood, the stronger the object. Squashing the object until it breaks gives a measure of its **compression strength**, while pulling or stretching it shows its **tensile strength** and bending its **bending strength**. Strength is an object property (7.1): it depends on the size and shape of the object as well as on the materials of which it is made. This means that if we wish to compare the strength of two materials, such as the bending strength of two samples of concrete, it is essential in order to make the comparison fair that the objects tested should be of the same size and shape, as well as being tested under the same conditions.

The third example above uses the word 'strong' in a potentially confusing way, because it refers, not to strength in the scientific sense, but to stiffness: (7.1.4): how large a force is needed to change the shape of an object. Confusion between stiffness and strength is very common, and comes about partly because the two are often associated: many useful objects such as steel nails and wooden beams are both strong and stiff, whichever way forces are applied to them. The confusion can be avoided by remembering that stiffness is related not to strength but to flexibility. For example, compare a rubber band which stretches a lot and can support a load of 50 N (5 kg), with a cotton thread which does not stretch but can support only 25 N (2.5 kg) before it breaks. The band has low stiffness (it stretches easily) and higher tensile strength, whereas the thread has high stiffness (it resists getting longer) but only half the tensile strength of the band: the two properties are quite independent of each other.

Activity 7.7.1 helps children to compare and measure strength and Activity 7.7.2, to investigate the tearing-strength of paper.

7.1.7 Brittleness and toughness

An object made of a strong material may withstand a large force before it breaks, but its strength does not tell us how the fracture is likely to occur. Using a material which breaks suddenly and without warning could be (and all too often is) disastrous. Two properties which can help us to understand and predict the breaking of materials are brittleness and toughness.

A brittle material breaks suddenly and completely, for example a china plate dropped onto a hard floor. Either it breaks, or it doesn't. Another characteristic is that fractures are usually fairly smooth and 'clean', not rough, splintery or jagged, because of the way in which cracks spread through the material. Once a crack starts in a brittle material, only small forces are needed to make it spread until the fracture is complete. When window-glass is cut to size, the glazier uses a glass-cutter (made of a very hard material) to make a light, even scratch on the surface of the glass. Once the glass has been scratched, only a very small force, tapping on the underside, is needed to spread the fracture through the glass and break it.

The property which contrasts with brittleness is toughness. In a tough material, cracks will not spread easily, so the material breaks more slowly and often shows signs of breaking before it fractures completely.

Brittle materials can seem weak and easily broken, having low strength, but this is not always true. It may take a large force to make the first crack in a brittle material and if so, the material is strong. Glass and the very hard steel used in files are examples of strong materials which are also very brittle: they break suddenly if they are bent, but it takes a large force to do it. Similarly, there is a tendency, both among children and adults, to think that all materials which break suddenly are hard. This association probably comes from experience with brittle materials such as glass, china and brick, but it is false.

Investigating hardness, brittleness and toughness

Dried, uncooked pasta and board chalk are not hard, but both are brittle materials which are useful because children can experiment with them safely and observe how they break. There are, however, much softer brittle materials. A plastic eraser, for example, is springy when squashed (elastic in compression) and may appear to be quite tough, but if it is bent it shows elastic deformation up to a point and then cracks suddenly with no warning. The crack spreads very quickly into a clean fracture which splits the eraser in two. An even softer material is jelly. It may seem odd to refer to it as being brittle but, as many cooks attempting to turn jelly from a mould can testify, once a crack has started the weight of the jelly alone is usually enough to make it spread until it falls apart.

A good way to observe the breaking of a tough material is to hold a thin garden cane (made from bamboo) in both hands and bend it slowly, watching it carefully until it breaks. Cracks can be seen, and sometimes heard, long before the final break, which usually happens slowly. The fracture itself is very ragged and splintery, quite unlike the clean break characteristic of brittle materials.

Polythene sheet is also useful as an example, because it shows very clearly that cracks do not spread readily in a very tough material. Cut strips 2 x 20 cm from a polythene bag, make a small cut in one long side and pull the ends apart. The fracture will spread from the cut, but only very slowly, in complete contrast to the behaviour of glass and other brittle materials. Polythene also provides an example of deformation which is partly elastic and partly plastic. The stretched strip will recoil a little when it is released, but most of the increase in length is permanent.

Activity 7.8.1 helps children observe brittleness and toughness.

In nearly all materials brittleness is a disadvantage, and can be seen as the price paid for other useful properties such as the hardness of steel files, the transparency of glass and the easily cleaned surface of china. Toughness, on the other hand, is very often a major advantage. Much of the usefulness of materials such as wood, cloth, string, paper, polythene and many metals comes from their toughness. In buildings toughness can be critical. Wood is very tough and good for smaller buildings, but in comparison with other materials such as steel and concrete it is not very strong in relation to its size. Concrete on its own, however, is not a good material for beams (in ceilings, or over windows and doors) because it is very brittle and under bending forces it can break entirely without warning. As a result, concrete used for pillars, beams and floors in large structures such as multi-storey buildings and bridges is reinforced with rods or meshes of steel, which not only increase its bending strength but also its toughness, so that if it does crack, the cracks should not spread right through. It also means that the structure should give warning signs long before it actually breaks.

7.2 LINKING THE PROPERTIES OF MATERIALS TO THEIR USES

Young children are likely to have learned from their life experience that some kinds of materials are useful for particular kinds of things. They will laugh when their teacher suggests that tissue paper would be a good material to make a hat for Teddy to keep his head dry in the rain, and say 'It will get all soggy and let the rain in'. As their range of experience grows, the teacher can teach them more and better ways of understanding this connection. A basic knowledge of the properties of materials makes it possible to understand much more clearly how and why materials and objects are used in different ways. An effective way to do this is, firstly, to identify the materials which are used together for a particular purpose. Secondly, identify the properties which make each one useful and list them under 'advantages'. Thirdly, identify any properties which may limit the usefulness of each material and list them under 'disadvantages'. It is then possible to compare the contribution which each one makes with the way in which it behaves and changes, and justify a decision about which one to use for a particular purpose.

Children can investigate packaging materials by being set a challenge. We wish to send a glass bowl (a very brittle object) in a parcel by post, possibly using plastic foam 'chips' for packing, a cardboard box, strong brown wrapping paper, adhesive plastic tape and string. We can assemble these materials in the classroom and ask children to investigate and list their properties as described above. A set of results is given in Table 7.2.

This investigation can act as the starting-point for many other enquiries such as: what would happen if some of the properties of the materials were changed and, for example, string and paper became elastic? Where do all the materials come from? Are they natural (7.3), and if they are not, how are they made? How does packing a glass bowl in this way protect it? Children can carry out similar investigations into many sets of materials. Those used in houses and bicycles are particularly interesting and have the added advantages that children are already acquainted with many of them at first hand, and work on them can be linked up to many other areas of the curriculum.

7.3 NATURAL AND MANUFACTURED MATERIALS AND OBJECTS

A good starting point for investigating materials is to classify a collection of objects made of different materials, into natural or manufactured. Natural materials are substances which are produced by natural processes and changes, either chemical or physical (Chapter 8). Examples include animal materials such as bone, ivory, wool and silk; plant materials such as cotton, wood and olive oil; and mineral materials

Table 7.2 Comparing the properties of packing materials

Material	Advantages	Disadvantages
Plastic foam 'chips' (packing)	Very soft, flexible, compressible, elastic, tough, very cheap and lightweight.	May shift in transit, so need to be packed firmly in a thick layer.
Cardboard (box)	Fairly soft; strong and rather stiff in bending and compression; tough.	Not waterproof
Soft polythene sheet	Soft; very flexible in bending and tough; waterproof	Not very stiff in tension; may deform plastically
Brown paper (wrapping)	Fairly soft, very flexible and mainly plastic in bending; very stiff and fairly strong in tension; tough.	Not waterproof
String (tying up)	Soft, very flexible and plastic in bending; very strong and stiff in tension; very tough; not affected by water.	None
Plastic adhesive tape (sealing)	Soft, flexible in bending; strong and fairly stiff in tension; adhesive (sticky).	Not waterproof; glue may come off if wetted; very brittle

such as granite, salt and slate. Natural materials may be changed physically and shaped by human activity in a wide variety of ways to make them useful (see below), but the nature of the material itself is not changed. In contrast to these are manufactured materials, made by processes which result in a raw material being transformed into a different kind of substance by chemical changes. In a few cases, chemical processes are used to make materials which occur naturally but are rare: the smelting of some metals such as copper is an example; but most manufactured materials do not occur naturally at all. For example, stone is a natural material, and a stone pebble on a beach is a natural object, because it was not shaped by human activity. Cut stone building-blocks and roofing slates are manufactured objects, although both are made of natural materials. Manufactured materials which children investigate are likely to be in the form of manufactured objects, such as bricks, polythene bottles or cardboard boxes. Naturally formed objects of manufactured materials are less common, and are usually worn away or corroded, such as heavily rusted steel or beach pebbles of brick and glass.

	Object	
Material	Natural	Manufactured
Natural	*Stone pebble on a beach*	Slate in a roof
Manufactured	*Brick pebble on a beach*	Brick in a wall

Natural materials may be changed physically in a wide variety of ways to make them usable, and care may be needed to distinguish such changes from the chemical changes involved in making manufactured materials. Children may be familiar with:

• **cutting, carving and splitting**	wood, slate and stone
• **crushing and grinding**	clay, chalk, metal ores, coal, roadstone, foodstuffs (especially cereals and spices)
• **sieving and sorting**	sand, gravel, roadstone, flour (8.2)
• **sedimentation**	clay for ceramics (8.2)
• **spinning, weaving and knitting**	cotton, wool, linen, silk
• **dissolving, filtering and evaporating**	extraction and purification of salt and sugar (8.1.2, 8.2)
• **pulping and sieving**	paper (glue is also added)

Children learn how and why materials are used as they are by obtaining information about their properties and origins. Productive investigations use a topic approach (1.4) to familiar and interesting processes and products.

Activity 10.1.1 explores suggestions on materials and objects suitable for sorting activities and Activity 10.1.2 helps children investigate the origins of materials.

7.4 ROCKS AND SOILS

Sorting and classifying rocks that children are familiar with in their local environment can be linked to investigating habitats and ecosystems. The materials found in buildings and the landscape can then be used as the basis for case-studies of how rocks are formed, used and changed.

Section 11.7 provides more information on how this might be approached.

Children can investigate the texture and fertility of topsoil, particularly the range of size among the mineral particles which make it up. Having compared textures, they can carry out a simple analysis of particle size in the same soils, by suspension and sedimentation. Each weighed sample is put into about twice its own volume of water in a jar with a secure lid. After any lumps have been broken up, the mixture is shaken vigorously and left to settle. Because large particles settle out faster than small ones it is usually possible, if similar containers are used, to make accurate visual comparisons of the particle range in the different soils. The range of particles, shown by the depth of the various layers, can then be linked to the earlier observations on texture.

Activity 11.10.1 and Activity 11.10.2 investigate soil textures and particle sizes.

7.5 WATER AND WEATHER

Weather and climate   Weather is the name given to the events and changes which take place from day to day within the Earth's atmosphere. Short-term changes and events are referred to as weather; longer-term changes and patterns describe the climate of a region.

When investigating weather, it is necessary, in order to begin developing an understanding of what is observed, to interpret observations in terms of the properties of liquids and gases (6.1) and changes of state (evaporation, condensation, freezing and melting, 6.2, 6.3). One effective overall strategy is to begin by concentrating on changes the children can observe for themselves and to develop explanations of them. These can then be used to develop an understanding of the water cycle as it is experienced both locally and on a wider scale (7.5.6), and to interpret common short-term weather patterns such as depressions, anticyclones and thunderstorms (7.5.4, 7.5.5). The aspects of weather which children can usefully observe, and for which explanations can be developed, include: temperature; wind (direction and speed); cloud (type and amount of cover); condensation at ground level; and precipitation (type and amount).

Section 11.6 gives ideas on observing and recording patterns in the weather.

7.5.1 Temperature

Temperature, measured in degrees Celsius (°C, 9.3.2) is a measure of how hot or cold things are. In weather study, it is the temperature of the air which is usually measured. Air temperature has profound effects on children's lives, which they can describe and understand. These effects are both direct (comfort, clothing, patterns of activity) and indirect (use of heating in home and school). Broad seasonal variations in air temperature are caused by changes in the amount of energy reaching any particular part of the Earth's surface from the Sun throughout the year (14.4). At all times of the year it is useful to record air temperature at intervals during the day and, if possible, to record maximum and minimum temperatures for a succession of 24-hour periods using a special thermometer.

Activity 11.2.1 and Activity 11.2.2 give ideas and information on measuring and recording air temperature.

7.5.2 Wind

Wind is the name given to any movement in the atmosphere. Children can make two main kinds of observations and measurements of wind: its direction and its speed. Both are likely to be affected near the ground by obstacles such as buildings, trees and hedges. Measurements should therefore be carried out in large open spaces wherever possible. Wind direction is measured by finding the compass point from which the wind appears to be blowing, using a windsock or weathervane, both of which can be made by the children themselves. Wind speed is measured using an anemometer. Accurate portable anemometers are very expensive, but if one can be borrowed they are very useful for calibrating simpler instruments. Designing and making an anemometer is an effective technological exercise, and at least two basic kinds can be made by children: those which are deflected by the wind (flaps, flags and windsocks) and those which rotate (propellers or cups on arms).

Wind speed, like other speeds, should strictly speaking be measured in metres per second (ms^{-1}), but children may be able more easily to visualize the speed if it is quoted in kilometres or miles per hour, which they can then compare with speeds they have experienced when watching or travelling in cars or trains.

The speed of the wind is directly related to the forces it exerts on objects in its path, such as buildings and trees, and on the surface of water in lakes and at sea. This in turn is related to effects which children experience and can observe. In 1806 a naval officer, Commander (later Admiral Sir) Francis Beaufort, devised a 12-point scale which linked the speed of the wind to the effects which it is likely to have, at sea and on land. The Beaufort Scale is still used to communicate predicted wind speeds in shipping forecasts, and is very useful for estimating wind speed when accurate measurement is not possible.

Activity 11.3.1, Activity 11.3.2 and Activity 11.3.3 help children observe and measure wind speed and direction and include the Beaufort Scale.

7.5.3 Water in the atmosphere

When liquid water is exposed to air it usually 'dries up' or evaporates (6.2.2), and is converted to water in the cool gas phase, known as water vapour. Air containing a lot of water vapour is said to be humid. If evaporation continues for long enough, a point will be reached at which the air can hold no more water vapour and is said to be saturated. Exactly how much water vapour is in saturated air depends on the temperature: the higher the temperature, the greater the amount. This means that if saturated air is cooled, it will not be able to hold all the water vapour in it and some will change back to liquid water by condensation (6.2.2). For condensation to occur, humid air must be cooled. In the atmosphere this occurs in two main ways: first, when humid air comes into contact with a cold surface (for example, condensation on cold windows); and second, when the warm, humid air is itself cooled (for example, breathing out on a cold day; vapour trails from jet air-craft). Cooling a humid air-mass leads to the formation of tiny water droplets. These are so small that they do not fall down through the air and settle out, but remain suspended in the atmosphere as a natural aerosol known as cloud, mist or fog. If the air is cold enough, the cloud will consist not of liquid water droplets, but of tiny crystals of ice.

Cloud is the general name for an air-mass, well above ground or sea-level, in which water vapour has condensed to form tiny, suspended droplets of liquid water or crystals of ice. For cloud formation to occur, a humid air-mass has to be cooled, by rising up into the atmosphere, by coming into contact with cooler air, or by both at once.

Mist, fog, dew and frost If humid air near the ground is cooled enough, some of the water vapour in it will condense. This can happen like cloud formation, but just above ground level. The most obvious effect is that light passing through the air is scattered (13.5.3), reducing visibility and making it difficult or impossible to see distant objects clearly. If visibility is between 1 and 2 km the cloud is referred to as **mist**; if it is less than 1 km, it is referred to as **fog**. If humid air comes into contact with cold surfaces at or near ground level, particularly in still air conditions, it condenses. If the surface and the air are above 0°C, then **dew** forms. If the ground temperature is below 0°C but the air temperature is just above there will be a **frost** as the water vapour condenses directly into ice without forming liquid water first. This happens on the ground and so it is called **ground frost.** But if both ground and air are below 0°C there will be an **air-frost**, which may form not only at ground level, but also on trees and telephone wires well above it. Frost is always most likely when the air is still, cold and stable; conditions associated with clear skies and rapid cooling of the land surface at night.

7.5.4 Precipitation

Precipitation is the general name for water falling to the ground from clouds in the atmosphere, either as solid or as liquid, including rain, snow, sleet and hail. Outside the tropics, almost all precipitation begins to form inside clouds as very small ice crystals. Once these tiny crystals have formed, they grow quickly as water vapour freezes onto them, and growing crystals may cling together as they collide. Inside the cloud, the air is rising. While the ice crystals are small, the upward movement of air prevents them from falling, but as they grow a point is reached at which this is no longer possible. What happens as the ice crystals fall depends on the height of the cloud and the air temperature. If the ice crystals fall for long enough through air above 0°C they will melt and fall as raindrops, whereas if the air is cold enough, they will reach the ground as snowflakes. Children may be able to observe how the size of snowflakes is related to temperature: powdery snow is associated with colder conditions than large, feathery flakes. When melting flakes pass through a layer of very cold air near the ground they may re-freeze, forming sleet; a term which is also used to describe mixed rain and snow falling when the air temperature is about 1.5°C.

Activity 11.5.1 shows how to observe and measure precipitation.

Raindrops lose water by evaporation as they fall below the cloud. The intensity of rainfall (i.e. how much water falls in a period of time) depends mainly on the size of raindrops, varying from very fine drizzle to very large raindrops, from a thundercloud (7.5.5). Thunderstorms may also produce a distinct kind of precipitation: hail.

7.5.5 Thunder and lightning

The exact cause of lightning is not known, but very large electrical charges are built up within thunderclouds. In any thunderstorm, most lightning occurs inside the clouds and may be visible as sheet lightning. Cloud-to-ground lightning occurs when a downward discharge, like a faint lightning stroke, is met by a small upward one as it nears the surface of the Earth. When the two meet, a pathway is created down which the bolt or stroke of lightning, like a gigantic spark, can travel. This lasts for less than 0.1 sec., but in that time it generates very high temperatures (estimated at 25,000°C, much hotter than the surface of the Sun), causing the air to glow white-hot and giving the flash of lightning which we see. The lightning conductors on buildings are an attempt to provide a route through which the very large current generated by the cloud can travel harmlessly to Earth. The intense local heating of the lightning flash causes the air around it to expand violently, sending out the shock-waves which we hear as thunder (13.1.4).

7.5.6 The water cycle

Earth is the wet planet. Its character and the conditions on its surface are largely a result of the abundance of water, which in the form of seas and oceans covers about two-thirds of its surface. Children need to know and understand something of the processes which create the conditions making life on Earth possible, of which the most important is the circulation of water between the oceans, air and land which is known as the water cycle.

The water (or hydrological) cycle is the evaporation of water from the ocean into the atmosphere – the energy required for evaporation or latent heat (9.2.2) coming from the Sun, followed by condensation of the water vapour as cloud, which may produce precipitation in a liquid form (rain) or a solid form (snow or hail). Precipitation falling into the ocean (about 77 per cent of the total, worldwide) is recycled directly, but the remainder which falls on land returns by less direct routes which may be rapid or take a very long time to complete. In mountains and polar regions, for example, snow turns to ice in glaciers and ice-caps where it may remain, slowly moving downwards or outwards towards the sea for thousands of years before it melts and re-enters the active part of the water cycle.

Apart from weather and precipitation, the parts of the water cycle which affect the lives of children most obviously are likely to be those which influence water supply and human activities such as farming. Water falling on land may be recycled to the atmosphere very quickly by evaporation from the soil surface and from the leaves of plants. Some of the water which goes deeper into the soil will move sideways, draining into lakes or rivers, including the artificial lakes we know as reservoirs. Much of this will return to the sea in a relatively short space of time – a few weeks or months – even if it is diverted on the way for human use. In areas with porous rocks, however, water often percolates much deeper and remains, in some cases for a very long time, as ground-water which may be extracted by drilling boreholes and pumping it to the surface.

The pattern of water supply, use and replenishment varies widely in different parts of Britain and Europe, but in densely populated areas all the major sources (rivers, lakes, reservoirs and ground-water) are exploited. In Britain there is a particularly clear pattern of population in relation to water supply. In general, the highest concentrations of people live in the areas of low rainfall, while areas of high rainfall are relatively sparsely populated. This has given rise to the need for large-scale storage of water in reservoirs and its long-distance transportation by pumping through pipes. Children should be aware of the need to conserve water and the dangers of pollution and over-exploitation, both of rivers and ground-water resources.

8 CHANGING, COMBINING AND SEPARATING MATERIALS

INTRODUCTION

Some of the awe and wonder of science in our cultural heritage comes from the amazing ways in which we have learned to gain control over materials and make many new ones to improve our personal and social lives. Young children begin to appreciate this as they learn to change materials. We need to encourage them to observe and describe changes in materials and to think about fundamental scientific ideas such as change, no-change, sameness, similarity, difference, cause and effect. They need plenty of investigative experience of many different changes including melting, freezing, boiling, condensing, changes in shape, mixing, combining and separating materials. The teacher's role is to ensure that they have ample opportunity to discuss the evidence they gather and that scientific ideas and language are carefully introduced as explanations to discipline and deepen their thinking.

In sections 6.3 and 6.4, as part of the background knowledge for primary teachers, a distinction is made between physical and chemical changes and we see how scientists can explain them using the atomic theory. Most primary children are not able to understand scientific ideas about atoms until they understand more of the abstract reasoning behind the theory and learn more about the indirect evidence that scientists have gathered which justifies believing in atoms. This situation calls for fine judgement on the part of primary teachers about what to teach and how to teach it. This chapter offers guidance about these decisions. It is based on a principle of becoming scientific that, just like scientists themselves, **children should be encouraged to think about evidence critically when deciding whether to believe in an explanatory idea**. The National Curriculum requires that during Key Stage 2, children should learn about the ease or difficulty with which a change can be reversed. This may be associated with the distinction between physical and chemical changes but they are not the same. As teachers we need to decide how best to introduce scientific explanations of changing, combining and separating materials by knowing our children, bearing in mind that the National Curriculum does not require us to teach them the differences between physical and chemical change.

Physical changes may alter the appearance and other properties of materials and objects, but the scientific idea is that **the actual substances involved remain the same**. Children are familiar with changing ice into (liquid) water and water into steam as well as the reverse of these. However, they may not believe that they are all the same substance, water. (Of course it does not assist clear thinking about this when we use the same word, water, to refer to the kind of stuff itself, and also its state when a liquid.) There are many other examples of physical change in everyday life experience. And a change which *does* result in the formation of a different kind of substance is a chemical change. Children are familiar with many everyday processes which involve chemical change, such as cooking, rusting of steel, decay and burning.

For scientists, an important part of the idea of physical change is that however the materials seem to change, they do not change in themselves at all. They are actually the same *stuff*. This is not an idea that is obvious to children. Their intuitive interpretation of this evidence is likely to be that water and ice seem to be so different in their characteristics because they really are different materials, made of different *stuff*. Children also have much life experience of bringing about other kinds of physical changes such as mixing and separating materials. We need to help them to notice that it is relatively easy to make these changes, adding or taking away relatively small amounts of heat. We do not need to give abstract theoretical explanations in terms of atoms. At primary level, investigating processes which involve chemical change cannot lead children to an understanding of the nature of chemical change itself.

8.1 MAKING AND SEPARATING MIXTURES

8.1.1 Mixing different materials

A mixture is made when two or more substances are physically combined or mixed together to make what appears to be a single substance, while remaining chemically separate and distinct. For example, air is a mixture of gases, mainly nitrogen and oxygen. It has more or less the same composition throughout the atmosphere, but the different gases are not chemically combined. Mixtures are made by physical changes and can, at least in theory, be separated by physical changes, though this may be very difficult. For example, to separate the gases in air it is necessary to make the gas so cold that it condenses into a liquid (at about −200°C) and then allow it to warm up gradually so that the different gases boil off in turn as their boiling-points are reached. This is the main way in which nitrogen and oxygen are produced for industrial use.

Children should make mixtures, observe the resulting changes and also use (and if possible devise) a variety of methods to separate them again. The main kinds of mixture which children may encounter, use or investigate are:

- solid dispersed in solid: a mixture of particles, e.g. sand and salt
- solid dispersed in gas: e.g. smoke, dust suspension
- liquid dispersed in liquid: an emulsion, e.g. milk, PVA glue
- liquid dispersed in gas: an aerosol, e.g. hair lacquer
- solid or gas dispersed in liquid: a solution or suspension (8.1.2)
- liquid dispersed in porous solid: absorption (8.1.3)

Activities 6.4.1, 6.4.2 and 6.4.3 give ideas on separating a variety of mixtures.

Solid–solid mixtures are made when granules or powders are mixed together.

Solid–gas mixtures A suspension of very fine solid particles in a gas is known as a smoke. The solid particles in a smoke are so fine that they do not settle out, so if they are breathed in they go right into the lungs and are likely to irritate and damage them. Tobacco smoke is particularly harmful because it is not only an irritant but also contains many chemicals which can cause cancer (3.12). Smoke, mixed with larger solid particles suspended in the air, is also part of the air pollution produced by vehicle engines and some industries. Unlike the smoke, the larger suspended particles will settle out slowly, but can still be very harmful, not only by creating a dirty urban-industrial environment, but also by contributing to bronchitis and other respiratory diseases when they are breathed in. Larger solid particles separating out of the air can be trapped and used as a measure of air pollution.

Liquid–liquid mixtures A suspension of very small droplets of one liquid in another is known as an emulsion. The emulsion children will be most familiar with is milk, which is a suspension of fat droplets in water. In whole milk, some of the fat droplets are large enough to separate, and rise to the surface to form a layer of cream, which may be skimmed off to make butter. As a result, skimmed milk has a much lower fat content than whole milk. Another example of an emulsion is PVA or white glue, made by dispersing a synthetic resin in water.

Liquid–gas mixtures A suspension of liquid droplets in a gas is known as an aerosol. Pressurized cans which produce aerosols are very commonly used to spray liquid chemicals, including hair lacquer, car paint and household insecticides. By far the most common and widespread aerosols, however, are natural suspensions of tiny water droplets in air, usually known as cloud, mist or fog (7.5.3).

8.1.2 Solutions and suspensions

When a solid is mixed with a liquid, the mixture produced is either a solution or a suspension, depending on whether or not the solid will dissolve in the liquid. Children gain an understanding of dissolving by comparing two mixtures, one of which forms a true solution while the other does not.

> Children can compare pottery clay with instant coffee by mixing them (separately) with water and stirring until no lumps remain. Both mixtures are brown, but the clay–water mixture is cloudy, whereas the coffee–water mixture is clear. After a while the clay will probably begin to settle out at the bottom of its container, but the coffee never will. Finally, if the clay–water mixture is filtered through filter paper or paper towel, the clay will remain in the paper whereas the coffee mixture passes through the paper unchanged and leaves no solid residue. This comparison shows three characteristics of a true solution (coffee) as opposed to a suspension (clay). A **solution** is clear, will never settle out however long it is left, and is unaffected by filtering; a **suspension** is cloudy, usually settles out to give a sediment and can be separated by filtering.

A solution is formed when a substance (solute) dissolves in a liquid (solvent). Any substance which will dissolve is called soluble; one which will not is called insoluble. A true solution is different from a suspension because the suspension is a mixture of very small, solid and insoluble particles in a liquid. These scatter light passing through the mixture, making it appear cloudy, are usually large enough to sink and settle out and can be removed by filtering, which is a kind of sieving. However, a true solution consists of individual particles (molecules, 6.4), which are thousands of times smaller.

> Children should learn that dissolving a substance such as sugar or salt in water simply makes a mixture: the solid has not disappeared and no new substance has been made. This is an idea they can easily test by tasting the solutions, using short disposable straws to ensure hygiene.

Activity 6.5.1 helps children compare solutions with suspensions.

Solubility If we add increasing amounts of a solute such as salt to water and stir, a point will be reached at which no more will dissolve. For any solute there is a definite amount which can be dissolved in a certain volume of solvent. This is a measure of its solubility. When as much solute as possible has been dissolved, the solution is said to be saturated. In nearly all cases solubility increases with temperature, so far more salt or, particularly, sugar can be dissolved in 100 ml of hot water than if the water is cold. This can be shown by making a saturated solution in a small volume of hot water. When this is allowed to cool, the solid will recrystallize, even though the solution has lost very little water by evaporation in such a short time.

Speed of dissolving When a solid dissolves, it does so only at its surface. Because of this, a single lump of solid will dissolve much more slowly than the same amount crushed to powder. This can be shown by taking two similar small lumps of soap, cutting one into tiny pieces and comparing the amount of time these and the larger lump take to dissolve in the same amount of water at the same temperature and stirred to the same degree. The difference shows why soap pow-der is preferred for washing clothes and a lump of soap for personal hygiene. A similar investigation can be done by using crystals of rock-salt or coffee-sugar: two similar crystals are selected, one is crushed and the time taken for the two samples to dissolve is compared. This also explains why sugar lumps dissolve much faster than one might expect. They are porous (8.1.3), made up of small grains of sugar pressed together, with air in between them. Water gets between the grains, softens and breaks up the lump, and then dissolves the individual grains very quickly.

Activity 6.5.2 investigates solutions and their separation.

Solvents other than water Many useful substances which cannot be dissolved in water, such as fats, waxes, resins, oils and gums, can be dissolved by other sol-vents which evaporate much more quickly. Various resins, both natural and synthetic, form the basis of fast-drying glues and varnishes, which are very useful technologically but whose solvents can, if inhaled, cause permanent injury or death. Many are also highly inflammable, and for these reasons their sale to chil-dren is restricted or prohibited. Perfumes, eaux-de-toilette and colognes are made by dissolving oils, some of which are distilled from flowers, in alcohol (ethanol). Dry-cleaning is a process which uses and recycles a powerful fat solvent capable of removing deep-seated dirt and stains without damaging fabrics which would be ruined by water-based cleaning.

Liquids other than water Children may assume that any transparent, colourless liquid that they haven't been able to investigate is water, even the melted wax that forms just underneath a burning candle flame. On the other hand, they are likely to suppose that liquids which are not pure water, such as drinks, are not water at all. Milk, for example, seems to be quite a different material from water, and yet it is mostly water in its composition. As indicated in the previous section, many liquids which are not water are dangerous for children. There are investigations which would benefit from having another kind of liquid with which to compare water. For example in learning about floating and sinking: *does it make any difference to how something floats on, or sinks through different kinds of liquid?* In these situations it is good to be able to use liquid paraffin (the clear, colourless oil, not the paraffin made from petroleum) and cooking oil. They have different properties from water in several ways.

Soap and detergents   Most of the dirt on our clothing comes from our skin, which is greasy. Fats and greases will not dissolve in water and are in fact water repellent. Soap and detergents can clean clothes and skin because they are able to break up a film of greasy dirt into tiny droplets which are then washed away in suspension by the water.

Gases dissolved in water   Gases as well as solids can dissolve in water and other solvents. Air dissolves in water, but unlike solids such as sugar and salt, much more air can dissolve in cold water than in hot. This explains why bubbles of air appear in cold tap-water when it is heated up, as children can notice if they fill a drinking glass with cold water and put it in a warm place for a while. Fish and most other water-dwelling animals rely on oxygen dissolved in water for respiration. Fish breathe by taking water in through the mouth and pumping it over the gills on either side of the head. The warming of water by electricity generating stations and the dumping of waste such as sewage can reduce the amount of dissolved oxygen in river water to the point where fish and other animals die. Children may also be familiar with carbon dioxide gas dissolved in water, in the form of fizzy drinks. Because the gas is put in under pressure, much more can dissolve than normally would do at that temperature. When the bottle is opened, the pressure is released and the excess gas comes out of the solution as bubbles.

Activity 6.5.3 helps children explore solutions of gases.

8.1.3 Absorbency and waterproofing

Many common materials, both natural and manufactured, are solid (they keep their form when unsupported) but have many small cavities in them which can be filled with liquid or gas. Such materials are described as porous. They include paper, cloth, sugar lumps, most woods, soil and soft rocks such as chalk, some sandstones and limestones. All these materials, in differing degrees, have the property of absorbency, which means that when in contact with a liquid they will soak it up or absorb it. Children can investigate the properties of an absorbent material by cutting a strip from a paper towel and dipping one end into water. The water does not simply wet the paper in contact with it, but moves up the strip to a much higher level. This happens because the water is attracted to the paper fibres. The narrower the gaps in the paper, the greater the force of attraction will be and the higher the water will rise. This is a mixture in which the liquid is dispersed in the solid and tends to stay dispersed in it, a property used in towels and babies' nappies. If the wet material is squashed or twisted the liquid may be removed, as for example when squeezing a wet sponge or spinning washing in a spin-dryer. Paint-brushes are specially made to exploit this effect: paint is held in the small spaces between the bristles while these are relaxed, but when they are bent and squeezed together the paint is forced out.

Activity 6.6.1 helps children investigate absorbency.

Absorbency is an important property in many everyday materials. It is an advantage in paper towels and kitchen rolls and children can devise fair tests to measure and compare the absorbency of different kinds and brands. In other materials such as brick, absorbency is a disadvantage if it allows rising damp in the walls of a house. The ability of porous solids to hold liquids is very important to life on Earth, because most land plants depend on it for their water supply. Soils are porous, and water can move into them both from above (rainfall) and from below (ground-water). Plant roots grow into the soil, and root-hairs (4.2) penetrate between the particles, into the spaces where water is held. They are then able to take up water for use by the plant. The spaces between the particles of clay soils are much smaller than those in sandy soil, so the forces holding water in them are much larger. As a result, clay soils hold more water and dry out much more slowly than sandy soils do (7.4).

Waterproofing   Sometimes we need to use a porous material such as cloth or paper but do not want it to absorb water. To make a porous material waterproof it has to be coated, or the spaces in it filled up with another material which will not attract water but repel it. Wax is an example of a material which repels water very strongly. This can be seen by dropping water onto leaves which have a waxy coating, such as those of cabbage or nasturtium. The water can neither wet the wax nor spread out over it, and either runs off or contracts into a round globule. A similar effect can be seen by dropping water onto the feathers of water-birds.

Children can investigate the coating of a porous material such as paper with a water-repellent substance as a way of making it waterproof. They can investigate waterproofing paper with a layer of wax crayon, testing it to see how long water takes to seep through and comparing it with untreated paper.

Activity 6.6.3 helps children explore waterproofing.

8.2 SUMMARY OF WAYS OF SEPARATING MIXTURES OF MATERIALS

Separating a mixture of different solid materials If the particles are of different sizes it is usually possible to separate them, at least to some degree, by sieving. This is a useful method for rough analysis of some soils, particularly sandy and stony ones, and is commonly used in the building industry to assess the suitability of gravels and aggregates for particular kinds of concrete. Sets of sieves with different meshes are available for this purpose. If the particles are finer and will not dissolve in water it may be possible to separate them by sedimentation. The solid mixture is shaken up with water and left to settle to form a sediment layer. The smaller the particle the longer it takes to sink, so fractions of the mixture with different particle sizes are separated into layers when the sedimentation is complete. This is a standard method of soil analysis (7.4) which is also used in the purification of sewage and in the refining of clay for pottery.

Activity 6.4.1 helps children separate particulate mixtures by particle size.

If a mixture is made of two solids, one of which will dissolve in a liquid while the other will not, they can be separated by shaking the mixture in the liquid, then filtering out the one which will not dissolve.

Activity 6.4.2 helps children separate mixtures by dissolving and filtering.

The dissolved solid can then be recovered by evaporating or boiling away the dissolving liquid (6.2.2). A mixture of sugar and sand can be separated in this way. It is, however, much more difficult to separate a mixture of two substances which both dissolve in water, such as salt and sugar. This is in fact a useful example because it serves to emphasize that some simple physical changes can be very difficult to reverse.

Activity 6.5.2 helps children separate solutions.

If a mixture is made of two solids such as sugar and salt, both of which dissolve in water, it can be very difficult to separate them. In some cases, a method which depends on absorbency, known as chromatography, can work. Chromatography means, literally, writing with colour, and the best way for children to investigate it is to separate mixtures of water-soluble dyes.

Children can investigate chromatography using interesting mixtures found in felt- and fibre-tipped pens with non-waterproof inks. They put a concentrated spot of dye onto a white absorbent paper such as blotting-paper, by repeatedly loading the spot with ink and letting it dry. Then they dip the paper into water, or carefully drip water onto the spot of dye. As the water spreads across or outwards, it dissolves the dyes and carries them over the paper, but at different speeds. The different dyes in the mixture become separated into spots or rings. Children can do their own detective work to answer many questions, such as, do different manufacturers use different dye mixtures? Comparing black inks is particularly interesting and the technique has been used to investigate forgeries.

The teacher can explain to the children that different dyes are carried over the paper at different speeds because they are attracted to the paper fibres to different degrees. A dye which is strongly attracted to paper will move only slowly and leave a streak behind the main spot, whereas one which is attracted more weakly will move more quickly and leave no streak. Chromatography is a very important technique in industry, research and forensic science for separating complex mixtures of chemicals in solution.

Activity 6.6.2 shows how children can investigate chromatography.

If one of the ingredients of a solid particle mixture is magnetic (12.3), it can be separated from the others using a magnet. Ceramic magnets (12.7) are particularly useful for this. Children can separate iron filings from (dry) sand using a magnet inside a thin plastic bag, so that the iron powder does not cling to it directly. This method is used to separate iron and steel from other metals in mixed scrap metal.

Separating a mixture of solid and liquid materials

• *Suspensions of solid in liquid*: The suspension of solid particles needs to be passed through a filter which has holes that are smaller than the size of the particles of the suspended solid. This is similar to sieving, with the tiny holes in the filter paper acting as a sieve.

• *Suspensions of liquid in liquid*: The droplets of one liquid suspended as an emulsion in another liquid are very difficult to separate.

• *Solutions*: Because a true solution cannot be separated by filtering, other physical changes have to be used. Children at primary level usually use water as the solvent to make solutions, so separating the water from the solute can usually be done either by evaporation or, if necessary, by boiling.

Children can leave a concentrated salt or sugar solution exposed to the air in a shallow dish, covered with a sheet of paper to exclude dust. As the water evaporates the solute will recrystallize, but gentle heat (for example from a room heater) will usually be needed to make the last of the water evaporate. Children can be taught that this kind of solute recovery is used on a large scale in the extraction and refining of salt and sugar. On a very small scale it is also what happens when fibre-tipped and other pens with liquid ink are used. The ink is a solution of dyes, and when deposited on the paper the solvent, usually water, evaporates and leaves the solute as a visible mark.

If we want to recover the solvent from a solution, it is boiled or evaporated and the gas or vapour collected, cooled and condensed. This is the process of distillation, and is used not only to recover industrial solvents from processes such as dry-cleaning, but also to produce pure fresh water from sea-water or contaminated supplies, particularly in dry areas of the world where the process can rely on heating from the Sun.

> Having made solutions and suspensions in water and separated the solutes and solids from them, children can experiment with the separation of more complex mixtures such as salt and sand, sugar and chalk or instant coffee and cornflour.

Separating a mixture of solid and gas materials   Solids which are suspended in gas, such as smoke, may separate spontaneously if the particles are big enough to fall out of suspension over a period of time. Otherwise they are removable by moving the air through a filter with holes that are fine enough to trap the particles.

Separating a mixture of gas and liquid materials   Liquids which are suspended in gas, aerosols, may separate spontaneously if the droplets get big enough to fall out of suspension over a period of time. Otherwise they are removable by moving the air through a filter with holes that are fine enough to trap the droplets. Gas which is dissolved in liquids can separate if the temperature rises.

> Children can observe a drinking glass of cold water freshly drawn from a tap for a while. They will notice that as the water temperature increases towards that in the room, air bubbles often form on the inside of the glass. If a Sodastream is available, with a cylinder of carbon dioxide for making fizzy drinks, the same kind of phenomenon can be investigated.

Activity 6.5.3 gives more information on investigating gases dissolved in water.

8.3 CHANGING MATERIALS CHEMICALLY

8.3.1 Food and cooking

Food is like most of the major groups of materials we use: a range of natural and manufactured substances. In preparing many kinds of food, natural raw materials are cooked to make them more palatable, more digestible, or both, and most cooking processes involve at least some chemical changes. Basic cooking relies, at least in part, on changing raw ingredients by heating.

Children can investigate changes to food chemicals such as carbohydrates, fats and proteins (3.4). Boiling water does not affect a fat such as olive oil at all. A dry starchy carbohydrate such as pasta or rice swells up, becomes soft and therefore more easily chewed and digested, but the changes it undergoes are largely physical and can be reversed simply by drying. However, a high protein food such as egg-white is changed chemically by heating, and the changes are obvious, drastic and irreversible.

Boiling an egg   When heated, the proteins in foods change irreversibly: they become coagulated, which means that their structure becomes tighter and they cling together in a mass much more firmly than before. Egg-white, which is mostly water with about 9 per cent of protein (albumen) is useful to investigate. Coagulation of the protein is easily shown by dropping a little egg-white into hot water.

> Children can find the lowest temperature at which this coagulation will occur by making small boats of aluminium foil, putting a little egg-white into each and floating them on water at different temperatures.

Activity 9.2.1 helps children to observe cooking egg-white.

Cakes and baking powder   Cakes and breads have a distinctive, spongy texture. A firm but soft 'skeleton' traps thousands of small, gas-filled bubbles. The 'skeleton' is made mainly of proteins in the flour (gluten) which are coagulated in baking. In some cakes, protein from eggs also helps to make a firm, soft structure.

The process of making bubbles in the dough or cake mixture is traditionally known as leavening. Sponge cakes for example are naturally leavened, the air bubbles made by beating eggs and sugar until they make a foam and then cooking immediately. This uses a combination of chemical and physical changes. The cooking expands the air bubbles (physical change) helped by steam produced from water (physical change) squeezed out of the gluten as it coagulates (chemical change), to form the structure of the cake.

An alternative way of providing gas bubbles uses mixtures of chemicals (known collectively as baking powder) which undergo a chemical change to produce bubbles of carbon dioxide gas within the mixture. This can be observed by putting a spoonful of baking powder into very hot water. All of the chemical mixtures use 'bicarbonate of soda' (sodium hydrogen carbonate) as the source of carbon dioxide with acidic chemicals such as 'cream of tartar'. When mixed into the dough, both chemicals dissolve in water and react with each other, producing carbon dioxide (chemical change). The carbon dioxide expands and mixes with steam just as the air in a naturally leavened mixture does, and again the gas bubbles are trapped as the protein coagulates. Some kinds of flour for domestic use are sold with baking powder already mixed with them in the correct proportion. These are known as self-raising flours.

Activity 9.2.2 helps children to investigate sponge cakes.

Yeast and bread   To be easily digestible, bread needs to have the same light, bubble-filled texture as cakes. The bubbles in bread are carbon dioxide mixed with steam, but they are generated using chemical changes brought about by yeast (5.3).

Activity 9.2.3 helps children to investigate baking bread.

Cheese and yogurt   Making cheese and yogurt also depends on the coagulation of proteins. Here, the proteins in milk are coagulated, not by heating but by other chemical changes which produce acids. Acids are a very large group of chemicals, with a characteristic sharp taste: for example in lemon juice, it is caused by citric acid. Many mild acids are found in foods and, like heat, they make proteins coagulate, and the ones which give cheese and yogurt their solidity and texture are made by microbes (bacteria, 5.3).

Activity 9.2.4 helps children to investigate making yogurt.

8.3.2 Reactions with oxygen: burning

All changes, including chemical reactions, involve transfers of energy (9.1). Some reactions transfer energy to the environment, usually as thermal energy (9.2.2). Others require a transfer of energy from the environment, for example eating fizzy sweets and sherbet powder tastes cool because the reacting chemicals need to be heated by the mouth.

Chemical changes which release energy are an essential part of everyday life, and children will be familiar with several which involve reactions with oxygen in the air, including burning and rusting. Investigating them together can be a useful way to understand the conditions under which each occurs and the ways in which they may be controlled or prevented.

The wax candle: an example of burning   Children's fascination with candles provides motivation for extended and intense observation. The changes involved in burning can be observed safely using wax candles fixed firmly, using molten wax, to metal lids or dishes. Provide additional protection by putting the candles on a tray containing sand or damp paper. Avoid loose clothing, particularly sleeves, and pupils with long hair should tie it back securely. The burning of a candle is a complex process which involves physical as well as chemical changes. When a match is applied to the wick, the heat of its burning causes the wax first to melt, then to vaporize (physical changes) and finally to burn (chemical change).

Activity 9.4.1 helps children to observe the burning of a candle.

A flame is a region of burning gases (Fig. 8.1). When a candle is first lit, the flame is usually small because only a little wax vapour is available. This, however, produces enough heat to melt the wax in the exposed part of the wick and then in the top of the candle. Because the heating effect is greatest near the wick, a 'cup' forms in the top of the candle, which becomes filled with molten wax. As wax is vaporized and burnt at the top of the wick, more hot liquid wax moves up by capillary action. After the candle has been burning for a short time, the flame usually becomes bigger than at first, because the melting of the wax in the main part of the candle increases the fuel supply. Sometimes a small flame produces too little heat to continue melting the main part of the candle. This is usually because the wick has been broken off short. The burning process is starved of fuel, the flame becomes smaller and finally goes out.

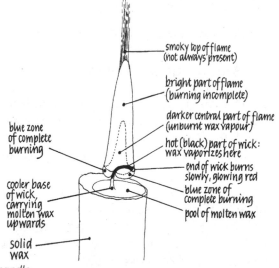

smoky top of flame
(not always present)

bright part of flame
(burning incomplete)

darker central part of flame
(unburnt wax vapour)

blue zone
of complete
burning

hot (black) part of wick:
wax vaporizes here

end of wick burns
slowly, glowing red

cooler base
of wick,
carrying
molten wax
upwards

blue zone of
complete burning

pool of molten wax

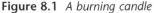

solid
wax

Figure 8.1 *A burning candle*

Children can observe many things as a candle burns. Heat from the flame sets up a pattern of movement in the air around it. Heated air, together with gases produced by the burning process, rises in a vertical stream above the flame, while at the same time cool air is drawn in at its base. The flame has three main parts. A dark area immediately around the wick is occupied by hot wax vapour which has not begun to burn and does not give out any light. At the base of the flame is a small blue zone, where the oxygen supply is greatest because air is being drawn in towards it. Here the burning process is rapid and complete, that is, the carbon in the wax vapour being burned here is converted completely into carbon dioxide. In the main, bright part of the flame, wax is at first only partly burnt because the oxygen supply is lower. In the partial burning process some of the carbon occurs as tiny, very hot particles which are burning, glowing brightly. This is what causes the candle flame to give out light. The presence of carbon in the flame can be shown by holding a tin lid in the bright part of it for a few seconds. Carbon particles are cooled and deposited as very small particles of carbon (sometimes called lamp-black) which is still used to make ink, for example by Muslim scribes.

8.3.3 Reactions with oxygen: rusting

Corrosion is the general term used to describe chemical changes which 'eat away' metals. There are many different kinds of corrosion, but most of those observed in everyday life occur when metals are exposed to weathering. Rusting is one example of corrosion, which affects impure iron and steel. Economically and technologically it is by far the most important kind of corrosion in the industrialized world, causing enormous amounts of damage and dilapidation to installations, machinery, civil engineering works, shipping and buildings, both public and private. Great amounts of material and labour are expended annually on trying to prevent rusting or even slow it down.

Tarnishing and corrosion   When investigating the chemical changes at the surfaces of metals, it is useful to distinguish between corrosion and tarnishing. Any of the commonly used metals except gold (i.e. steel, aluminium, zinc, silver, copper and its alloys) become dull when a freshly polished surface is exposed to the air, even in conditions which seem quite dry. This effect is one form of tarnishing, caused by a chemical reaction between the metal and oxygen in the air, which results in the formation of a very thin layer of metal oxide on the surface. Other reactions cause different forms of tarnishing. For example, a silver or silver-plated spoon turns black by silver oxide or silver sulphide tarnish. The layer of tarnish can be removed by the fine abrasives in metal polish. Tarnishing is not destructive if the oxide layer protects the metal from further change. If conditions such as weathering break down the oxide layer, the destructive changes which we call corrosion are likely to set in. When investigating the rusting of steel, the main interest lies in finding the conditions under which the corrosion occurs and ways in which it may be prevented or slowed down.

Children can easily investigate the conditions under which iron and steel rust: a chemical reaction in which the iron combines with oxygen and water to form a chemical complex of iron oxide and water. Investigations will help children understand more about rust prevention, as well as providing excellent opportunities for prediction, 'fair testing' and the use of controls (1.8, 1.10).

Activity 9.5.1 helps children to investigate the conditions under which rusting occurs.

Children should be given a standard material to investigate, such as 2.5 cm (one inch) steel nails which are cheap and convenient. Before each test, they need to clean the nails with a fine abrasive sheet until they are shiny. They can try observing newly cleaned nails kept in dry air: they will lose their brightness and become dull, slowly tarnishing, but will not rust. This shows that air alone causes tarnishing but not corrosion, and provides an opportunity to distinguish between the two. Only when the steel is in contact with both water and air will corrosion set in, and it is then likely to be rapid. A nail in a little water at the bottom of an open jar will be rusty within 24 hours, and the first signs may be visible much sooner. The contact between liquid water and steel does not, however, need to be direct: rusting will occur in humid air. A nail suspended in air above water in a sealed jar will rust rapidly even though no liquid appears to touch it, because very small amounts of water vapour condensing (6.2.2) on the metal are enough to start the process of corrosion. In contrast, a nail in water with no air dissolved in it will not rust. This can be shown by boiling water for ten minutes to expel all the dissolved air, cooling it, pouring it gently into a jar, dropping in a nail and then sealing the water surface with cooking oil. Air cannot penetrate the oily layer to dissolve in the water, so the nail will not rust. A control set up using unboiled tap water with a sealing layer shows some rusting, though this is limited by the small amount of oxygen dissolved in the water. Once this has all been used up, no further rusting can occur.

Chemicals such as salt dissolved in the water speed up the process, so steel exposed to sea-water or spray rusts very rapidly indeed; a major problem for ships with steel hulls and superstructure.

The difference between steel and metals such as copper and aluminium, which tarnish quickly but corrode much more slowly, is that the oxide layer formed as steel tarnishes is very easily broken, allowing water and air into contact with the metal. Rust forms a loose and flaky layer which is very easily broken and disturbed by stress and bending, so that it cannot protect the metal in the way that copper and aluminium are shielded by their oxide layers. As a result, water and air continue to penetrate and the steel continues to corrode.

Control and prevention of rusting   It is very difficult, if not impossible, entirely to prevent rusting in any steel object which is in use, but there are several different ways in which the process can be slowed down.

Children can investigate applying a protective coating which seals the surface of the steel and so impedes or prevents contact between water, air and the metal. The coatings have to be waterproof and adhere closely enough to the steel to prevent oxygen reaching it. Most are relatively short-lived because if the steel object is in use it will be subjected to abrasion which wears any coating away, bending which will tend to loosen or crack it, or both. Apart from other metals plated onto the steel, the main coating materials are paints, oils and greases. Paints are relatively cheap and flexible, but most have low resistance to impact or abrasion. It is also very difficult to make paint adhere well to the surface of steel, so that complex surface treatments and multiple coatings are needed, as in car body finishing, if paint on steel is to be durable for more than a short time. Grease and oil are very effective in rust prevention as long as the steel is completely covered. Steel can also be protected by coating it with other metals which corrode less easily, such as zinc, making 'galvanized' steel.

Comparing rusting and burning   Rusting and burning are both chemical changes which involve oxygen from the air, produce chemicals containing oxygen (oxides) and transfer energy to the environment. In all other ways, however, they are very different. It can be an instructive exercise for children to work out the differences from their own observations and experience. The main differences are summarized in Table 8.1.

Table 8.1 Summary of the differences between burning and rusting

Aspect of chemical change	Burning	Rusting
Energy transfer to environment	Large and usually very rapid in the form of heat and light	Very slow: no detectable heating
Temperature of reacting materials	Usually 500–1,500°C	Air temperature, i.e. rarely over 40°C
Products	Oxides, usually gases; some ash	Iron oxide-water complex; no gases or ash
Role of water	Slows down or stops reaction	Necessary for reaction to occur

PART 4

PHYSICAL PROCESSES

Part 4 is about the Science National Curriculum Attainment Target 4 (Sc4). Chapter 9 provides background scientific knowledge about energy which underpins the teaching of all parts of Sc4 which are covered by: Chapter 10, electricity; Chapter 11, forces and motion; Chapter 12, gravity and magnetism; Chapter 13, sound and light; and Chapter 14, the Earth and beyond.

When children are being scientific, learning about the changes they experience in their lives, their teacher needs to make sure that the ideas and evidence in the classroom are challenged and enriched by scientists' knowledge about how and why these changes happen. This knowledge should be used to help the children to think about their experiences more deeply.

Investigating changes by finding out how they happen in different ways, and noticing their characteristics in everyday events, will enable young children to learn about electricity, forces, light, sound, the Earth and beyond. After a lot of learning about these things, it will be possible for them to see how scientists' ideas about energy make sense.

The key ideas presented in Chapter 9 are about energy, its different forms and various sources. These powerful ideas in science are straightforwardly presented here to help teachers understand what lies behind the teaching they do in Attainment Target 4. You can read Chapter 9 before or after reading the subsequent chapters, according to your learning style and immediate purposes of reading. Some learners like to have the big, organizing idea in their minds as they read about the examples and illustrations, while other learners prefer to go through lots of examples and illustrations first.

Refer to the CD-ROM for a QUICK GUIDE to Sc4.
Refer to the CD-ROM for Progression in learning SCIENTIFIC ENQUIRY (Sc1) through PHYSICAL PROCESSES (Sc4) levels 1 to 6.

BEFORE WE BEGIN

Scientists use the word **energy** in a particular way which may not easily relate to its everyday use in ordinary conversation. Young children are often likely to associate the word with physical energy, for example: whether a person feels lively or tired. But scientists' meaning of energy is about helping to understand and explain changes in objects and materials, particularly when they are part of an interacting group or *system*. As noted in Part 3, many teachers see every lesson as a language lesson – an opportunity to clarify the usage of words as part of clarifying thinking. They value spending time talking about the children's prior understanding of words which can have different connotations for different children. The same is true here, as good teaching involves the teacher using expert knowledge and clear language to challenge, develop and refine the emergent thinking and language of young children.

As with materials, the question may arise about where to begin teaching. Is it wise to start with the fundamental idea? In this case, energy. It may seem logically attractive to teach what seems to be the idea that links all parts of the National Curriculum Sc4. Electricity, force, light and sound (as well as heat and movement, etc.) are all different forms of energy. However, this apparently fundamental idea is one which is very unlikely to be grasped meaningfully by young children until they have gained a great deal of experience and knowledge about all the contributory parts of this huge piece of understanding. If introduced too soon, children may just please the teacher by parroting the word *energy* with little understanding. Instead, following the curriculum planning principles for young children that it is good to *start where the children are*, and that new direct experience of everyday events and material is the best starting point to stimulate learning, the concept of energy as a unifying idea will need a long time and much learning before it gains credibility. Nevertheless, it is part of the scientific understanding needed by a primary teacher throughout this long period of 'conceptual gestation'. For much of this time, in the early stages, the concept of energy is best kept in the back of the teacher's mind as s/he teaches, to enable young children to build up rich and varied experiences of energy in all its diverse forms, but with the focus of attention on gaining experience of the ideas and evidence of the changes themselves. Explicit teaching of energy as a concept is not specified by the National Curriculum at Key Stages 1 or 2, however it can be appropriate to the scientific learning of high-achieving children.

9 ENERGY

9.1 ENERGY AND CHANGE

It is amazing to think that most of science, and most investigations carried out by children at primary level, are about change. Observing and learning about change enables us to distinguish living things from non-living (2.1), to find out how the human body works (3.1–3.11), how plants grow, feed and reproduce (4.3–4.5) and how living things interact to form communities (5.7–5.8). The properties of materials, both physical and chemical, are concerned almost entirely with how they change, or can be made to change other things, while Earth science investigates change and its results in the atmosphere, on land and in the oceans.

For both scientists' own learning and the scientific learning of young children, an essential part of science is observing, describing, measuring and understanding change. The crucial message of Chapter 9 is that it is impossible fully to understand the changes we observe without a concept of energy. Although it is said that energy is an abstract idea which is difficult to define, its basic concept is quite straightforward, and teachers can have it in mind when they teach many areas of experience which are meaningful to children. At times it may be difficult to apply the idea of energy to some of the changes which children observe and investigate. However, it is an essential part of their education in science for children gradually to develop and use the idea of energy to explain and understand much of what they experience.

9.1.1 Energy as a property of objects and systems

Energy is the property or characteristic of material things (or, to be more exact, of systems) which enables them to change. It shows itself in different ways in different objects and systems, so that these are said to have different forms of energy (9.2). In this context, a 'system' is a group of objects which interact as changes take place. For example, we can understand and explain the changes in an electrical circuit, which is made up of a battery, wires, lamps and other objects, by understanding the energy changes which are taking place. The different energy forms and the different amounts of energy in an object or system determine the kind and extent of the changes it can bring about or undergo. When a change occurs, energy is transferred from one part of the system to another, often in a different form.

For example, when a battery (an object) is connected to form part of a circuit (a system) which includes a lamp, chemical changes in the battery cause some of its energy (chemical-potential energy, 9.2.8) to be transferred to the rest of the system as electrical energy. Most of this electrical energy is transferred in turn to the filament of the lamp as thermal energy (9.2.2), making it so hot (9.3, 10.7) that it glows. The hot filament transfers energy to its environment as light and by heating the air around it.

> Astonishingly, ANY change in any object or system, whether it be a microbe or a motor car, a person or a planet, involves transfer of energy, and the reverse is true: any transfer of energy brings about change. Another way of saying this is that the changes we observe in the material world and the transfer of energy are two aspects of the same happening or phenomenon.

When we think about change, energy and energy transfer, and when we communicate our ideas, it is important to avoid the suggestion that energy is a substance which is generated, moved around and transformed as changes occur. For example, a battery in a circuit does not generate energy when the circuit is switched on. What it does generate is electric current (10.3). Because current is flowing, the circuit has the property that it can bring about changes, such as making a lamp light up, so we say that energy has been **transferred** to the circuit from the battery, in the form of electrical energy.

The idea of **energy as a property and not a substance** is also shown by the way in which some energy transfers do not change objects at all, but simply their position or the way they are moving. If I lift a brick from the floor by pulling it up on a rope, energy from my food (chemical-potential energy, 9.2.8) is transferred to the muscles of my arms (by way of respiration, 3.6) as energy of movement (kinetic energy, 9.2.1), and from them to the brick, which is lifted and gains energy as a result (gravitational-potential energy, 9.2.6). The energy in my body has been reduced; that of the brick has been increased. If I let the brick fall, it could bring about changes which it could not do while it was still on the floor, so it has the property we call energy in greater degree, but the only change is its position in relation to the Earth. As an object the brick has not changed at all. The higher the brick is raised, the more energy it gains and the more change it can bring about. If, for example, the brick fell onto your foot from a height of 1 cm you would feel it but it would be unlikely to hurt, whereas if it fell from a height of 1 m you would suffer severe pain and probably some injury as well.

9.1.2 Energy and forces

Lifting a weight is an example of a very important kind of change which involves forces. When a force changes the movement or position or shape of an object (11.1), energy is transferred. It is, however, important to realize that the transfer of energy is not the cause of the change, it is an effect. **Do not confuse the idea of energy with the idea of force**. Forces are causes: they make things happen. They determine whether and how objects move or stay still, and may determine their shape. When the movement or shape of an object changes, this is an effect caused by forces acting.

9.2 FORMS OF ENERGY

Energy is a characteristic of a system. It is the property which enables systems to change. The energy may change in form when it is transferred from one part of a system to another as a change occurs. Examples involving a simple electrical circuit and lifting a brick have already been mentioned in section 9.1. Good teaching of these ideas can use the 'describe–explain' strategy (1.11.2). Concentrate first on the observable changes which are taking place and then explain these in terms of the transfer of energy.

Children at primary level can investigate changes involving the main forms of energy:

9.2.1 kinetic energy;
9.2.2 thermal energy;
9.2.3 electrical energy;
9.2.4 light energy (one form of radiant energy);
9.2.5 potential energy;
9.2.6 gravitational-potential energy;
9.2.7 elastic-potential energy;
9.2.8 chemical-potential energy;
9.2.9 nuclear energy.

9.2.1 Kinetic energy

As an object is made to move, energy is transferred to it. The object can then bring about changes because it is moving, which it could not do if it were at rest.

Scientists say that a moving object has energy because it can bring about changes. The energy which was transferred to it when it was made to move is called energy of movement or kinetic energy. The heavier the object and the faster it is moving, the more energy has been transferred to it in making it move and the more kinetic energy it has.

Kinetic energy is observable when something impedes the movement of an object, slowing it down or stopping it. When this happens, kinetic energy is transferred to another part of the system. For example, water in a pond is at rest and has no kinetic energy, but water flowing downhill has kinetic energy which can be transferred to water-wheels or turbines (again as kinetic energy) and used to bring about changes such as the grinding of grain or generating electric current. Other systems which transfer kinetic energy include windmills, which are becoming increasingly important for the generation of electricity, electrical generators, which when they are rotated transfer kinetic energy to electrical circuits as electrical energy, and any object which makes a sound (13.1).

Children are familiar with systems in which energy is transferred to an object as it is made to move, including: a moving animal (using chemical-potential energy in food); a car or steam engine (using chemical-potential energy in fuel); falling water (using gravitational-potential energy); a spring, catapult and air-gun (using elastic-potential energy); and an electric motor (using electrical energy).

Friction is the most widespread means by which kinetic energy is transferred, and is explored in section 11.4. It occurs when two moving objects or materials come into contact. It is most obvious when solid surfaces slide over one another, but it also occurs when objects move through air or water. When two surfaces or materials move past each other, it is a frictional force which impedes their movement and slows them down. The most obvious effect of this is that the moving objects and their surroundings are heated (9.3). This happens because kinetic energy is transferred to the objects in the form of thermal energy (see below) as the movement becomes slower.

> Children investigating the braking of a bicycle (11.7) notice that the brake-blocks grip the wheel and slow the bicycle down. Kinetic energy is transferred to the blocks, the wheel-rims and the air around them, which are heated as a result. The heating effect of overcoming friction can be felt even more simply, by rubbing hands together.

Section 14.3 contains a range of activities that help children explore friction in a variety of situations.

9.2.2 Thermal energy

All materials are made up of very small particles (atoms and molecules, 6.4), which are constantly moving. In a gas they move about freely and collide with one another, whereas in a liquid they are in contact and move past each other much more slowly. In a solid the particles cannot move past each other at all (this is why it is a solid), and simply vibrate. If energy is transferred to a material its molecules move more, and move faster. In most situations the most obvious effect of this is that the temperature of the material goes up and it becomes hotter (9.3). The exceptions are when changes of state are occurring, by melting, boiling or evaporation (6.2.1, 6.2.2). In these situations, the energy transferred to the material results in a change of state rather than a rise in temperature. This 'extra' energy transferred to the material is known as **latent heat**.

A hot object brings about change by heating whatever is around it. This is usually called the thermal energy of the object, though it is sometimes incorrectly called heat. The more violently its molecules are moving and the higher its temperature, the more thermal energy an object has. Heating, cooling, thermal energy and temperature are explained further in section 9.3.

Section 12.3 contains a range of activities to help children explore thermal energy.

9.2.3 Electrical energy

When an electric current (10.3) is generated, energy is transferred to a circuit in the form of electrical energy. There are two main ways of doing this: by batteries (10.4) which have chemical-potential energy, and by generators which transfer kinetic energy as electrical energy when they are forced to move. Lightning (7.5.5) is a violent event in which electrical energy is transferred to the environment as light, thermal energy and kinetic energy in the form of sound. Electrical energy is widely exploited in technology because electric current can activate appliances which bring about a wide variety of useful changes and transfers of energy. Examples include the transfer of energy as kinetic energy by electric motors, as thermal energy by heaters (10.7) and as light energy by lamps. Electric current and its effects are explained further in Chapter 10.

Chapter 13 contains a range of activities to help children explore electricity.

9.2.4 Light energy

This is the form of **radiant energy** with which children are most familiar: others include radio waves, microwaves and X-rays. Light is a very important form of energy to us, partly because we can detect it directly through vision (3.10) and gain information about the world around us. Because of this, understanding how light interacts with materials is a major branch of science (13.8). Light is a form of energy that seems as real as material things. We can literally and metaphorically see it, unlike electricity, which by comparison seems more imaginary or like an idea invented to explain changes.

When materials are heated to a high enough temperature they glow (become incandescent) and transfer energy to the environment as light. The colour of the light emitted depends on temperature. Light from a star like the Sun, whose surface temperature is about 6,000°C, is white, while cooler stars appear yellow or red and hotter ones appear blue. A lightning flash generates temperatures comparable with those of the hotter stars, about 25,000°C, and so the light it emits also appears blue. The same effect can be seen in an electric filament lamp. If the current for which the lamp was designed is passed through it, the filament is heated to about 2,300°C and gives a yellow light. If the current is reduced (10.3), the filament is at a lower temperature and so appears dimmer and more red, whereas a larger current gives a whiter light but overheats the filament, which usually breaks in a short time.

Fluorescent tubes, neon strip-lights and yellow (sodium vapour) street lights work by passing an electric current through a mixture of gases in a tube. The gas molecules are activated by the electrical energy and transfer some of this energy to the environment as light, a process known as gas discharge. The colour depends on the gases used in the tube, not the temperature to which they are heated. Light is also emitted at much lower temperatures by chemical changes carried out by living organisms, including animals (glow-worms, fire-flies and some jellyfish), and a few fungi and bacteria. This is known as bioluminescence.

Light energy can be transferred in a variety of ways. It may be absorbed as thermal energy so that the material is heated, as in the solar panels on some houses in which water is heated by sunlight. Light falling on water can also evaporate it (6.2.2). Transfer of energy in this way makes possible the series of changes in the atmosphere and hydrosphere which we know as weather and the water cycle (7.5.6). Materials are now made which can generate electric current when light falls on them, transferring some of the energy to circuits as electrical energy. These are solar cells, used in calculators, in satellites such as the Hubble space telescope and unmanned spacecraft for exploring the Solar System. They may become more important as energy sources in the future (13.8).

As far as life on Earth is concerned, however, by far the most important transfer of light energy occurs during photosynthesis (4.4), in which light is absorbed (13.8) as part of a process which produces foods with high chemical-potential energy (see below). It is almost the only way in which energy can be transferred to the biosphere, so nearly all life depends on it.

Activity 12.3.5 helps children compare the characteristics of filament bulbs with energy-saving bulbs.

9.2.5 Potential energy and energy storage

The four forms of energy discussed so far are all characteristic of systems which are undergoing change. If a change is taking place in a system, one or more of these forms of energy is involved. There are, however, other forms of energy which are characteristic of materials and systems which, while they are capable of change (because they have energy), are not changing at the moment. Examples include suspended weights, coiled springs, foods and fuels. Energy of this kind is referred to as potential energy.

When energy is transferred to an object or system as potential energy it is in effect stored, but in referring to storage of energy, care is needed to avoid any suggestion that energy is a material. It is more accurate and less misleading to say that through the transfer of energy, the system has acquired the property of being able to change under certain conditions, for example if the weight is made to fall, the spring to uncoil or the fuel to burn.

9.2.6 Gravitational-potential energy

Like kinetic energy, this form of energy is connected with movement and work, but is a result of an object's vertical position within a system rather than its movement. For example, a brick suspended from a rope has gravitational-potential energy, transferred to it as work was done in pulling it up. The heavier the object and the higher it is lifted, the more energy is transferred to it in the lifting and the more gravitational-potential energy it has.

Activity 14.2.3 and Activity 14.3.4 help children explore gravitational-potential energy.

Any object or material moving spontaneously from a higher to a lower level in relation to the Earth, whether falling, rolling, sliding or flowing, is transferring some of its gravitational-potential energy to the system as kinetic energy. Some will also be transferred as thermal energy, because friction and heating are always involved in any movement. Gravitational-potential energy is already an important renewable energy source in hydro-electric installations and tidal barriers, both of which use water flowing downwards to rotate turbines.

9.2.7 Elastic-potential energy

An elastic object is one which regains its original shape when the forces deforming it are released (7.1.5). This is a change, so the deformed object must have potential energy. This is part of the (kinetic) energy transferred to it when forces were applied to change its shape, and is known as elastic-potential energy. The greater the force needed to deform the object and the greater the change of shape, the more energy is transferred to it during deformation and the more elastic-potential energy it has. Examples of familiar elastic objects include bouncy balls (elastic in compression), rubber bands (elastic in tension) and the springs of clockwork toys (elastic in bending).

Activity 7.2.1, Activity 14.1.4 and Activity 14.2.1 help children explore elastic-potential energy.

The energy transfers involved in dropping a ball and allowing it to bounce are summarized in Table 9.1. When an elastic object regains its shape, some of its potential energy is transferred as kinetic energy, but not all. This is shown by the bouncing ball, which will never bounce as high as the point from which it was dropped, because some of its potential energy has been transferred as thermal energy, both as air-resistance (friction) is overcome, and as the ball is deformed and recoils. This explanation predicts that a ball would be very slightly warmer after it had bounced than before, and this has been detected using very sensitive temperature probes.

Table 9.1 Summary of the main energy transfers in a falling and bouncing ball

Position and movement of ball	Forms of energy (arrows show energy transfer)		
	Gravitational-potential	Kinetic	Elastic-potential
1. Ball held suspended	Is at a maximum	None	None
2. Ball falling	Is decreasing	→ Is increasing	None
3. Ball hits floor and is deformed	None	Is decreasing	→ Is increasing
4. Ball fully deformed and momentarily at rest	None	None	Is at a maximum
5. Ball recoils	None	Is increasing	← Is decreasing
6. Ball rises	Is increasing	← Is decreasing	None
7. Ball at top of bounce	Is at a reduced maximum	None	None

Note that the potential energy of the ball decreases with each change and energy transfer, so maximum at stage 1 is the greatest and maximum at stage 7 is less. The energy is transferred as thermal energy in the ball and its surroundings.

9.2.8 Chemical-potential energy

All chemical changes involve transfer of energy, either to or from the environment (9.1.1). Any chemical substance which transfers energy to the environment as it undergoes chemical change has chemical-potential energy and some are very widely used as energy sources both by humans (e.g. batteries and fuels) and by all living things in the form of food.

Batteries are small, sealed tanks of chemicals (10.4), which generate electric current when connected as part of a circuit, transferring energy to the circuit as electrical energy. As they do this, their own chemical-potential energy is reduced until the chemical changes are complete and current can no longer be generated. In some batteries the chemical changes can be reversed by passing current through the battery in the reverse direction, transferring electrical energy to it as chemical-potential energy so that it is 'recharged'. Note, however, that no kind of 'rechargeable' battery is safe for use in primary schools (10.4).

Fuels are chemicals, produced by the activities of living things either recently (wood) or in the past (fossil fuels), which can be chemically combined with oxygen in the chemical changes known as burning (8.3.2). Burning transfers energy to the environment or the system very rapidly, so that it is characterized by powerful heating and high temperatures.

Foods are complex chemicals which are used as a source of energy by living things, in the process of respiration (3.6). This is quite unlike burning, because it is a low-temperature process in which chemical-potential energy is transferred in a complex series of controlled chemical changes. All foods have their origin in the process of photosynthesis (4.4), in which light energy is absorbed by plants (13.8) and transferred as chemical-potential energy by building up substances such as sugars, starch and oil.

9.2.9 Nuclear energy

Sometimes incorrectly called 'atomic' energy, nuclear energy is different from the other energy sources considered in this chapter. In all the examples discussed so far, energy is transferred to a system by some kind of change, and sooner or later is transferred from it again as further changes take place. But in the changes which result in the transfer of nuclear energy, instead of one form of energy being transferred as another form, a very small amount of matter is transformed into a very large amount of energy, so that after the changes, the mass of material involved has been very slightly reduced. There are three main ways in which nuclear energy affects the lives of children: radioactive decay, and two kinds of nuclear reaction – fission and fusion.

In the late nineteenth century some naturally occurring minerals were found to emit radiation which changes photographic materials just as light does, but in complete darkness. These radioactive materials undergo a process known as radioactive decay, slowly transferring nuclear energy as thermal energy. It is the process thought to cause the heating of the Earth beneath its crust. The results of this heating can be illustrated for children in the form of earthquakes and volcanic eruptions.

Unlike the gradual decay of radioactive materials, nuclear reactions involve sudden and drastic changes which do not occur naturally on Earth. They are of two kinds. **Nuclear fission** involves the splitting in two of the atomic nuclei of certain radioactive materials. This occurs in a very rapid, uncontrolled and catastrophic way in atomic bomb explosions, and in a much slower and (hopefully) more controlled way in atomic power stations. **Nuclear fusion** occurs when two light atomic nuclei join to form one heavier one. In hydrogen bombs and in the centre of the Sun, the nuclei fused are those of hydrogen and the material produced is helium. The process needs very high temperatures, so it has not yet been possible to use it as a controlled energy source. The Sun is in effect a gigantic nuclear fusion bomb, which does not explode because it is so massive. The Sun is the major energy source for the Earth (internal heating being the only other one) and the radiant energy transferred from it includes light, which is the only source of energy for almost all living things.

9.3 HEATING, COOLING AND TEMPERATURE

If one part of a system is hotter than the rest, there is always a tendency for thermal energy to be transferred from the hotter parts to the cooler ones. This is the process of heating, which can take place by conduction, convection and radiation (see below). It is scientifically correct to describe objects as being hot or cold, and to observe that they are made hotter or colder by heating and cooling. Teachers should avoid speaking as if objects contained heat, or as if heat were gained by or lost from a system, as if a substance. This would encourage the misunderstanding that heat is a substance. Always use the word 'heat' as a verb, not a noun.

9.3.1 Heating and expansion

Almost all materials become bigger (expand) as their temperature rises and smaller (contract) as it falls. The only common exception is water, which expands as it freezes. This evidence is explained by the idea that when an object is made hotter, its thermal energy is increased, making its molecules (6.4) move more violently. Gas molecules move faster and collide with each other more frequently. The molecules of liquids and solids move or vibrate over greater distances as the material is made hotter, so that on average they are further apart. Cooling a material makes the reverse happen: the movement of molecules is reduced and they are closer together. Increases and decreases in molecular movement cause the size of an object to change with temperature.

Activity 12.3.1 investigates thermal expansion and contraction of air.

9.3.2 Temperature and thermometers

Temperature is a measure of how hot or cold an object is. This is an indicator of its thermal energy. Three temperature scales are in common use, the most useful for primary science being the Celsius scale, sometimes incorrectly referred to as the centigrade scale. Temperature is measured in degrees with reference to fixed points, which in the Celsius scale are the freezing- and boiling-points of water. The difference between them is divided into one hundred degrees, so we say that water freezes at 0°C and boils at 100°C.

Activity 12.3.2 contains more information about thermometers.

Thermometers are devices which measure temperature. Children can sense hot and cold through skin receptors which respond to relative *differences* in temperature rather than sensing *absolute* temperature, making them very unreliable as a thermometer (3.10). The commonest thermometers in primary science are made of a thick-walled glass tube with a very narrow bore, sealed at one end and with a thin-walled reservoir of liquid at the other. Changes in temperature cause the liquid to expand or contract, so it rises or falls in the tube. Even a small change in the volume of the liquid in the bulb produces a visible rise or fall in the tube, because of its narrow bore. The liquid must be a non-toxic coloured mixture. Mercury thermometers should never be used in primary schools. Digital thermometers work by measuring changes in an electrical circuit as it is heated or cooled and giving a readout on an LCD display.

9.3.3 Heating by conduction

If the violently vibrating molecules of a hot material are in contact with those of a cooler material, thermal energy will be transferred until the temperature of the two is uniform. This is known as thermal conduction. As a result of conduction, thermal energy always tends to spread throughout a system. How rapidly this occurs depends on the temperature difference and the materials involved. Materials such as metals which transfer thermal energy very rapidly are said to be good thermal conductors, whereas materials such as wood and air, which are very poor conductors, are known as thermal insulators. Note that how hot or cold a material feels to the skin often has as much to do with its conductivity as with its temperature.

Indirect observations of the conduction of thermal energy

Place wooden and metal objects in a refrigerator for an hour, or hot water for a few minutes, and then hold them. Feeling the objects from the refrigerator, the metal one feels colder than the wooden one because a metal transfers thermal energy by conduction away from your hand more rapidly. Feeling the objects from the hot water, the metal one feel hotter than the wooden one again because the metal transfers thermal energy by conduction into your hand faster than the wood. So even though in both cases the objects were at the same temperature, it is the different rate of transfer of heat which causes the different sensation.

Make simple comparisons of the conductivity of different materials by using hot water (never use flames or heaters). Obtain suitable objects for comparison such as large (15 cm) steel nails, wooden dowels and plastic utensils of about the same length. Stand these in a mug so that they lean outwards. Place a small blob of margarine or other fat near the end of each, at the same height and facing outwards. Pour very hot water into the mug. How quickly the fat melts will show how good a thermal conductor each material is. This evidence can be linked both to ideas about the use of materials as related to their properties, and to work on safety in the home, for example by examining a variety of kitchen utensils.

Activity 12.3.3 describes this practical activity in more detail.

9.3.4 Heating by convection

Heating in liquids and gases usually makes a pattern of movement called convection, which begins when the materials expand as they are heated. This means that a certain volume of liquid or gas weighs less when hot than it does when cold. The result is that hotter material rises through cooler material around it. In a system being cooled, movement sets up in the reverse direction, cooler material sinking down through warmer layers. These movements are called convection currents.

Convection currents circulate on a very large scale in the atmosphere and oceans, redistributing much of the energy reaching the Earth from the Sun, and playing a major part in generating changes we call weather and climate (7.5). On a small scale, heaters and central heating systems which circulate hot water through 'radiators' rely on convection to transfer and distribute thermal energy in rooms. The 'radiators' in such systems would more logically be termed convectors.

Children can observe convection of thermal energy in air and water by noticing currents in the air above heaters, made more obvious by using paper spirals suspended from threads. Patterns of convection currents in water can be observed by filling a heat-resistant glass container with water, heating it gently and then dropping in a few grains of dye powder.

Activity 12.3.4 gives more information on these practical activities.

9.3.5 Heating by radiation

All warm and hot objects transfer energy by radiation. They do this by emitting a form of radiant energy called infra-red radiation, which behaves like light although we cannot see it. Infra-red emitted by a hot object does not heat the air through which it passes, but is absorbed by solid objects in its path, which are heated as a result. This explains why a large fire can be felt even when one is too far away from it to be affected by the hot air rising from it. Heaters such as electric fires transfer some energy by conduction and convection, but far more by radiation, with the result that they can give an immediate sensation of warmth to someone sitting in front of them while the room itself remains cold.

Activity 12.3.5 gives practical help in providing children with experience of these ideas.

9.3.6 Thermal insulation

This slows down the transfer of thermal energy from hotter parts of a system to colder ones. This can include both reducing the rate of energy loss from a hot object such as a person, an oven, a hot-water tank or a house, and reducing the rate of energy gain by a cold object such as a refrigerator or freezer. Apart from reflective foil layers (see below), most common insulation systems work by slowing down conduction and convection, which usually occur together, and rely on materials which are very poor thermal conductors.

One way to improve the insulation of a building is to reduce conduction by making a basic element of construction double-layered, with air trapped in between: cavity walls and double or secondary glazing are examples. The effectiveness of this is limited, however, because air can still circulate in the cavity and so transfer energy by convection between the inner and outer layers.

More effective is the kind of insulation engineers call lagging. This consists of layers of fibrous or foam material, itself a poor conductor, which trap a thick layer of air, prevent it moving and so reduce convection as well as conduction. A familiar form of lagging is warm clothing, and examples in the home include carpets and under-felt, loft insulation, jackets for hot-water tanks and insulation of pipe work to prevent freezing. Oven-gloves are like lagging working in the opposite way, to protect against burning. All kinds of domestic insulation are of great importance in view of the need to reduce consumption of fossil fuels and the demand on energy resources generally.

Slowing down energy transfer by radiation requires a kind of insulation which reflects the infra-red radiation and prevents it being absorbed. This is achieved using a very thin layer of metal foil. A substantial proportion of the energy transfer from the human body to the environment occurs by radiation. If the infra-red is reflected back to the body it is re-absorbed, energy loss is substantially reduced and skin temperature rises. This explains the effectiveness of reflective 'space blankets' (foil-lined plastic sheets) to treat victims of hypothermia, shock or accidental injury.

The most efficient thermal insulation children are likely to encounter is the vacuum ('Thermos' or Dewar) flask. This is a double-walled glass vessel with the inside of the cavity silvered like a mirror. After shaping, the air between the walls is sucked out by a vacuum pump. This means that there is nothing in the cavity to transfer energy by conduction or convection, and the silvering reflects outgoing or incoming infra-red. Transfer of energy is very slow, being limited to conduction through the insulated stopper and the glass walls around it. Stainless steel vacuum flasks, though robust, are less efficient because the metal walls are much better thermal conductors than glass walls are.

Activity 12.3.6 suggests ways that children can investigate these ideas.

ELECTRICITY

INTRODUCTION

Young children can learn much about electricity in the primary school by building simple circuits, finding out what their properties are and learning about the safe use of mains electricity. Their understanding of electricity itself is limited by the abstract nature of the necessary concepts (electron, charge, electrical forces and charge separation). However, they can understand important scientific ideas about electricity, such as current, voltage and resistance, which explain evidence of how circuits behave. In this situation, achieving a degree of understanding becomes much easier and confusion less likely if, alongside first-hand investigation, a clear mental picture of electric current can be developed (10.3, 10.4).

10.1 SIMPLE CIRCUITS

Young children's investigative learning about electricity is likely to begin by making simple circuits such as in Figure 10.1 which shows a drawing (a) and a diagram (b). Young children begin with drawings and progress to show the layout of circuits with diagrams. These do not show details, such as the actual shape of the circuit, the lengths of the wires or whether crocodile clips have been used, but they do show the positions of the essential components in relation to one another. Electrical engineers have developed a wide range of symbols for use in circuit diagrams, but only a few are needed in primary science. These are shown in Figure 10.2.

Children's practical investigation of this circuit may begin with the switch open. When the switch is closed (Fig. 10.3a), the circuit is 'switched on' and the lamp normally shines. This obvious change means that energy is being transferred to the environment and children will probably identify the battery as the source of energy. It appears that something reaches the lamp from the battery which leads to energy transfer (10.4), but can reach it only when the switch is closed. If either wire is detached from the battery (Fig. 10.3b) the lamp goes out, and repositioning the switch (Fig. 10.3c) makes no difference to the way it works. Children need to carry out a great variety of similar and related investigations to develop the idea that a complete pathway is needed from the battery, through wires, (closed) switches and devices such as lamps, motors or buzzers, before anything will 'work', that is before energy transfer can take place. This complete pathway is an electrical circuit, and once the idea of the circuit as a complete pathway has been established, other concepts can more easily be developed.

Activities 13.1.1 and 13.1.2 contain guidance on investigating simple circuits.

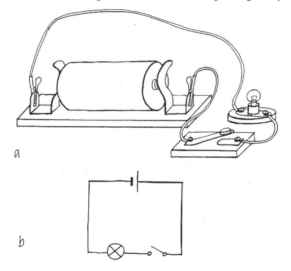

Figure 10.1 *A simple circuit represented by a drawing and a diagram*

10.2 CONDUCTORS AND INSULATORS

Materials which can form part of an electrical circuit are called electrical conductors. Children can test a wide variety of materials to find out whether they are conductors or not, using a simple circuit with a gap in it instead of a switch (Fig. 10.4). Bridging the gap with various materials and observing whether or not the lamp glows allows a simple classification to be made. Children will find that all the metals they test are conductors, and that nearly all non-metals are not. One exception which they can usefully use is graphite, in the form of thick pencil 'leads'. This acts as a conductor, but it is not a very good one and it may be noticed that the lamp is dimmer. This is a useful observation when developing the concept of electrical resistance (10.6).

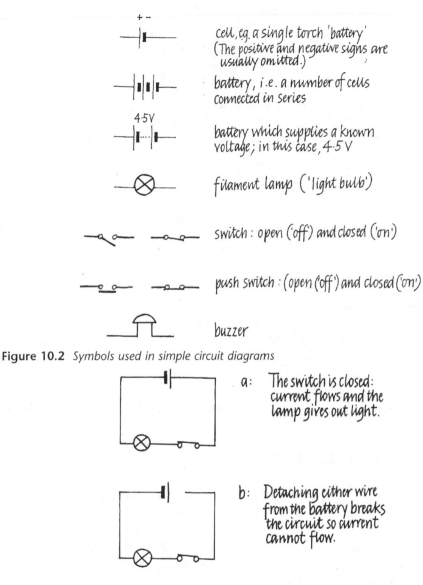

cell, e.g. a single torch 'battery'
(The positive and negative signs are
usually omitted.)

battery, i.e. a number of cells
connected in series

battery which supplies a known
voltage; in this case, 4·5 V

filament lamp ('light bulb')

switch : open ('off') and closed ('on')

push switch : (open ('off') and closed ('on')

buzzer

Figure 10.2 *Symbols used in simple circuit diagrams*

a: The switch is closed:
current flows and the
lamp gives out light.

b: Detaching either wire
from the battery breaks
the circuit so current
cannot flow.

c: Repositioning the
switch has no effect.

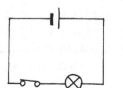

Figure 10.3 *Changing a simple circuit*

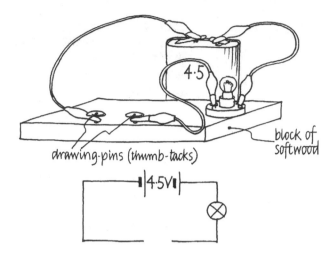

drawing-pins (thumb-tacks)

block of softwood

4·5VI

Figure 10.4 *Testing electrical conductivity*

Materials such as wood, plastic, rubber and paper, which cannot form part of an electrical circuit, are called electrical insulators. Some insulators, especially plastics, are very important technologically because they allow mains electricity to be used safely (10.13). An incomplete circuit with an open switch or a gap in it will not 'work' because air is an insulator.

Section 13.2 gives ideas for children's investigation of conductors and insulators.

10.3 ELECTRIC CURRENT

In a complete circuit, it is the flow of electric current, brought about by the battery, which transfers energy to devices such as lamps, motors and buzzers, causing them to emit light, move or make a noise. The use of terms such as 'energy', 'electricity' or 'electric power' to refer to electric current should be avoided. Children's understanding of what electric current is and how it behaves, is helped if the teacher knows a little about atomic structure.

All matter is thought to be made up of very small particles called atoms (6.4), each of which consists of a central nucleus surrounded by a cloud of very rapidly moving, even smaller particles called electrons. In electrical conductors such as copper, about four per cent of the electrons are free to move from atom to atom. Normally they do not do this, but if they are acted on by electrical forces they can be made to move. It is the flow of these so-called 'free' electrons, acted on by electrical forces within a conductor, which is electric current. Developing this mental model of current flowing in a circuit can be difficult, and like most difficult ideas it cannot be built up all at once, but develops by making sense of much experience and discussion about how observations relate to each other. There have been many attempts to help this learning process by using **analogies**, such as suggesting that electrical current is like water being pumped around in pipes. The problem with analogies is that while each makes it easier to understand part of the behaviour of current and circuits, they tend to produce confusion about another part of the understanding, so it is probably best to use them with great care.

Once the basic idea of an electrical circuit is understood (10.1, 10.2) through investigations in Key Stage 1, older and more able children can learn more about electric current by investigating three of its properties. Although these investigations are simple in themselves, they need logical thinking to understand their significance and to avoid common misconceptions about electric current, for example that it flows in part of a circuit only, or in different directions in the same simple circuit.

Section 13.3 gives guidance on investigating electric current.

Three characteristics of electric currents to investigate

1. *Evidence that current flows in all parts of the circuit*: Children can move the lamp in a simple circuit (Fig.10.1) to each of the five possible positions in relation to the battery and switch. The lamp lights up in the same way regardless of where it is, so a logical deduction is that current must flow in all parts of the circuit.

2. *Evidence that current has direction*: Children can insert a buzzer, a light emitting diode or electric motor instead of a lamp. A different battery may be added as well. Most buzzers only sound when connected correctly. If the connections are reversed, no current flows and there is no sound. If a buzzer is placed in different positions in a simple circuit (Fig.10.1) and correctly connected it will sound every time, showing that current flows in the same direction throughout. This can also be shown using a light emitting diode. A small electric motor will rotate whichever way it is connected, but if the connections are reversed, so is the direction of rotation (clockwise or anti-clockwise).

3. *Evidence that current can vary in amount*: Children cannot directly observe electric current flowing in a conductor such as a wire: it is invisible. Electrons are so small that they can move slowly through the solid structure of the conductor without changing its appearance at all, unless they make it very hot (10.7). The greater the rate and speed of electron flow, the greater the current; the greater the current, the greater the rate at which energy can be transferred to devices such as lamps, motors and heating elements. The heating of a lamp filament when current passes through it is a particularly important example. As current in the circuit is increased,

Continued

Continued

the filament begins to glow and becomes hotter and brighter, changing colour from black (no light given out), through red to yellow and finally to white. These changes in brightness and colour are very important for investigating electricity in primary science because they mean that the lamp can be used as a simple current measuring device. If a lamp is moved to different positions in a simple circuit, its brightness will not change. This shows not only that current flows in all parts of the circuit, but also that the amount of current is the same throughout. Lamps used as simple current measuring devices also make it possible to compare the behaviour of different circuits (10.9, 10.10).

How much current flows in a circuit is the result of two other factors: the electrical forces making electrons move (measured as voltage, 10.5), and opposition to their movement around the circuit (resistance, 10.6). Before discussing how voltage and resistance affect current, however, it is necessary to develop the concept of electric current further by learning something of how batteries work.

10.4 BATTERIES AND ELECTRIC CURRENT

The batteries used to generate current in experiments with electricity in the primary classroom are small sealed tanks of chemicals. When the chemicals react together, they produce a concentration of electrons in one part of the battery (the metal base of the case) and a deficiency of electrons at another (the metal stud in the middle of the other end). When a battery is connected to a circuit, the concentration of electrons in the case (the negative terminal) repels the 'free' electrons in the conductors of the circuit, pushing them away from the battery. This electrical force acts all round the circuit almost instantly, so as soon as the circuit is completed (switched on), current is moving in all parts of it (10.3). The flow of electrons is from the negative terminal to the positive, so the same number of electrons flows into the battery at the positive terminal (which has a deficiency of electrons), as is forced out from the negative terminal.

The chemical reactions which enable the battery to make electrons move, continue only as long as the circuit is complete. As soon as it is disconnected or switched off and current ceases to flow, the chemical changes stop. Once the chemical changes in the battery are complete it can no longer generate current and must be replaced. The generation of current is an example of energy transfer (9.1). Chemical-potential energy in the battery is transferred to the circuit by way of chemical changes and the movement of electrons. It should be emphasized that the battery does not generate energy: it generates electric current and in so doing causes energy to be transferred. Rechargeable batteries, in which the chemical reactions are reversible, should not be used in primary schools because they can become very hot if short-circuited (10.11).

A technical point about naming batteries is that the single 'battery' is properly called an electrical cell. Joining two or more cells together, to produce a higher voltage or current (10.5), is how a battery of cells is made.

There are two common misconceptions about electric current. The first is that current 'gets into the circuit' from the battery. In fact, electrons which can be made to move are already in all the conductors of the circuit. What the battery does is to generate an electrical force which makes them move, setting up a flow of current. It is not possible using ordinary equipment in the classroom for young children to see evidence of this idea, so teachers need to justify it by saying that scientists believe in it because of the evidence they obtain using more complex equipment. When electrons are moving in the circuit, they can transfer energy (9.1) as they pass through devices such as lamps, light emitting diodes and motors, producing changes such as light, heating and movement. Secondly, it is often assumed that electrons move round a circuit very fast. However, although the electrical force making them move is propagated round the circuit with almost the speed of light, the electrons themselves move through the solid structure of the conducting materials only slowly: a few millimetres each second at most. A similar effect can be seen by lining glass marbles up along a metre rule, almost touching one another, then giving the end one a sharp push. Each marble moves hardly at all, but the one at the other end will move out almost immediately, showing that the force has been transmitted very quickly.

10.5 VOLTAGE

In order to concentrate electrons at its negative terminal (the case), a battery has to exert an electrical force on them which in turn acts on the 'free' electrons in the conductors of the circuit, making them move and so generating current. The bigger the force, the faster the electrons move through the conductors (though they always move quite slowly) and the bigger the current. The property of the battery which determines the size of the 'push' is measured in units called Volts (symbol: V) and is one of the factors affecting current in a circuit which children can investigate. A standard dry cell generates current at about 1.5 V. If more than one cell is joined **in series** (10.9), with the negative terminal of one connected to the positive terminal of the next, the electric forces they produce reinforce each other and the voltages across the terminals simply add together, so that a battery of three 1.5 V cells produces a total of 4.5 V, and one of six cells, 9 V. Special symbols are used in circuit diagrams to show that batteries of this kind are being used (Fig. 10.2). If two cells are connected the wrong way round, with negative or positive terminals joined (Fig. 10.5), the electrical forces they produce will be in opposition and cancel each other out, so no current will flow in the circuit.

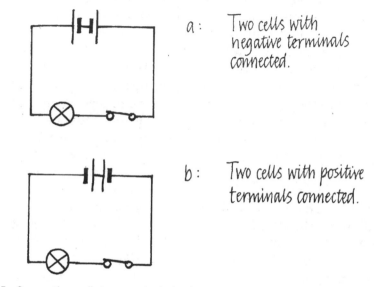

a: Two cells with negative terminals connected.

b: Two cells with positive terminals connected.

Figure 10.5 *Connecting cells incorrectly: in both cases the electrical forces exerted by the two cells are in opposition, so no current flows*

10.6 RESISTANCE

Conductors vary a great deal in how easy or difficult it is to make current flow through them. In a good conductor such as copper wire, current flows very easily, so the conductor is said to have low electrical resistance. In a poor conductor such as graphite, current will still flow but much less readily, so graphite has much higher resistance than a copper wire of the same thickness. Insulators, which will not let current flow at all, can be thought of as having very high resistance indeed. Resistance is an important concept because it is a major factor affecting current flow in circuits which children can investigate (10.12).

The resistance of a conductor does not depend only on the material of which it is made: it is also affected by shape and size. A long, thin wire will have higher resistance than a short, thick one of the same material. This is important when developing ideas about the heating effect of current (10.7) and fuses (10.13).

10.7 THE HEATING EFFECT OF ELECTRIC CURRENT

When electrons are made to move through a conductor as electric current, they do not move entirely freely. Their movement is impeded by the material through which they are moving, transferring energy to it and heating it. If the conductor has low resistance (good conducting material, thick wire or strip) it does not impede the current much, so there is little heating and the rise in temperature may be undetectable, as with connecting wires in the circuits which children investigate. But if resistance is high (poor conducting material, thin wire), the current is impeded much more, energy is transferred rapidly and the temperature of the conductor rises. Children will be familiar with the filaments of lamps and the heating elements of toasters.

Section 13.7 gives guidance on investigating the heating effect of electric current.

For any particular conductor, the rate of heating and therefore the rise in temperature depends on the current and resistance: the larger the current and/or the higher the resistance, the hotter the conductor becomes. It is this relationship which makes it possible to use the brightness of lamps as a simple measure of current, as long as the lamps used for comparison are of similar type (10.3). If the current is large enough, even a copper wire can become hot enough to start a fire (10.13).

10.8 THE RELATIONSHIP BETWEEN VOLTAGE, RESISTANCE AND CURRENT

Once children understand that the relative brightness of a lamp can be used to compare current (10.3), their further investigations of circuits can establish simple, logical, cause-and-effect relationships between the number and type of batteries and bulbs on the one hand and current on the other. This enables them to develop the concepts of voltage and resistance, together with an understanding of their relationship to current. In simple circuits, the amount of current is determined by the voltage (a property of the battery) and the resistance (a property of the whole circuit), and not the other way round. To put it another way, voltage and resistance are causes and the current is the effect they produce between them.

The voltage of the battery determines the size of the 'push' the battery gives to electrons in the circuit, so if the rest of the circuit stays the same (i.e. if resistance remains constant), increasing the voltage will cause an increase of the current. Resistance is a measure of how difficult it is to make current move in the circuit, so if the voltage stays the same (i.e. the battery is not changed or run down), decreasing the resistance will increase the current and vice versa.

Children in the early stages of finding out about the properties of circuits need to follow the rules of fair testing (1.10). For any particular design of circuit they should experiment by changing either the voltage (number or type of batteries) or the resistance (e.g. the number of lamps) but not both at once. All lamps used for making comparisons must be of the same type. Once they have developed some understanding of the relationship between voltage, resistance and current, children can observe a change in current and seek the cause of it, or change the properties of a circuit and predict what the result will be (1.8).

10.9 SERIES (UNBRANCHED) CIRCUITS

The simplest type of circuit is an unbranched or series circuit. All investigations benefit by keeping a simple series circuit set up (Fig. 10.6a), to show a standard of brightness against which lamps in other circuits can be compared. The filament of a lamp heats up when current flows through it because it has a fairly high resistance. This means that adding a second lamp in series with the first (Fig. 10.6b) increases the total resistance of the circuit. The voltage of the battery is unchanged, so current is reduced and the lamps glow more dimly. Because the current is reduced, the battery will 'last' (i.e. continue to generate current) for longer than if only one bulb were in the circuit. Notice, however, that adding the second lamp does not change the basic character of the circuit: it is still unbranched, so the lamps are said to be connected **in series**. As in all series circuits, removing any component (lamp or wire) will create a gap so that current ceases to flow throughout the whole circuit.

If two cells or batteries are connected in series, the total voltage is equal to their separate voltage values added together. Adding a second battery to a circuit with a single lamp (Fig. 10.6c) means that the voltage, and also the current, will be greater than in the simple circuit (Fig. 10.6a). The single lamp will glow very brightly and will probably overheat, so that the filament breaks and therefore also breaks the circuit. If a second lamp is added to the circuit, however (Fig. 10.6d), the resistance is increased, so the current is reduced to about the same level as that in the simple circuit (Fig. 10.6a) and the lamp will be as bright. Reversing one battery, as shown in Figure 10.6e, puts electrical forces generated by the two batteries in opposition, so they cancel each other out and no current flows in the circuit.

Section 13.9 gives guidance on investigating unbranched (series) circuits.

10.10 PARALLEL (BRANCHED) CIRCUITS

The second basic type of circuit which children need to investigate includes more than one pathway for electric current by making the circuit branch as in Figure 10.7. There are two possible conducting pathways through which current flows. This is called a **parallel circuit** and the lamps are said to be connected in parallel. What may be unexpected is that each lamp glows as brightly, and therefore has the same current flowing through it, as the single lamp in the simple circuit (Fig. 10.6a) unlike the two lamps connected in series (Fig. 10.6b).

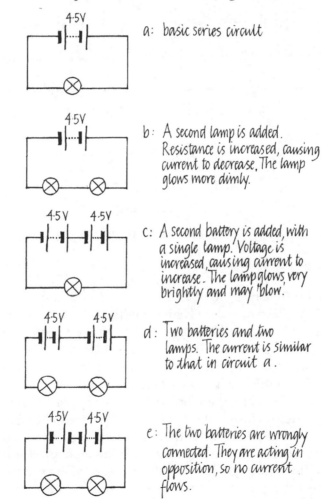

a: basic series circuit

b: A second lamp is added. Resistance is increased, causing current to decrease. The lamp glows more dimly.

c: A second battery is added, with a single lamp. Voltage is increased, causing current to increase. The lamp glows very brightly and may 'blow'.

d: Two batteries and two lamps. The current is similar to that in circuit a.

e: The two batteries are wrongly connected. They are acting in opposition, so no current flows.

Figure 10.6 *Simple series circuits*

The characteristics of a parallel circuit can be explained by thinking about the relationship between voltage, resistance and current (10.8). The brightness of the lamps shows that each branch of the parallel circuit has the same current flowing through it as flows in the simple circuit. So the current at points A and B in Figure 10.7a must be twice that in the simple circuit. Since the voltage has not changed, the increase in current must have been caused by reducing the resistance of the circuit. This can be explained by remembering that resistance is how difficult it is for current to flow in a circuit and that, if two pathways are provided rather than one, current can flow more easily.

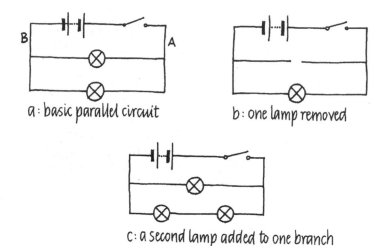

a: basic parallel circuit   b: one lamp removed

c: a second lamp added to one branch

Figure 10.7 *Simple parallel circuits*

Children who find it difficult to understand how a circuit with two lamps can have a lower resistance than a circuit with one may find an analogy of one-way traffic in a city to be useful. Figure 10.8 shows a model of current flow. In the model, the two-lane roads represent the unbranched, low-resistance wires in the circuit and the single lane roads, the lamps with higher resistance. In slow, nose-to-tail traffic, will more vehicles be able to pass points A and B if both single-lane roads are open, or if only one is open? Obviously, if both are open; but opening or closing the road at point C will not affect the amount of traffic which can pass point D. If there are two lamps through which current can flow, the resistance of the whole circuit is lowered and the battery can make more current flow through it. This does mean, however, that the chemical changes in the battery will take place faster, so it will have only about half its normal active life. When working with parallel circuits it is important to use fresh batteries, since old ones generate insufficient current to make both lamps glow brightly, producing confusing observations.

Children can investigate another characteristic of parallel circuits: that their branches behave as if they were independent circuits, so changing one branch has no effect on the others (unless one branch is a short circuit, 10.11). One obvious example of this is provided by removing the lamp from one branch of a parallel circuit (Fig. 10.7b) and observing what happens in the other. There is no change: the lamp continues to glow and its unchanged brightness shows that the current through it is the same as before, because the active part of the circuit is now behaving just as a simple series circuit does. The same principle is shown when a slightly more complex circuit is built (Fig. 10.7c). The single lamp continues to glow as brightly as before, but the two in the other branch behave exactly as we would expect of two lamps in series (see Fig. 10.6b): both glow, but more dimly. It is also noticeable that removing a lamp from one branch has no effect on the lamp(s) in the other. If removing a lamp from a parallel circuit does affect the brightness of those in other branches, it is probably because the batteries are nearly exhausted.

Section 13.10 contains guidance on investigating branched (parallel) circuits.

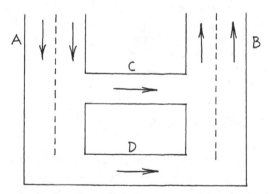

In a crowded one-way traffic system, more traffic can circulate past points A & B if both single-lane roads C & D are open. C & D are like lamps in a circuit, which limit current. Two lamps in parallel allow more current to flow (as at A & B in Fig 10.7a) than one.

Figure 10.8 *Modelling current in a parallel circuit*

10.11 SHORT CIRCUITS

If terminals of a cell or battery are directly connected by a low-resistance conductor such as a copper wire, the resistance of the circuit is very low, so a large current can flow in it. This situation is called a short circuit and should normally be avoided. The short circuit allows the battery to generate a large current so that it will be rapidly discharged and rendered useless. Also, the conductor itself will be heated by the large current and may become hot enough to burn the skin. The effect of a short circuit can be shown by building a simple circuit (Fig. 10.6a) and connecting the terminals of the battery with a length of copper wire for a moment (not more than a second). This makes what is in effect a parallel circuit, but because the resistance of the wire is so low, nearly all the current flows through it rather than through the lamp, which goes out.

Safety note

Children need to be aware of short circuits because they are not only wasteful: they can be dangerous and should be avoided. Some batteries discharge very quickly and generate large currents when short-circuited, becoming very hot, with a danger of severe burning. This is one reason why 'rechargeable batteries' and car batteries should never be used in primary schools. Many of the dangers of using mains electricity are associated, in one way or another, with short circuits, and most of the measures needed to use electric appliances safely are aimed at preventing them or limiting damage if they do occur. See also 10.13.

10.12 CONTROLLING CIRCUITS

Circuits are controlled by regulating the flow of current in them either by using some kind of switch to allow or prevent the flow of current or by changing the resistance of the circuit to increase or decrease the current.

Simple switches   A simple switch is a gap in the circuit which can be closed by a conductor. It works because air is an insulator and will not normally allow current to pass across the gap. To understand the idea of switches, children need to make their own from materials such as paper fasteners, paper-clips and drawing-pins mounted on card. In a series circuit the position of the switch is immaterial (Fig. 10.3a, c): it switches the whole circuit on or off wherever it is. In parallel circuits, however, switches can be positioned to operate the whole array or any part of it. This is the basis of control in circuits such as traffic-lights and motor car lights. Children can also make two- or three-way switches by using a swinging arm (such as a paper-clip) between two or three contacts, so that as one circuit is switched on, another is switched off. This provides a useful link between science and technology.

Variable resistors   Switches give all-or-nothing control of current in a circuit: either the current is flowing or it is not. A different kind of control can be exercised by changing the resistance of the circuit to vary the current gradually and continuously. The principle of variable resistors can be shown by bridging a gap in a simple circuit (Fig. 10.4) with varying lengths of fairly high-resistance conductors, such as graphite (pencil 'leads'), or nichrome wire, and observing the effect on the brightness of the lamp. The greater the length of material inserted, the greater the resistance, the lower the current and the dimmer the lamp.

Commercial variable resistors work by rotating a contact on a coil of wire or a strip of material containing carbon. By moving the contact, a variable length of the high-resistance conductor is included in the circuit, controlling the current.

10.13 MAINS ELECTRICITY AND SAFETY

All the work on electricity discussed so far has used batteries and low voltage current. Apart from short circuits (10.11) and the possibility of heating a very thin wire, these are perfectly safe: there is no danger of fire or electric shock. In their homes and at school, however, pupils regularly use electric appliances whose energy source is mains electricity. They do not need to understand the difference between battery current (DC) and mains current (AC), but they do need to know and understand enough about mains electricity to use it safely. This means knowing the main causes of danger, the basic safety measures built into circuits and appliances, and some simple rules for using them safely.

The first thing to emphasize about mains electricity, without being alarmist, is that potentially it is lethal. When properly used with well-designed and maintained appliances it is safe, but when safety measures fail it can and does kill people, directly through electric shock, and indirectly through causing fires. One reason why mains electricity can be dangerous is that the voltage is much higher than that generated by batteries. In Britain, mains voltage is 240 V, which means that even quite a small current can transfer a large amount of energy very quickly.

Electric shock   Because the human body contains a large amount of water in which chemicals such as salt are dissolved, it can act as an electrical conductor, particularly if the skin is wet. If an electric current passes through the body it will bring about changes which, depending on the size of the current and how it moves through the body, may range from a slight tingling sensation to uncontrollable jerking and spasm of muscles, severe pain, burning, heart failure and death. Apart from burning, electric current has this effect because it disrupts the normal control of the body by the brain, spinal cord and nerves.

Electric shock can occur only if there is a conducting pathway through the body, usually to the earth. There are two common causes of this: touching bare wires or faulty appliances with a metal object or bare hands, especially if they are wet, and using appliances in damp or wet conditions. Impure water conducts electricity sufficiently well to provide conducting pathways between a mains circuit, the body and the earth. Because of this, it is extremely dangerous to use electrical appliances in a bathroom unless, like electrically heated showers or electric razors, they have been specially designed and installed for that purpose. If a mains appliance such as a radio were to fall into a bath while switched on, anyone in the water would receive a severe and probably fatal shock.

Fire caused by electricity   Electric current passing through a conductor heats it (10.7). If a mains circuit or appliance is faulty and a short circuit develops (10.11), a large current may flow, causing wiring or other metal to be heated, so that inflammable material in contact with it may ignite. The main precautions against fires caused by electricity are the regular testing and inspection of appliances and wiring, and the use of correctly rated fuses (see below).

Basic concepts of control   The purpose of mains electricity and the technologies which depend on it is the transfer of energy. When this is controlled, appliances are safe. When control fails or is rendered ineffective by wrong usage, a dangerous situation is always created. When electrical circuits and appliances are properly installed, maintained and used, accidents are very rare. The overwhelming majority of danger and accidents associated with mains electricity result either from incorrect installation or neglect, so that the circuit or appliance is faulty, or from carelessness and deliberate misuse.

There are three basic means of controlling mains electricity and so ensuring safety: insulation and earthing; the use of circuit breakers and fuses; and correct usage of circuits and appliances.

Insulation and earthing. Mains electricity has been described, perhaps overdramatically, as being like a raging giant who has been imprisoned and is always trying to get out. The 'prison' is insulation. If conductors are properly insulated, current cannot reach the outside of the wiring or appliance, so they can be touched safely. If insulation is damaged there is always the danger of a short circuit leading to electric shock, or fire, or both. In modern circuits and appliances the commonest insulators are plastics where the working temperature is low, and ceramics where it is high.

Children will be familiar with the rigid insulating covers of plugs, sockets and switches, and the flexible covers of supply leads and cables. Any signs of wear or damage to insulation should be checked and if necessary repaired by a qualified electrician.

Some appliances which children may use have uninsulated wires. The most familiar examples are the heating elements of electric heaters and toasters. When the appliance is switched on these are not only very hot, but are carrying large currents and so should never be touched.

If insulation fails, the whole appliance may become 'live', that is, connected to the mains circuit and capable of carrying current. Touching the casing of the appliance could then result in a short circuit through the body to earth and electric shock. To help prevent this, many appliances are earthed. This means that the casing is connected to the third (long) pin on a standard mains plug. This in turn is connected, through the earth wire in the mains wiring, to the earth. Failure of the insulation in the appliance sets up a short circuit by way of the earth wire, through which a large current flows to earth, overloading the circuit breakers or fuses (see below) so that they break the circuit, cutting off the main current and preventing further damage.

Circuit breakers and fuses. These are damage-limitation devices, to break the circuit if the flow of current becomes too high, and cut it off. Circuit breakers are always used in modern wiring at the distribution box in a building such as a house. If there is a surge in current the circuit breaker detects this, a switch is opened and that particular circuit is deactivated. The circuit can be reactivated only by closing the switch at the distribution box.

Fuses work by overheating and breaking if too large a current flows in a circuit. If circuits and appliances are properly installed, maintained and used, mains fuses are not activated. Simple fuses are lengths of thin wire in a cartridge made of heat-resistant and insulating ceramic material, inserted into a circuit. When current flows in a circuit, the conductors are heated (10.7). If a short circuit occurred (10.11), the current could increase, possibly to a dangerous level, if the circuit were not protected. Because the fuse wire is very thin in relation to the current it carries, it has enough resistance to heat up and melt if it is overloaded, so breaking the circuit and effectively switching it off.

Current is measured in amperes (abbreviated to amps; symbol: A). Children may be familiar with the cartridge fuses used in standard three-pin plugs. These are the 'front-line' defence, giving protection from short circuits arising in individual appliances. Domestic power circuits are rated at 13A, which is therefore the maximum current which they should carry. Many appliances require much smaller currents than this, and fuses should be used in their plugs which match their maximum requirement. For example, a TV set needs a maximum current of less than 2A. If it developed a short circuit and had a standard 3A fuse fitted, this would quickly 'blow', breaking the circuit, but if a 13A fuse were fitted, a faulty set would probably overheat and might catch fire before the fuse melted. Plugs are usually sold fitted with 13A fuses. These should be replaced when plugs are fitted to appliances which require a smaller current. To calculate the kind of fuse required, find the power rating of the appliance in watts (W) and divide this by the mains voltage (240V). This gives the current in amps (A): use the next highest rating of fuse. For example, a microwave oven rated at 650W will have a current of 2.7A, so should be fitted with a 3A fuse.

Safe use of mains circuits and appliances. Once the basic principles are understood, using mains electricity safely becomes a matter almost of common sense. The following is simply a list of the major points as they relate to children. More comprehensive advice and information can be obtained from electricity supply companies.

1. Never use appliances with damaged leads.
2. Never poke anything into a mains socket.
3. If a socket is seldom used it should be protected by a dummy plug-cap.
4. Never try to use mains electricity to operate a home-made circuit or one designed for use with batteries.
5. Never use appliances in wet conditions or with wet hands.
6. If anything seems to be wrong with an appliance (e.g. strange noise, malfunction, smell of burning) switch off immediately and unplug it. Do not use it again until it has been checked and repaired if necessary.

11 FORCES AND MOTION

INTRODUCTION

Like all scientific ideas, the ones included in this chapter have been developed by scientists through thought and discussion regarding a great deal of evidence over a long period of time, to help us explain what we observe, and predict what might happen in the future. Concepts of forces and motion are used to help us explain and predict the movement and shape of objects, both when they change and when they remain the same. Scientists cannot say what forces are, only what they do, so in order to learn about them, their effects have to be experienced. This chapter is about how forces make things move or stay still. A range of pushing, pulling and twisting forces which children frequently experience are considered here. More discussion and investigation of how forces change the shapes of things is found in Chapter 7.

Careful attention to clear meaning is necessary as soon as a teacher uses the word force with young children. They may associate it with parental discipline in utterances such as 'I will force you to do that', for example. Or they may have heard of the police force or armed forces. These meanings existed in our language before scientists started to use the word in a specialized way.

As soon as an idea about a phenomenon is clarified, scientists seek ways of categorizing and measuring many examples in many contexts. Similarly, young children can develop language such as hard/big pushes and small/gentle pushes, as they progress from sense experience towards trying out ways of measurement. This chapter gives careful attention to some scientific ideas which can be difficult for many children and some adults to understand if they seem counter-intuitive: that is, in conflict with our life experience as interpreted intuitively. Knowing about this will guide teaching to be progressive in its conceptual challenge to children's thinking. A clear example of this is provided by the attention given to floating and sinking. Very young children's learning is the playful gathering of much experience of a rich variety of different objects and materials, together with a lot of descriptive talk about their observations and questions about which float and which sink. Later, when this experiential base is linked with other learning about forces, children can develop a more complex scientific understanding of why things float or sink, using more critical and creative talk about how ideas explain their evidence.

11.1 PUSHES AND PULLS: THE BASIC PROPERTIES OF FORCES

In order to learn about forces, their effects have to be experienced as pushes and pulls. Particularly with young children, this is a good starting-point, because it is easy to develop a simple and intuitive concept of forces in relation to the sensations in one's own body of exerting forces to affect things. For example, they can push or pull a table and move it, or squash clay and change its shape.

Children can use their bodies to be more aware of forces during familiar activities in physical education and art, and learn how forces are involved every time we move something (including ourselves) or change its shape. Children need to learn two basic characteristics of forces: they have both direction and size.

Activity 14.1.1 gives guidance on experiences of forces and movement in physical education.

Forces act in particular directions   If an object is pushed or pulled, any changes in its movement or shape occur in the direction of the forces acting on it. Children experience this in many ways, such as a game involving pushing a ball by throwing, kicking or hitting it. Especially when the ball is still to begin with, as in a shot in netball or a penalty, corner or free kick in football, it can clearly be seen and felt that the ball travels in the same direction as the force with which it is kicked or thrown, although it is also affected by gravity (11.5; Fig.11.5c). When we write and draw, we push or pull the pen or pencil in a particular direction, so what is drawn or written is a visible record of changes in direction of the forces applied to it. If plastic or elastic materials are squashed or stretched (7.1), their changes of shape also show the direction in which forces acted on them.

Activity 14.1.2 has guidance on experiences of forces and change in art.

Forces have magnitude   Forces vary in size: they can be bigger or smaller causes, resulting in bigger or smaller effects.

Children can notice the connection between a change and the magnitude of the forces causing it by observing everyday activities such as walking, running or jumping, and by throwing and kicking balls. The greater the force exerted by the body, the faster or further the body itself or the ball moves. Similarly, when changing the shapes of objects, for example by squashing clay, stretching an elastic band or pressing on a brush to squeeze paint out, the greater the force applied, the more the object changes shape. Evidence of this kind should link to the important idea that 'the bigger the force, the bigger the change it brings about'. This learning provides children with plenty of examples of the cause–effect relationships which scientists value.

Measuring forces   It is possible not only to experience forces of different magnitudes but also to resolve disputes about size of forces by learning to measure them. The basic unit of force is the Newton (symbol: N). At the Earth's surface, gravity pulls down on a mass of 100 g with a force (weight, 12.2) of about 1 N. Children need to experience a wide range of forces in many ways, such as by holding a range of masses.

Forces can be measured using forcemeters, which are in effect spring-balances. Pulling on the forcemeter extends a spring and the length of extension shows how large a force is applied. If children find forcemeters difficult to read, or if the teacher wants to start off with arbitrary units before introducing the scientific ones, then a paper scale can be stuck onto the barrel.

Activity 14.1.3 has guidance on measuring forces with forcemeters.

11.2 PUSHING, PULLING AND PAIRS OF FORCES

The apparently simple idea of pushes and pulls is a good basis for thinking about forces in science in the early years. Beyond such early experiences, however, teachers should be aware that significant problems of understanding can arise for three reasons.

Activity 14.1.4 has guidance on experiencing pushing and pulling actions.

First, children may investigate situations where forces seem to be involved, but nothing is obviously pushing or pulling anything else. For example, when we stop pushing a moving trolley, it does not just continue to move but is slowed down by a hidden force: friction (11.4).

Second, any pushing (a force applied towards the object) or pulling (a force applied away from the object) does not involve one force, but a pair of forces acting in opposite directions. For example, as I push a trolley, whether it moves or not, the trolley pushes back at me with exactly the same force as I exert on it. A pulling action also involves two forces acting away from each other and sometimes this can be experienced directly. When I am carrying the shopping, for example, gravity pulls down on the bag while my arm pulls up on it. The two forces are in balance so the bag neither rises nor falls (11.3; Fig. 11.9b). The pair of forces can also be experienced when we push things that will not move. If I push on to a wall, the wall does not move, but I do, in the opposite direction. Similarly, if I want to jump up, I have to push down on to the floor with my legs and feet. My body moves in a direction opposite to the one I am pushing in because when I push on the floor or wall, it pushes back at me, and the object which moves is the one which is free to move, in this case my body. (See also the discussion of walking in section 11.4.)

Third, it can be difficult to identify correctly the pair or pairs of forces involved. This problem is most likely to arise when only one of the forces involved in an action can be observed and measured. For example, when the Earth pulls an object downwards with gravitational force, so that it falls, no second force seems to be involved. What also happens is that a falling object pulls on the Earth with the same force that the Earth pulls on it, but because the Earth is so massive there is no detectable effect on it. We notice only the falling object. In a similar way, when I throw a small object I push it, but I am not usually aware that it is pushing me with an equal and opposite force, because I am much more massive than it is. In both examples, as in any change of movement, pairs of forces (pushes or pulls) are involved, but gaining evidence for this is far from straightforward.

As teachers at primary level, we can avoid these problems if we look in more detail at how forces are related to change and realize that we never normally experience a situation in which no forces are acting.

11.3 FORCES IN AND OUT OF BALANCE

Because we live on Earth, everything in our world, including ourselves, is affected by gravitational force (12.2), and everything that moves encounters forces which resist its movement (friction, 11.4), generated by contact with the solid, liquid or gas around it. This means that the movement and shape of all the things we experience, whether they are changing or not, is a result of the forces acting on them. These are ideas that are not obvious to children, but important for teachers to think about. We need to consider two situations: either the forces acting on an object are in balance and so cancelling each other out, or they are out of balance.

Section 14.2 contains basic investigations of forces out of balance.

Forces out of balance   The forces acting on an object are out of balance if:

• its movement changes in speed;
• its movement changes in direction;
• its movement changes in both speed and direction;
• its shape changes.

Forces in balance   The forces acting on an object are in balance if:
• there is no change in its movement, either in speed or direction. (This includes both remaining stationary and moving at a constant speed in a straight line.);
• there is no change in its shape.

We must remember that on Earth we never experience a situation in which no forces are acting. A no-change situation does not mean that no forces are acting on the object, but that the forces acting on it are balanced, bringing about no change in shape or movement (11.6). We should think about forces in and out of balance by identifying the object and the change (or no-change) which is the focus of interest and remembering that it makes sense to speak of forces being in or out of balance only if they are acting on the same object (Figs. 11.4, 11.6, 11.9, 11.10).

Children can investigate changes of shape of a rubber band that is stretched and held between their hands. The pulling forces (inward by the band and outward by the hands at either end) are equal: the forces acting on the rubber band are in balance and nothing moves. Only when the pulling action of the hands is increased or decreased does the shape of the band change so that it becomes longer or shorter, and this can be felt directly. Changes in the forces and the response of the band can be measured using a forcemeter at one end. As the hands pull harder or relax, the change in length of the band can be experienced directly and measured at the same time. Such observations can also help to reinforce the important idea that the bigger the force applied, the bigger the change it brings about.

The same happens in a symmetrical beam balance in which the main forces are the weights of whatever objects are put into the pans, weight being the force with which an object is pulled towards the Earth by gravity (12.2). The object on which the weights act is the beam of the balance. If the weights in the pans are equal, the beam remains level and at rest: the forces acting on the beam are in balance and there is no change. The beam moves only when the force on one side is changed, either by adding weights or taking them away, showing that it is forces out of balance which cause change of movement. The beam balance is also useful because it shows that the change of movement always takes place in the direction of the larger force: it is always the heavier weight which moves down. The investigation of static friction (11.4) also shows forces in and out of balance very clearly.

Later, these four situations are considered in more detail and discussed in sections 11.5 and 11.6.

	Forces are	
The object is	out of balance	in balance
stationary	Go to 11.5.1	Go to 11.6.1
moving	Go to 11.5.2	Go to 11.6.2

First, however, we need to understand more about the force which, with gravity, has the greatest effect on the way we live: friction.

11.4   INVESTIGATING FRICTION

Friction is a force which tends to oppose or impede the movement of objects and materials past each other, regardless of whether they are solids, liquids or gases. Friction has a profound effect on everyone's lives because it almost always affects all moving objects on the Earth, and because a great deal of technology is directed towards reducing friction where it is a nuisance and exploiting it where it is useful.

11.4.1   Friction between solids: static friction

Children can develop their understanding of friction using an arrangement such as that shown in Figure 11.1. 'Sliders' are similar pieces of wood or laminated chipboard, which can be loaded with weights and covered with a variety of materials such as sandpaper, polythene sheet and carpet. They can be moved by hand, or by using a string, pulley and bucket as shown, or with forcemeters pulling horizontally. Children can move a slider with their hands, feeling and hearing the resistance to movement as it is pushed or pulled. They can make simple comparisons of friction generated by different pairs of surfaces, by feeling then measuring and finally recording.

Trying to start the movement of two surfaces in contact, by pushing or pulling, is resisted by a kind of friction called **static friction** because the surfaces are not moving. The smallest possible force which will start one surface moving past the other is known as the **limiting friction**. When a small pulling force is applied to the string attached to a slider, static friction and pulling force are in balance (11.3), so nothing moves. The slider will not move until the pulling force is increased so that it is greater than the limiting friction. At that point, friction and pulling force are not in balance (11.3) so the slider begins to move. As the pulling force is exerted, the string becomes taut. This shows that the friction force and the pulling force are acting in opposite directions: the pull is forwards and friction acts backwards, opposing movement as friction always does. This evidence is useful to understand the idea of friction as the reason for why moving things slow down and stop (11.6).

Moving sandpaper-covered surfaces over each other provides a helpful model of friction between solid surfaces. However smooth they appear to be, all surfaces have tiny irregularities which catch on each other, just as the grains on the sandpaper do, to impede movement. If the surfaces are pressed more closely together, for example by loading a slider or trolley, the limiting friction will be increased and a larger force will be needed to make the object move. If, on the other hand, the surfaces can be held slightly apart by a film of liquid, friction will be reduced and much smaller forces will be needed to move objects. This is the basis of lubrication, which is difficult to demonstrate with sliders but whose benefits are clearly felt in machines such as bicycles (11.7).

Activity 14.3.1 has guidance on static and limiting friction.

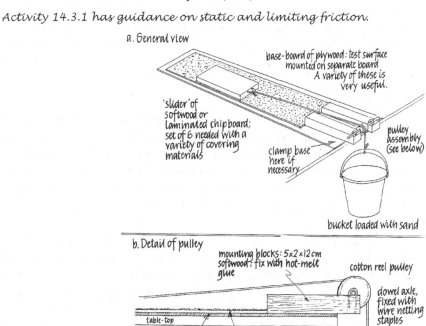

Figure 11.1 *Simple equipment to investigate limiting friction*

Making use of static friction   In many situations friction is a nuisance and much technological effort, such as lubrication and special bearings, is directed towards reducing it. And yet without friction, our normal modes of movement and transport would be impossible. When walking, the sole of the foot or shoe is placed on the ground.

Because it is pressed down by the weight of the body, the limiting friction between foot and ground is high, so the foot will not slip unless a large sideways force is applied to it. This can be experienced by trying to slide one foot across the floor while standing: it

Continued

> *Continued*
>
> cannot be done until the friction between foot and floor is reduced by transferring most of the body's weight onto the other foot. This high-friction contact without sliding is the key to walking and running. When we walk, the leg is pushed backwards, and because the foot does not slide over the floor, the body is moved forward as a result. This may be difficult to understand because walking is so habitual. If so, try walking backwards: the pushing action of the leg and the friction forces between the floor and the feet will be much more apparent.

Activity 14.3.2 has guidance on observing walking.

A similar effect makes bicycles and cars move. Forces applied by pedalling or by the engine make the wheels rotate. The rubber tyres, pressed down by the weight of the rider or the vehicle, make a high-friction contact with the road. The limiting friction between tyre and road is greater than the force needed to move the vehicle forward, so as the wheels rotate and push backwards, the road pushes on the wheels with an equal and opposite force and the vehicle moves forward. This action of the wheel on the road is a combination of rolling friction (see below) and high-friction contact. The tyre in contact with the road at any instant is the point at which the pushing force is being exerted. This may be easier to understand with a tracked vehicle such as a toy tank or bulldozer. The part of each track in contact with the ground is stationary. As a backward pulling force is exerted on the tracks by the driving wheels, high-friction contact prevents the tracks moving, so the body of the vehicle moves forward over them.

It is essential for both walking and the movement of vehicles that there is static high-friction contact with the ground. This becomes apparent when it is lost, for example on slippery floors or wet, icy and snow-covered roads. Feet slip, wheels spin and normal forward movement becomes difficult or impossible. High-friction contact is equally important when trying to slow down, stop or change direction. If it is lost, there is skidding and accidents to pedestrians and vehicles.

Friction between a tyre and the road can be increased by pushing the body of the vehicle down, towards the road surface. This is achieved in racing cars by a wing at the rear which acts as the reverse of an aircraft wing (see 11.4.3), creating downforce rather than lift as it is moved through the air. On wet roads, the patterned tread on tyres allows water to be squeezed from between the contact surface and the road. When the tyre is excessively worn, the channels of the tread are no longer deep enough to remove the water and the vehicle can 'aquaplane' – ride on a film of water which acts as a lubricant, so there is insufficient friction to prevent skidding if an attempt is made to brake or corner sharply (see section 11.5.2 under 'Changing direction').

Friction between solids: rolling   If spheres (marbles) or cylinders (rollers made from thick dowel) are placed between a slider and a hard surface, friction is greatly reduced, so a much smaller force is needed to make the slider move. If all the surfaces involved are hard, **rolling friction** is usually very much less than sliding friction, because there is very little sliding of surfaces over one another. As the curved surfaces rotate, they move towards and away from the flat ones with only a tiny area in contact at any moment. On soft surfaces such as carpet, much of the advantage of rolling friction may be lost because friction forces are generated as the rollers or marbles deform the material by compressing it. The reduction of friction by rollers, wheels, and later by ball- and roller-bearings, is of great importance both historically and in present-day technology.

Activity 14.3.3 has guidance on more ways to investigate sliding and rolling friction.

Children investigating toy cars, some of which move more easily than others, can use a standard push force from a catapult (Fig. 11.2) to find out which toy car is 'best' (least friction, travels furthest).

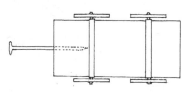

Fit head of nail onto rubber band, pull back and let go

Catapult made from a wood block with two nails and a rubber band, held down with other hand (not shown)

body: softwood, about 150 × 60 mm

nail: drill pilot hole and push in

wheels: ready-made plywood or fibreboard

axles: 2 mm dowel

axle-barrels: large plastic drinking straws

Fix axle-barrels to body and wheels to axles with hot-melt glue

Figure 11.2 *Simple trolley and catapult system*

11.4.2 Solid–liquid friction: streamlining

A solid object moving through a liquid or gas experiences friction forces which slow it down. This resistance occurs because there is friction as the liquid or gas moves over the solid surface, and also because the solid body pushes fluid aside. The overall resistance is called drag. The smaller the disturbance in the liquid or gas and the smoother the flow over the surface of the solid, the less the drag will be.

Children can investigate friction between solid and liquid using an arrangement as shown in Figure 11.3. Model boats of the same area and thickness but of different shapes can be pulled along, and the drag on each compared by measuring the force needed to keep it moving. This develops simple ideas of streamlining. The children can sprinkle very fine sawdust on the water surface to observe the pattern of movement and link it to the shape of each model. The more swirls and eddies, the greater the drag.

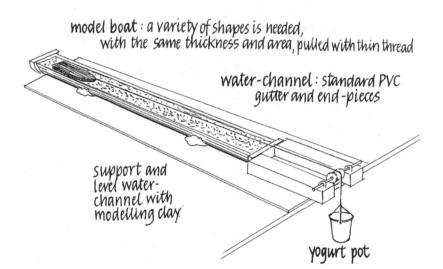

Figure 11.3 *Simple equipment to investigate friction between solids and water: baseboard and pulley are similar to those shown in Fig. 11.1; load yogurt pot with 10 g, 5 g and 1 g weights*

11.4.3 Solid–air friction: parachutes

An object falling through air experiences friction forces as drag, just as a solid moving through liquid does. This opposes the gravitational force of the Earth and slows the rate of fall. Increasing the drag reduces the rate of fall and the impact when the object reaches the ground, for example by using a parachute (see Fig. 11.4).

How parachutes fall is obviously related to the load and size of canopy and, less obviously, stability. Children who make a simple canopy by attaching strings to the corners of a square of fabric or plastic sheet find it will slow the fall of an object attached to it. As it falls the load will probably swing wildly: the parachute is unstable and this needs to be corrected. Close observation may show that air caught in the canopy cannot escape easily so the canopy tilts to release it, making the load swing like a pendulum. This is particularly noticeable in parachutes made with plastic sheet, which allows no air to flow through it. The problem can usually be cured by making one or more small holes in the centre of the canopy, or by using a fabric which allows a slow flow of air through it.

Children investigating parachutes can learn that when forces are out of balance, it is the difference between them which determines how fast change occurs. The drag created by the parachute acts against the pull of gravity. The higher the drag, the smaller the difference between the two forces and the slower the rate of change. This is explained diagrammatically by Figure 11.4.

Activity 14.3.4 contains investigations on solid-air friction and parachutes.

An aircraft or glider in a shallow descent achieves a gradual rate of fall in a different way from a parachute. Instead of the gravitational pull being opposed by friction between the parachute canopy and the air, the forward movement of the aircraft wing through air creates an upward force known as lift, which opposes the pull of gravity. A stable parachute can fall vertically, but a gliding aircraft can descend slowly only if it keeps moving forward through the air. Powered aircraft are propelled through the air by their engines, so that much more lift is generated than when gliding. The lift is greater than the weight of the aircraft so the imbalance of forces is reversed and it gains height.

11.5 FORCES OUT OF BALANCE

11.5.1 Object stationary

Unbalanced forces acting on a stationary object will either move it, or change its shape, or both. Changes of shape are discussed in Chapter 7.

Movement from rest   A stationary object experiencing unbalanced pushing or pulling forces will move in the same direction as the larger force. Children can observe the effect of pulling an object at rest with the 'sliders' used to investigate friction (11.3, Fig. 11.1). The pulling force and the friction force between slider and

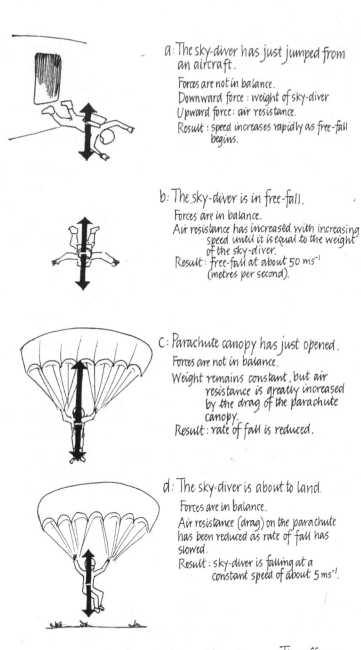

a: The sky-diver has just jumped from an aircraft.

Forces are not in balance.
Downward force : weight of sky-diver
Upward force : air resistance.
Result : speed increases rapidly as free-fall begins.

b: The sky-diver is in free-fall.

Forces are in balance.
Air resistance has increased with increasing speed until it is equal to the weight of the sky-diver.
Result : free-fall at about 50 ms^{-1} (metres per second).

c: Parachute canopy has just opened.

Forces are not in balance.
Weight remains constant, but air resistance is greatly increased by the drag of the parachute canopy.
Result : rate of fall is reduced.

d: The sky-diver is about to land.

Forces are in balance.
Air resistance (drag) on the parachute has been reduced as rate of fall has slowed.
Result : sky-diver is falling at a constant speed of about 5 ms^{-1}.

Notice that the forces acting in (b) and (d) are the same. The difference made by the parachute is to reduce the speed at which the sky-diver's weight is balanced by air resistance.

Figure 11.4 *Forces acting on a sky-diver*

base-board act in opposite directions. When the pulling force becomes greater than the friction, the two are no longer balanced and the slider begins to move. This can also be seen by holding up a ball and dropping it (Fig. 11.9d).

Children can investigate the action of a pushing force on an object at rest using a simple trolley propelled by a rubber band (Fig. 11.2). Toy cars can be used instead but are more difficult to observe in detail. When the trolley is fitted to the rubber band, pulled back and held, the situation is one of no-change, showing that the forces acting on the hand, the rubber band and the trolley are all in balance. When the trolley is released the rubber band straightens out, exerting a pushing force on the trolley. This is much greater than the friction forces impeding the trolley's movement, so it moves forward in the direction of the push force.

Children can vary the amount of stretch in the band, and load the trolley with modelling clay, to investigate two important aspects of movement from rest. First, the bigger the pushing force, the faster the trolley travels. Second, the greater the weight of the trolley and its load, the larger the force needed to make it move at the same speed. The reasons for this are that increasing the weight of the trolley increases friction, which tends to impede movement (11.4), but the greater mass of the trolley (12.2) also needs a greater force to get it moving. What happens when the trolley slows down and stops is discussed in the next section.

Section 14.2 supplies more ideas on investigating forces out of balance.

11.5.2 Object moving

Three kinds of change in movement   When a moving object is acted on by unbalanced forces, its movement will be changed. How the movement changes depends on the direction and size of the forces in relation to the way the object is moving. There are three situations in which children at primary level are likely to experience this which are summarized by Figure 11.5. When observing and trying to explain changes in the movement of objects, the 'describe–explain' strategy (1.8) provides a useful framework for thinking.

Situation 1: an object is falling vertically downwards. The downward force (due to gravity) acts in the same direction as the object is moving. Result: the object speeds up, but does not change direction, that is, it continues to move in a straight line (Fig. 11.5a).

Situation 2: a trolley is moving but slowing down. The (frictional) force (in the wheels) acts in the direction opposite to the object's movement. Result: the object slows down, but its direction does not change (Fig. 11.5b).

Situation 3: an object that has been thrown into the air starts to fall. Forces (from the downward pull of gravity and the friction between the object and the air) act in directions different from the object's movement. Result: the direction of movement is changed and, depending on how large the forces are and their direction, speed is likely to change as well (Fig. 11.5c).

The second situation is the most difficult for most children and many adults to understand. If an object is slowing down in a straight line, then a force must be acting on it in the opposite direction to its movement. This is discussed further below, in the context of objects slowing down.

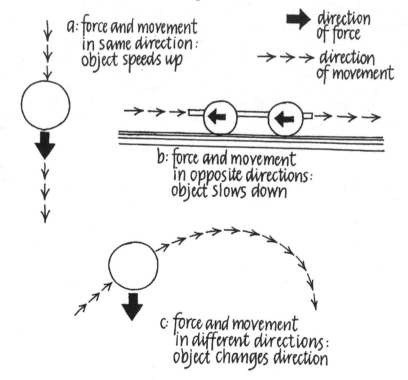

Figure 11.5 *Unbalanced forces acting on moving objects: in a and c the unbalanced force is gravity; in b it is friction*

Speeding up If an object moving in a straight line speeds up without changing direction, then an unbalanced force is acting on it in the direction in which it is already moving (Fig. 11.5a). If nothing else changes, the longer the force continues to act on the object, the more its speed will increase. This can be shown by investigating the effect of gravity (12.2) on the speed of falling objects. Gravitational force acts on everything on Earth all the time, so as an object falls its speed increases, although air resistance means that it will finally reach a constant speed (Fig. 11.4).

Two ways of observing the effects of speeding up

1. Try dropping spheres of soft modelling clay from different heights between 0.5 and 2 m on to a hard, level surface. A longer fall means that gravitational force acts on the sphere for a longer time, so that it is moving faster on impact. This in turn means that the force of the impact will be greater so the sphere will be squashed more. Spheres of the same size dropped from different heights will have differently sized flat faces after impact, which can be recorded by brushing them with paint and printing them on a prepared chart.

2. A similar effect can be seen by dropping a steel ball-bearing from different heights into a layer of dry silver-sand at least 2 cm deep in a shallow tray. The size of the splash crater depends on the force of the impact and so varies with the length of the fall and the speed of the ball-bearing.

How much a moving object speeds up depends on how long the force acts, and also on how large the force is. Gravitational force (i.e. its weight, 12.2) is constant, but when riding a bicycle, pedalling hard speeds up much more rapidly than pedalling gently, and pedalling for longer does the same.

Slowing down   If an object moving in a straight line slows down without changing direction, then an unbalanced force is acting in the direction opposite to its movement (Fig. 11.5b). Children can investigate a simple trolley that is moved from rest by a rubber-band catapult on a level floor (Fig. 11.2) observing that it rolls across the floor, getting slower all the time until it stops, and then does not move any more. Explaining what happens when the trolley is released and is moved from rest is very simple (11.5.1). The critical question, and the one which makes this a very useful investigation is, Why does the trolley slow down and stop?

Children's answers to this question reveal their thinking about forces and their ideas about why things move. A common misconception is that if an object is moving, a force must be acting on it to keep it moving. Children say something like 'The trolley slows down because it is running out of push', indicating that it is natural for things to slow down – there is no causal force to slow it down, just an absence of the force to keep it moving. This is an understandable, intuitive assumption which is based upon our everyday life experience (11.8). The idea was also held by Aristotle in ancient Greece, however in modern science it is seen as mistaken. Closer observation provides evidence for deeper thinking. Once the trolley has moved forward away from the elastic band, nothing is pushing it. However, the trolley's movement is changing, so the modern view is that the forces acting on it must be out of balance. It is slowing down, so there must be a force acting on it which is opposing its movement, acting in the opposite direction.

Children can find out what the slowing-down force is with a simple thought-experiment, which could be carried out in reality. Imagine you are pedalling your bicycle on a level road. You stop pedalling: no force is now acting to move you forward. What happens? You gradually slow down, as the trolley does. How could you slow down more suddenly, in a shorter distance? By putting the brakes on. Because the brakes change your movement, making you slow down more suddenly, they must be exerting a force on the bicycle and you, as they grip and rub on the wheel-rims (11.7). This is the force called friction (11.4), which tends to slow down moving things by acting in the direction opposite to movement, that is backwards (11.4; Fig. 11.1). Even without the brakes on, there are other friction forces acting on you and your bicycle, which also slow you down. One of these is friction in the wheels rubbing on the axles. Another is air resistance, which you can feel, pushing you backwards as you and the bicycle move forwards. When you apply these ideas to the simple trolley, you can see what could be generating friction: mainly the axles rubbing on the body as they rotate.

As with speeding up (see above), the greater the force opposing movement, the more rapid and obvious its effect will be; and the longer it acts, the more the moving object will be slowed down. Again this relates to children's own experience with bicycles and as passengers in other vehicles. If the brakes are applied gently, the force opposing movement is small so the bicycle slows down more gradually, and usually more safely, than if braking is fierce. The reverse is also true: if a vehicle is travelling fast it will take longer for braking forces to stop it than if it is moving more slowly, and it will travel a greater distance while it is slowing down. All these observations have fundamental relevance to education in road safety.

Changing direction   If an object moving in a straight line changes direction, then a force must be acting on it in a direction different from the one in which it is travelling. The curved path of a ball thrown or kicked into the air is a very familiar example of this effect (Fig. 11.5c). As the ball travels through the air there are no longer any forces propelling it forward, though air resistance (friction, not shown in Fig. 11.5c) is tending to slow it down. Gravity, however, is acting vertically downwards all the time, so the ball's direction is continually changing and it moves in a curved path. This change of direction continues until the ball is falling vertically (i.e. in the same direction as gravity) or it hits something.

As in snooker or billiards, rolling balls across a surface so that they collide with each other or fixed objects provides more examples. The ball moves in a straight line until it hits something, which it will push, and be pushed by, at the same time (11.2). Unless the push is in a direction exactly opposite to its movement, the ball will move off at an angle in a new direction.

Road vehicles use forces acting at an angle to their direction of travel to change direction. When cars or bicycles are steered round a corner, their front wheels are turned so that they are at an angle to the direction of movement, while continuing to rotate. This generates friction forces between the tyre and the road which push the front of the vehicle sideways, making it change direction. If this sideways force becomes greater than the friction forces between the tyres and the road (wheels turned too much, or speed too great), the car or bicycle will skid.

11.6 Forces in balance

11.6.1 Object stationary

When children look at a book sitting on a table, they find it puzzling to be told that there are forces acting on the objects. Yet scientists believe that when the movement and shape of an object on Earth remain the same, there are always forces acting on it but they are in balance. Refer to sections 11.3 and 11.4 for other examples of forces in balance acting on stationary objects.

Activity 14.5.1 shows investigations with beam balances and Activities 14.5.2 and 14.5.3 illustrate experiencing forces in balance.

A teacher can help children's thinking by asking: 'What would happen if the table did not support the book?' (it would fall to the floor) followed by: 'What prevents it falling?' To find out, try supporting a heavy object such as a brick in your hand. To keep it steady, you have to press up on it. This means that you are exerting an upward push force on it. This force opposes the downward pull of gravity and if they are in balance it does not move. If you either relax your muscles or push harder, the forces are out of balance and the brick moves down or up. The next stage is to measure the force needed to support the brick, with a weighing machine. The weight of the brick changes the shape of the spring until it pushes back with an equal force, and the mechanism tells us how large that force is. But the weight of the brick stays the same, so the table must exert an equal force to keep it from falling. Balanced forces can be difficult to detect because most of the structures we have are rigid as far as normal forces are concerned (7.1) and show no apparent response when loads are placed on them.

> Children engage in many physical education activities: pushing and pulling on partners, tug-o'-war contests and developing balance on the floor and on apparatus, which provide useful experience of the idea of forces in balance. Devices for measuring weight can also serve as useful illustrations. Rubber bands can be used as simple forcemeters by carefully measuring the extension produced when known weights are suspended from them. If a card scale is constructed using these measurements it can be used with the band to measure unknown weights or forces, remembering that the weight of a 100 g mass is about 1 N (11.1). Floating is a very important example of forces in balance with no movement and it is discussed as a separate topic in section 11.8.

11.6.2 Object moving

An object moving in a straight line at a constant speed, so its movement is not changing, has forces acting on it in balance with each other. Model parachutes have the downward force of their weight balanced by the upward force of air resistance which inflates the canopy. Cyclists can experience constant speed when freewheeling down a gentle slope. The gravitational force of the Earth moves the cycle and rider forward and would, if unopposed, cause their speed to increase (11.5.2). Friction forces in the bearings, and from air resistance, oppose the forward movement. While the two forces are in balance, speed remains constant. If either changes, for example because of a change in the slope or wind-speed, the speed of the cyclist will change.

Similarly, a car driven at a steady speed in a straight line on a level road, has a pushing force from the engine making the car move forward (11.4) which is balanced by friction and air resistance (Fig. 11.6b). However, a trolley with no engine is slowed and stopped by friction (11.6).

Activity 14.5.4 gives guidance on investigating forces in balance: object moving.

11.7 FORCES AND MACHINES

A device which enables a person to do something they cannot do unaided, by applying and transferring forces, is called a **machine**. Children can investigate hand tools as simple machines, by actually working with them.

Try removing a tightly fitting can lid with a screwdriver. The frictional forces holding the lid in place are much too large to be overcome by the unaided hand. A screwdriver used as a **lever**, **pivoting** on the rim of the can (Fig. 11.7a), shows many properties of a simple machine. A force is transferred from one place (the screwdriver handle) to another (the lid of the tin). The force applied, which scientists call the **effort**, is changed to a much larger force, which scientists call the **load**, when the effort is moved through a greater distance than the load. In this example, the effort moves about 12 times as far as the load, and the force used to move the load is about 12 times the effort.

Another good example is to use a claw hammer to pull a nail from a piece of wood (Fig. 11.7b). The **load** is the frictional force between the nail and the wood, the **effort** is the force applied to the hammer handle. Using a typical hammer the effort moves through about 300 mm to pull a nail 30 mm out of the wood, so the machine generates a force of about ten times the effort, to move the load. The hammer is acting as a **lever**, its **pivot** being the curved surface of the head in contact with the wood. It is worth noticing that the effort required to move the load is least when it is applied at the end of the handle; that is, as far away from the pivot as possible.

Activities 14.4.1 and 14.4.2 give more guidance on investigating simple machines.

a: Van moves off from rest.

Forces are not in balance. Driving force from the road on to the rear wheels is much larger than friction forces and air resistance. Result: van moves forward and speeds up.

b: Van travels at a steady speed.

Forces are in balance. Friction forces and air resistance are larger because the van is travelling faster, but a smaller driving force is needed to balance them. Result: van's speed is constant.

c: Van brakes and slows to a standstill

Forces are not in balance. There is no driving force (clutch disengaged) and the brakes exert large friction forces in addition to air resistance. Result: van slows down and stops.

Figure 11.6 *Forces acting on a van which affect its movement. The total of all friction forces and air resistance are shown acting on the front of the van in (a) and (b). In (c), friction forces in the brakes are shown separately*

Even a door can be thought of as a machine in which the **effort** is a person's push, to open or close it, and the **load** is the force necessary to move it on its hinges – the **pivot**. Children can investigate the effect of applying the effort to this machine at different points. They will observe that the effort required to move the door is least when it is applied at the end away from the hinge. If it is applied part way along the door, nearer the hinge, a larger effort is required and it may not be possible to move it at all.

Another example of a lever-based machine is a pair of scissors, whose **pivot** is the rivet on which the blades turn, and whose **load** is the resistance of whatever is being cut. Scissors show another principle of lever-based machines: that while the effort needs to be as far away from the pivot as possible, the load needs to be as near the pivot as possible for maximum effectiveness. If the load is considerable, as, for example when cutting thick card, the scissors cut most effectively using the blades as near to the hinge as possible. A similar effect can be observed when cutting thick wire with pliers or wire-cutters.

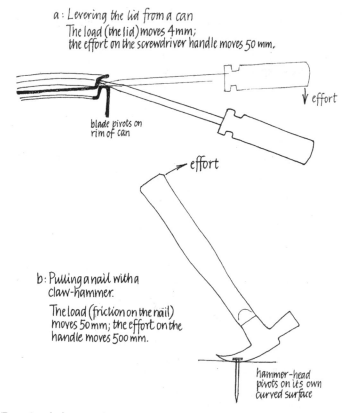

a: Levering the lid from a can
    The load (the lid) moves 4mm;
    the effort on the screwdriver handle moves 50 mm.

↓ effort

blade pivots on
rim of can

← effort

b: Pulling a nail with a
    claw-hammer.

The load (friction on the nail)
moves 50mm; the effort on the
handle moves 500 mm.

hammer-head
pivots on its own
curved surface

Figure 11.7 *Two simple lever systems*

All the machines mentioned so far have the property that they can, as it were, multiply force, having as their input a small force moving over a large distance, and producing as their output a larger force moving over a shorter distance. Other ways of doing this include pulley systems, gears and screw threads.

Most simple machines children can investigate are useful because they change a small force into a much larger one: we could call them **force-multipliers**. Some, however, work the other way round, and could be called **distance-multipliers**. Their input is a large effort moving over a short distance and their output is a smaller force moving over a larger distance. The most familiar examples are the limbs of animals. The human arm is a lever system in which a very small shortening of the biceps muscle (3.5) brings about a very much larger movement of the hand. Gear-systems can be used to do the same thing: rotary egg whisks and bicycles are examples.

The bicycle: a more complex machine Many basic concepts regarding forces and machines can be learned by investigating the transmission of propulsive force and the brakes. The leg is a distance-multiplying lever system, in which a very small movement of the muscles produces a much larger pushing movement of the foot. The foot presses down on the pedal, causing the crank and chainwheel to rotate. Teeth on the chainwheel engage the chain-links, pulling the upper part of the chain loop forwards. The chain transmits this pulling force to a smaller cog on the rear wheel, causing it and the wheel to rotate. The tyre makes a high-friction contact with the road, transmitting a backwards pushing force. Because the road is immovable and the tyre does not slip, the road pushes forwards on the tyre, so the bicycle and rider move forward.

Activity 14.4.3 has more investigations on the bicycle as a complex machine.

The brakes of a bicycle are a double lever system which is a force-multiplier. A small pulling force on the brake lever is changed to a large pulling force on the brake cable. The pulling force is transmitted by the flexible cable, running inside a sheath lubricated by grease, to the brake mechanism. This is another lever system, which in most cases further increases the force as it moves the brake blocks into contact with the wheel-rims. The blocks push inwards, gripping the rims and generating large friction forces as they slide past, so slowing the movement of the cycle and rider.

11.8 FLOATING AND SINKING

11.8.1 Thinking of floating as arrested fall

When an object floats in a liquid (e.g. a ball in water) or in air (e.g. a hot-air balloon), the object neither rises nor falls, so the forces acting on it must be in balance. Floating is when the object is prevented from falling.

Children can understand this by investigating objects floating in water. A table-tennis ball dropped into an empty bowl obviously falls to the bottom. But if the bowl has water in it, the ball falls to the water surface but then does not fall any further, because the water holds it up. This state of **arrested fall** is what we call floating. It does not continue to fall because the water is exerting an upward force on it, which balances its weight.

Activity 14.6.1 has fuller investigations on floating as arrested fall.

11.8.2 Displacement and upthrust

Children can investigate how water exerts an upward force on a floating object by standing a bucket in a bowl (to catch water that overflows) and filling the bucket completely with water. They gently push a large plastic ball into the water so that it pushes the water away, occupying part of the space within the bucket, and some water overflows. This displacement of some water causes the remaining water in the bucket to exert an upward force on the ball, known as an upthrust. This upthrust can be felt, because it is necessary to exert a downward push in order to balance it and keep the ball still. If the ball is pushed further down, the displacement and the upthrust increase: then more water overflows and a larger push is needed to prevent the ball rising. This shows that displacement is related to upthrust. In order to understand floating and sinking in terms of forces, it is necessary to find out what this relationship is.

Activity 14.6.2 gives simple investigations on displacement and upthrust.

Investigating the relationship between displacement and upthrust

Obtain a 2- or 3-litre plastic bottle, a bucket of water that is big enough to float the bottle in and a waterproof marker. Cut the top part from bottle, pour exactly 1 litre of water into the bottom part, stand it on a level surface and draw a line with a waterproof marker to record the water level. Bear in mind that 1 litre of water has a mass (12.2) of 1 kg, and a weight (it is pulled down by gravity with a force) of about 10 N (11.1). Put the bottle into the water and observe that it floats with the line more or less at the same level as the water in the bucket. The amount of water in the bucket that has been pushed aside or displaced by the bottle is also 1 litre. Empty the bottle, dry it and put exactly 1 kg dry sand in the bottom. Now float the loaded bottle again in the water in the bucket. Notice the level of the water again. The bottle should again float with the marked line level with the water (Fig. 11.8). The bottle is floating in the same way, even though the sand does not occupy as much space in the bottle as the water did. In both situations, the same size of downward force is acting on the bottle and its contents, their weight is about 10 N. Because the loaded bottle floats, the upthrust must be equal to this. It too is about

10 N. We know that the line on the bottle was drawn to show how much of it is occupied by 1 litre, and we observe that it is level with the water surface. This shows us that 1 litre of water has again been displaced. Remembering that 1 litre of water has a mass of 1 kg and a weight of about 10 N we can see that the upthrust on an object is exactly equal to the weight of the water it displaces. This is known as **Archimedes' Principle.**

Using Archimedes' Principle, if the weight of a floating object is changed, displacement and upthrust also change until the system is in balance again. This can be shown by changing the load in the marked bottle. If the weight is reduced, the bottle rises so that displacement and upthrust are also reduced. If the weight is increased, the reverse happens and the bottle sinks deeper. This self-adjusting property explains why similarly shaped pieces of different materials float with different proportions under the surface. If weight is very low in relation to volume, as in expanded polystyrene foam for example, a small amount of displacement generates enough upthrust to support it, so very little of the object is immersed. If the weight is greater in relation to volume, more upthrust is needed to support it and the object sinks deeper, displacing more water.

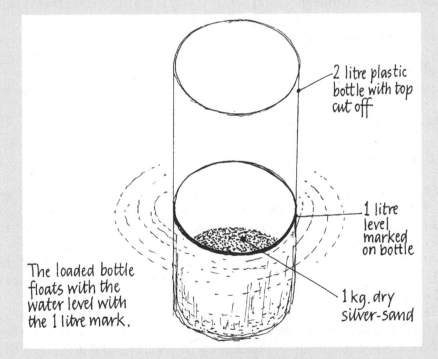

2 litre plastic bottle with top cut off

1 litre level marked on bottle

The loaded bottle floats with the water level with the 1 litre mark.

1 kg. dry silver-sand

Figure 11.8 *The relationship between displacement and upthrust*

Activity 14.6.3 has more investigations on floating and sinking.

11.8.3 Sinking – and more floating

Any object has to displace a weight of water equal to its own weight in order to remain afloat. If it cannot do this, the weight is greater than the upthrust, a balance of forces will not be achieved and the object will continue to fall: in other words, it will sink. An object which sinks in water does so because the water cannot give it *enough* support. However, support still exists, even though it is not obvious. It can be shown by hanging an object which sinks, such as a ball of modelling clay or Plasticene, from a thread attached to a forcemeter, and lowering it into water. The weight of the object appears to be reduced. Actually it is unchanged (12.2): the change in the reading on the forcemeter is caused by the upthrust of the water on the object. It is because the upthrust is less than the weight of the object when it is weighed in air (as shown by the forcemeter), that the water cannot support it fully and it sinks.

Modelling clay is particularly suitable for this investigation because its shape can be changed. Although it sinks when a solid lump, it is possible to make it float if it is formed into a hollow cup shape, as thin-walled and as large as possible. Its weight is unchanged, but in a cup shape it can displace more water than when it is a solid lump, so gaining more upthrust and, if it is large enough, remaining afloat. Similar experiments can be carried out with aluminium foil. They help to explain why ships made of steel can float and even carry heavy cargoes as well.

Activity 14.6.4 has more guidance on making a 'sinker' float.

11.8.4 Floating in air

Just like water, air has weight. Even though air has much less weight than water for the same volume, air that is displaced by an object will also exert an upthrust. Most objects are so heavy in relation to the air they displace, that this effect is not noticeable, but if an object is light enough in relation to its volume it will float in air. Children are likely to see examples such as balloons filled with helium, a gas which, litre for litre, is much lighter than air, or hot-air balloons.

Heated air expands, so a litre of heated air weighs less than a litre of cold air, and therefore hot air rises through colder air (9.3). If hot air is trapped in a large balloon, it eventually floats and rises in the cooler air around it. As with any object warmer than its surroundings, the balloon loses thermal energy by heating the air around it and becoming cooler (9.3), so the burner has to be ignited periodically to raise the temperature of the air inside the balloon and keep it afloat.

11.9 DIAGRAMS OF FORCES

Scientists use force diagrams to show how they understand forces in a particular situation, using arrows to represent the size and direction of the force (11.1). The length of the arrow shows how large a force it is, and its position shows where the force acts. Children can learn to use force diagrams, with care to avoid misunderstanding.

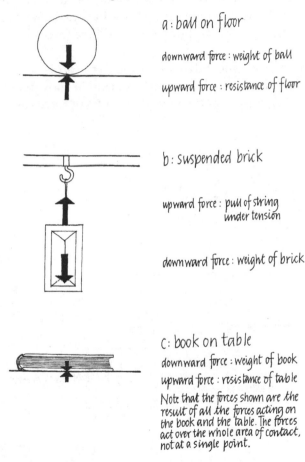

a: ball on floor

downward force: weight of ball

upward force: resistance of floor

b: suspended brick

upward force: pull of string
under tension

downward force: weight of brick

c: book on table

downward force: weight of book
upward force: resistance of table

Note that the forces shown are the result of all the forces acting on the book and the table. The forces act over the whole area of contact, not at a single point.

d: falling ball, which has just been released
upward force: air resistance (friction)

downward force: weight of ball

Figure 11.9 *Simple diagrams of forces*

Figure 11.9a is a diagram of a ball at rest showing how the forces on the ball are acting in opposite directions and are in balance. Notice in the similar situation shown by Fig. 11.9b. the force acting downwards (the weight of the brick) is represented by a single arrow from its centre. Also, only one pair of forces is shown, although similar pairs are also acting between the string and the hook, and between the hook and the beam above.

In the common example of a book resting on a table, although the forces involved act over the whole area of the book in contact with the table, it is usual to represent all the upward and downward acting forces by single arrows, as in Figure 11.9c.

An object falling for a short distance through the air is acted on by forces which are out of balance. Diagram 11.9d emphasizes that movement takes place in the direction of the larger force and shows the results of forces acting on the ball from both directions.

a: Trolley at rest

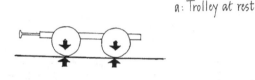

b: Trolley is pushed to the right

Force tending to make the trolley speed up: the push on the nail.
Force tending to make the trolley slow down: friction, mainly between the axles and the body.
Result: trolley speeds up and moves to the right.

c: Trolley moves to the right

Force tending to make the trolley speed up: NONE.
Forces tending to make the trolley slow down: friction, as in (b) above.
Result: trolley slows down and finally stops.

Figure 11.10 *Forces acting on a trolley*

A teacher needs to be aware of problems that may arise from using force diagrams. For example, the forces acting on a trolley at rest could be shown by a diagram such as Figure 11.10a. These forces continue to act on the trolley in the same way when it is moving, but to include them might make a diagram complex and confusing. They are usually omitted and only the forces affecting the movement of the trolley are shown (Fig. 11.10b). Once this convention is understood, such diagrams can be very useful. Figure 11.9, for example, emphasizes that friction forces opposing the movement of the trolley act in the direction opposite to its movement, and that when it is rolling across the floor, no force is tending to make it speed up, and only the friction forces are affecting its movement (11.6). The sequences shown in Figures 11.4 and 11.6 use most of the concepts discussed in this chapter to explain the changes observed.

 GRAVITY AND MAGNETISM

INTRODUCTION

Chapter 12 is about phenomena which seem to be forces that act-at-a-distance and may have a mysterious quality for young children. Children's familiarity with things falling when they are dropped encourages them to take gravity for granted and not question it. On the other hand, they often find fascination in the less familiar experience of magnets and their forces of attraction and even more strangely, of repulsion. A good teacher of science needs to be able to understand the scientific ideas and relate them sensitively to children's thinking through investigative experience.

12.1 ACTION-AT-A-DISTANCE

When investigating the forces we experience in everyday life and their effects (Chapter 11), much of our attention is directed towards finding out how objects interact when they are in contact with one another. From very early in life (including dropping toys from a high-chair!), we develop an awareness that not all changes of movement are caused by things directly pushing or pulling each other. If an object is held above the Earth's surface and released, its movement changes: unless it is prevented from doing so, it falls. Because we are so accustomed to this happening, it is easy to forget how mysterious an occurrence it is. An object which was at rest begins to move, and its speed increases. This means that a force must be acting on it all the time it is falling; but nothing, apart from air, is touching the object. A teacher who knows that scientists have observed that objects in a vacuum (in a container from which the air has been pumped out) fall just as objects in air do, may use this indirect evidence to challenge the idea held by some children, that an object falls because of the weight of atmospheric air pressing down on it.

Activity 15.1.2 gives guidance on observing action-at-a-distance by gravity.

The force which makes a falling object begin to move and speed up is gravitational force, and its effect is an example of what scientists call action-at-a-distance. The name action-at-a-distance emphasizes that we can explain such mysterious observations using the idea of forces, even though we cannot say exactly what they are, only what they do.

Children will be familiar with another example of action-at-a-distance: magnetism. Although magnets affect only certain kinds of materials (12.3) rather than all objects, as gravitation does, they also have the property of exerting forces on objects which are not in contact with them. This can easily be shown using a magnet and paper-clip, or ring magnets (Figs 12.1 and 12.4).

Activity 15.1.1 gives more guidance on observing action-at-a-distance by a magnet.

Fields The scientific idea of a field is helpful to explain evidence of the effects of both gravitation and magnetism. When action-at-a-distance occurs, how large the forces are depends partly on the distance between the objects involved. The smaller the distance between them, if other things remain the same, the larger the forces will be, as can easily be observed with magnets (12.4). It has also been demonstrated by many interplanetary flights: once the space vehicle is far enough away, the forces tending to pull it back to Earth are undetectably small. A field is the space around an object in which another object experiences a force. In the gravitational field around the Earth, any object experiences a gravitational force which tends to make it fall towards the Earth. The Moon is in the Earth's gravitational field, but is prevented from moving nearer to it by its movement in orbit, just as manufactured satellites are (12.2). The Earth–Moon system is in the Sun's gravitational field, as are all the other planets of the Solar System (14.1). When it is in a gravitational field, any object will experience a force. Magnets also have a field around them, known as a magnetic field, but this affects only magnetic materials (12.3).

Gravity and magnetism: two unexplained phenomena The aim of science is always understanding: knowing 'why', as well as knowing 'that' and knowing 'how to' (1.3). Teachers, who are seeking explanations which their pupils can understand, need to be aware that there are some phenomena which at present are unexplained by scientists. It is appropriate to tell children this, and convey a sense of science as an unending quest which includes awe and wonder. Gravity and magnetism are two examples. Scientists can measure forces which cause action-at-a-distance, relate them to mass (gravity, 12.2) and the orderly arrangement of atoms (magnetism, 12.3) and they can also make very accurate predictions of how objects in gravitational and magnetic fields will behave. And yet there is no scientific explanation of why they behave as they do that is generally agreed. In watching objects fall, or magnets attract and repel each other, we are experiencing mysteries which human ingenuity has so far failed to explain.

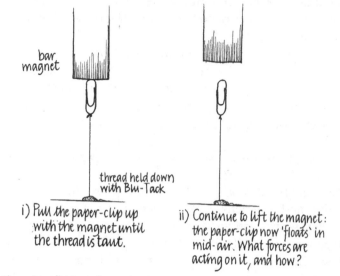

bar magnet

thread held down with Blu-Tack

i) Pull the paper-clip up with the magnet until the thread is taut.

ii) Continue to lift the magnet: the paper-clip now 'floats' in mid-air. What forces are acting on it, and how?

Figure 12.1 *Action-at-a-distance by a magnet*

12.2 GRAVITY, MASS AND WEIGHT

12.2.1 Observing gravitation

All objects have gravitational fields, but unless an object is very large (the Earth, for example), the field is so weak that it has no effect on human activities and can be detected only by using very sensitive measuring methods. An object in a gravitational field experiences a gravitational force which tends to make it move towards the large object creating the field, as a falling ball moves towards the surface of the Earth. This force is the weight of the object.

Activity 15.2.1 shows simple investigations with falling objects.

Children's observations of freely falling and suspended objects can develop two important general ideas: the gravitational force acting on any given object is always the same, and it always acts in the same direction. Objects tend to fall vertically, both when they are free and when they are suspended by a string or thread. Objects which are not falling vertically must either have been moving sideways when they began to fall or have another force acting on them sideways and changing their movement (11.6). Children have observed balls thrown or kicked and the bob of a pendulum pulled out of its vertical fall by the string. The fact that gravitational force always acts vertically downwards is the basis for using plumb-lines to measure verticals and liquid levelling devices to measure horizontals.

Activity 15.2.2 provides more investigations of changing direction in falling and Activity 15.2.3 investigates pendulums.

12.2.2 The distinction between mass and weight

Mass is a measure of how much matter or material is in an object (see the Introduction to Part 3). The unit of mass is the kilogram (kg). Weight is the force which acts on a mass as a result of its being in a gravitational field. The unit of weight, like that of any other force, is the Newton (N). At the surface of the Earth, any object of mass 1 kg is pulled down with a force of 9.81 N, so for most purposes the weight of 1 kg is taken to be 10 N.

There may be confusion between mass and weight because, in everyday experience and language, there is no distinction between them. Because we live within Earth's gravitational field, we never experience mass (amount of material) directly, but only through weight: the object is more or less heavy. Because of this, we measure the mass of an object by weighing it, measuring the gravitational force acting on it and comparing this with another, known, force. Thus, a statement such as 'I weighed out a kilogram of apples' simply means that a quantity of material (mass, measured in kilograms) was measured by finding its weight. In science, however, the distinction between mass and weight is of great importance.

Unless the amount of matter in an object changes, its mass remains constant, no matter where it is. When pieces of rock were brought back from the Moon to the Earth, the amount of material remained the same: their mass did not change as a result of being transported. The weight of an object, on the other hand, will change if it is moved towards or away from the Earth, because weight depends on the intensity of the gravitational field in which the object happens to be at any time. On the surface of the Moon, for example, a kilogram of rock would weigh about 1.6 N, whereas the same rock, brought back to Earth with its mass unchanged, would weigh 9.8 N. The difference comes about because the Moon, being much less massive than the Earth, has a gravitational field which is much less intense. On the surface of a planet more massive than the Earth, a kilogram would weigh much more than its weight on Earth.

12.2.3 Developing concepts of mass and weight

Primary teachers use the distinction between mass and weight when establishing the relationship between displacement and upthrust in a floating object (11.8). An object suspended from a weighing machine loses weight when lowered into water due to upthrust, but stays the same mass since nothing has been added or taken away.

12.2.4 Real and apparent weightlessness

On Earth, the weight of an object remains the same as long as its mass does not change. True weightlessness is quite different from the apparent weightlessness brought about by a balance of forces. The gravitational field around the Earth, and any other large object, varies with distance: the farther away one is, the less intense the field. This means that the weight of an object decreases as its distance away from the Earth increases. At a distance of 15,000 km, for example, 1 kg would weigh only 2 N, one-fifth of its weight on Earth. If an object travels far enough away from the Earth, until no gravitational field can be detected, it will have no weight. This is true weightlessness, which cannot be experienced on Earth.

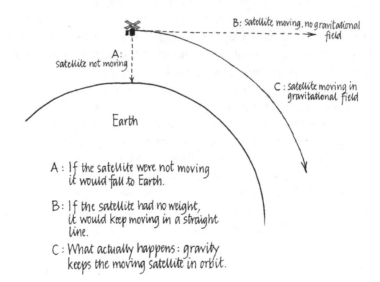

A : If the satellite were not moving it would fall to Earth.

B: If the satellite had no weight, it would keep moving in a straight line.

C: What actually happens: gravity keeps the moving satellite in orbit.

Figure 12.2 *The orbit of a satellite*

Humans in orbit around the Earth in space stations appear to experience true weightlessness and are often said to be living 'in zero-g'. Both statements, however, are misleading: they are not outside the Earth's gravitational field, and what they experience is another kind of apparent weightlessness, brought about by the way satellites move round the Earth, a condition known as free-fall. Figure 12.2 helps to explain the movement of a satellite. Because it is in the Earth's gravitational field the satellite has weight, so if it were not moving (A) it would fall towards the Earth. But the satellite is moving, very fast: Skylab travelled at about 28,000 km per hour, or nearly 8,000 ms–1 (metres per second). If a satellite were outside the Earth's gravitational field and therefore truly weightless (B), it would keep moving in a straight line. What actually happens (C) is that the satellite is continually falling towards the Earth, but its movement prevents it getting any closer, so both it and the people in it are in free-fall. One effect of free-fall is that the satellite, together with the people and objects in it, appear to be weightless, as do parachutists in free-fall before their parachutes open (Fig. 11.4).

12.2.5 Rate of fall

Because the Earth's gravitational field is constant, the rate at which any object falls towards it is also constant, unless other forces are acting on it. This means that, unless another force is acting against gravity, all objects fall towards the Earth at the same rate, regardless of their weight. This may seem to contradict everyday experience: feathers and stones, for example, do not fall at the same rate. The difference, however, has nothing to do with gravitational force. It comes about because air resistance (friction, 11.4) tends to slow down light objects with a high surface area, such as feathers, much more than compact objects such as stones. In a chamber with all the air pumped out (in a vacuum), a feather and a hammer would fall at the same rate, and this was demonstrated on the Moon during one of the Apollo missions and can be viewed on YouTube using the URL http://www.youtube.com/watch?v=PE81zGhnb0w.

12.3 MAGNETS AND MAGNETIC MATERIALS

It has been known for thousands of years from observations of natural magnets or lodestones that magnets attract iron to themselves and always point in the same direction if free to move. The magnets used by children today are either metallic, made of special alloys of iron with other metals such as nickel, or ceramic, made of a non-metallic material known as magnadur (12.7). Magnets are made in a wide variety of shapes for different purposes. The most useful for children's investigations are simple bar magnets. Horseshoe magnets show that magnetism as a property does not depend on shape.

Disc and ring magnets made of black ceramic are very useful for particular demonstrations and investigations (12.4, 12.7). Modern plastic-cased bar-shaped magnets are very robust and in most investigations behave much as simple bar magnets do. It is, however, important to realize that they are not simple, but are made up of a row of ceramic magnets held end to end in a tough case.

Consequently, they may give unexpected results when the shape of their magnetic field is observed (see below) and their 'strength' is measured (12.4).

Magnetic materials   Children learning to distinguish between magnets and magnetic materials find the concept of field (12.1) is very useful. Children can classify a range of materials into groups, depending on whether they are magnetic (attracted to a magnet) or non-magnetic (no attraction).

A **magnetic material** is one which, when placed near a magnet, within its magnetic field, will experience a force tending to pull it closer to the magnet. Children will find that all common magnetic materials are metallic, but not all metals are magnetic: aluminium and brass, for example, are unaffected by magnets. The only common magnetic materials are iron and its alloys such as steel, but some stainless steels are non-magnetic, and some special materials used to make ceramic magnets (12.7) are non-metallic. Although magnetic materials experience forces when they are in a magnetic field, they create no magnetic field of their own, unless they are magnetized (see below and 12.6) to become magnets themselves. This means that two objects of magnetic material normally have no tendency to cling together or attract each other.

Activity 15.3.1 shows ways of sorting magnetic and non-magnetic materials.

A **magnet** is always composed of magnetic material, which creates a magnetic field around itself, within which magnetic materials and other magnets experience forces. The process by which a magnetic material becomes a magnet is called magnetization. This may be achieved either by contact with a magnet (12.6) or electrically. Once the magnetizing process stops, different materials retain magnetism to different degrees. The magnets which children use retain their magnetism to a very high degree if handled properly and are known as permanent magnets (12.6). Distinguishing magnets from materials which are magnetic but unmagnetized is explained in section 12.4.

A magnetic material is magnetized when its internal structure becomes more ordered. The thousands of magnetic zones, known as domains, each acting like a very small magnet, are arranged in a disordered way in an unmagnetized object, so their magnetic fields cancel each other out. When the material is fully magnetized, all the domains within it become lined up in the same direction so that their magnetic fields reinforce instead of cancelling each other out, and a single magnetic field is created.

> *The shape of a magnetic field*   Children can investigate the field of a magnet by placing a piece of thin, stiff card over it and sprinkling a thin layer of finely powdered

iron ('iron filings') onto the card. Iron powder may be difficult to remove from magnets (use adhesive tape) and may stain clothes by rusting. The card is tapped gently to help the particles of powder line up in the magnetic field and show its shape. Differently shaped magnets usually have differently shaped fields (compare Figures 12.3 and 12.7). The iron particles concentrate in the places where the poles of the magnet are located in the magnet (12.4). Close observation shows that the particles nearest the magnet move less readily when the card is tapped than those farther away. This shows that the intensity of the magnetic field decreases as distance from the magnet increases.

Activity 15.3.2 contains more observations of magnetic fields.

Barriers to magnetic fields   Barriers to the field around a permanent magnet can be set up only by magnetic materials. The forces of attraction between a magnet and a magnetic object are unaffected by thin layers of wood, glass, paper, water, plastic and non-magnetic metals, so that (for example) a magnet can be used to remove a steel paper-clip from a cup of water without wetting the hands, by sliding the magnet up the outside of the cup. A thin sheet of iron or steel, on the other hand, does act as a barrier against a magnetic field, though the effectiveness of different kinds of steel may vary.

Activity 15.3.3 shows investigations of barriers to magnetic fields.

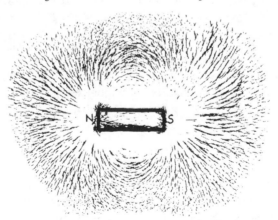

The lines of iron particles show the shape of the field and the direction of magnetic forces in it. These forces act towards the poles of the magnet at either end, but parallel to the sides in the middle.

Figure 12.3 *Observing the field of a simple bar magnet*

12.4 THE POLES OF MAGNETS AND THEIR BEHAVIOUR

12.4.1 Observing magnetic poles

The ancient Greeks, early Chinese scientists and Viking navigators all knew that magnets, if free to move, come to rest pointing in a particular direction. An early way of effecting this was to place the magnet on wood floating in water, but a more useful way for children's investigations is to suspend a bar magnet from a thread so that it hangs horizontally. Eventually, it comes to rest lined up in a north–south direction. When a bar magnet is free to move, one end always points north unless it is deflected by magnetic materials or magnets near it. This end is known as the north-seeking pole, or 'north pole' for short. The opposite end is the south-seeking or 'south pole'. Magnets which are free to move line up in this way because the Earth itself is a very large magnet (12.5).

Activity 15.4.1 provides investigations of magnetic poles and polarity.

Children observing the shape of a magnetic field (12.3) or making simple comparisons of the 'strength' of magnets (see below), will notice that the magnetic field and the forces of attraction which it produces appear to be concentrated at the poles of the magnet. Steel paper-clips will not easily cling to the middle of a bar magnet, though they are strongly attracted to the ends. Although the whole of the magnet is equally magnetized and all of it contributes to the magnetic field around it, the magnetic forces in the middle of the magnet are acting parallel to the magnet, not towards it (Fig. 12.3). To test this idea, magnetize a length of steel wire (12.6) and then cut it in two, you will find that each piece behaves as a separate magnet, showing that the middle of the wire had been magnetized just as much as the ends.

12.4.2 Attraction and repulsion

A material which is magnetic but is not itself a magnet is always attracted to a magnet. But when two magnets are close to each other, what happens depends on their positions. If the north pole of one magnet is brought near to the south pole of another, the two pull towards and attract each other. But if the north poles or south poles of two magnets are brought close to each other, there is a pushing force which tends to move them apart, known as magnetic repulsion. This gives rise to the rule that 'Unlike poles attract; like poles repel'.

Magnetic repulsion provides convincing evidence for the idea of a magnetic field and of action-at-a-distance (12.1). Ring magnets show this very clearly (Fig. 12.4).

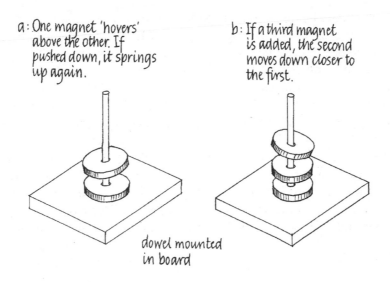

a: One magnet 'hovers' above the other. If pushed down, it springs up again.

b: If a third magnet is added, the second moves down closer to the first.

dowel mounted in board

Figure 12.4 *Repulsion by face-polarized ring magnets*

Activity 15.4.2 provides investigations of the attraction and repulsion of magnets.

12.4.3 Testing for magnetism

An object which is attracted to a magnet must be made of, or at least contain, magnetic material, but is it a magnet? This requires a more critical test: that of magnetic repulsion. One magnet and a piece of magnetic material will never repel each other: they will always be attracted. Only two magnets with like poles opposed will repel. If the magnet is weak (as for example a needle magnetized by stroking it with a magnet usually is) repulsion is difficult to observe. To overcome this, suspend the weak magnet from a thread or place it on wood floating in water. It is possible to move it with much smaller forces, so any repulsion can be detected when the magnet used for testing is much farther away.

Activity 15.4.3 shows more ways of testing for magnetism.

12.4.4 Measuring the 'strength' of magnets

Children and adults often refer to magnets as being 'strong' or 'weak'. Different magnets create magnetic fields of greater or less intensity, so that magnetic materials experience greater or lesser forces of attraction when near them. (12.6).

Magnets can be compared by attraction and by repulsion. Tests which use attraction are simpler but less accurate. The simplest test is to dip the magnets into a large box of steel pins or paper-clips. Compare how many each picks up to obtain a rough comparison of magnetic 'strength'. Alternatively, hang paper-clips from one pole of each magnet and see how long a chain each will support.

More accurate comparisons can be made using repulsion. Choose one magnet as the standard for all the tests. Place all the magnets to be tested on as smooth a surface as possible and bring the standard magnet slowly closer to each one, with like poles opposed. When the magnet being tested just starts to move by repulsion, record the distance between the two. The larger the distance, the 'stronger' the magnet under test. Refine this test by mounting the magnets on trolleys and pulling the standard magnet closer to the one under test until it and its trolley move. This test can provide not only technological challenges but much insight into forces, friction, lubrication and fair testing. An alternative method is to compare the 'strength' of the magnet with that of the Earth's magnetic field (Fig.12.5).

Activity 15.4.4 shows more ways of comparing the 'strength' of magnets.

12.5 THE EARTH'S MAGNETISM AND NAVIGATION

The idea that the Earth itself is a magnet is justified by evidence that magnets, if free to move, always come to rest pointing in the same direction (12.3). A swinging magnet shows the direction of the magnetic forces round the Earth.

There is no generally agreed explanation of why the Earth is a magnet. One theory is that material circulating in the Earth's core generates electric currents and, with them, the magnetic field. Like any magnet, the Earth has two poles. These are near the geographical north and south poles, but their position moves slowly all the time, so that magnetic north and true north are not in the same direction.

Magnetic compasses and navigation Magnetic compasses are an example of ancient technology still extensively used today. They are simply magnets which are free to move and so to become aligned with the Earth's magnetic field. To make a simple compass, suspend a magnet from a thread, or place it on wood floating on water, or balance it on a small spike. The most useful compasses for children to use are the modern fluid-filled type used by walkers and orienteers. These have a balanced compass needle whose swing is damped by the fluid around it, so that although it gives a quick reading and is stable in use, it is also sensitive and accurate.

A magnetic compass is affected by any magnetic material around it. Steel-framed furniture and buildings, for example, may make it impossible to obtain a consistent north–south bearing in the classroom. If this happens, compasses can be used for direction-finding only outdoors or in another room.

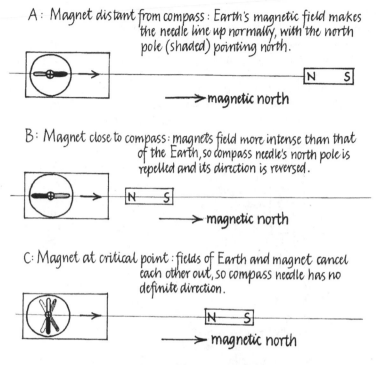

A: Magnet distant from compass: Earth's magnetic field makes the needle line up normally, with the north pole (shaded) pointing north.

⟶ magnetic north

B: Magnet close to compass: magnet's field more intense than that of the Earth, so compass needle's north pole is repelled and its direction is reversed.

⟶ magnetic north

C: Magnet at critical point: fields of Earth and magnet cancel each other out, so compass needle has no definite direction.

⟶ magnetic north

Figure 12.5 *Finding the strength of the Earth's magnetic field*

Activity 15.5.1 shows more investigations with the magnetic field compass.

The Earth's magnetic poles are not located at the geographical poles, so a magnetic compass does not point to true north. This means that when using a magnetic compass for navigation or locating one's position on a map, it is necessary to make a correction. This is further complicated by the fact that the magnetic north pole moves, so the correction needed varies with place and time. In Britain in 2002, for example, magnetic north lay about 6° west of true north, and this difference is being reduced by about ½° every four years.

12.6 MAGNETIZING AND DEMAGNETIZING

A magnetic material is attracted to a magnet because, when it is in a magnetic field, it becomes magnetized. This is called **magnetic induction**. Children can investigate this

Continued

Continued

by suspending two steel nails from a magnet, having first checked that they are unmagnetized by making sure that they will not repel a compass needle. When suspended from the magnet the nails will not hang vertically, because the poles which are induced at their ends repel each other (Fig. 12.6a), showing that the nails themselves are magnetized. This can be confirmed by bringing another magnet near the nails with like poles opposed, which will cause the nails to be repelled even further (Fig. 12.6b).

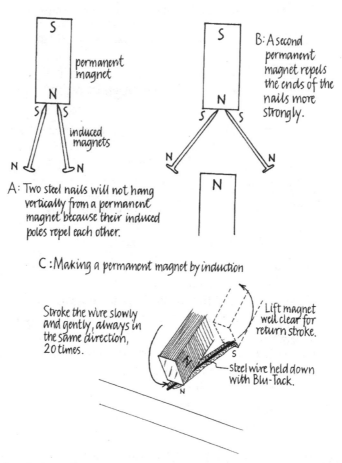

Figure 12.6 *Induced magnetism*

Temporary and permanent magnets When an object in contact with a magnet is magnetized by induction, the magnet's field makes some or all of the magnetic domains in the object temporarily line up in the same direction, so that the object develops poles and an overall magnetic field of its own (12.3). How much of this induced magnetism remains when the object is removed from the magnet depends on the material of which it is made. Soft iron, such as iron 'filings' or florist's wire, is very strongly magnetized when in contact with a magnet, but when it is removed, it loses all its magnetism because its magnetic domains immediately go back to their original disordered state. As a result, soft iron can be only a temporary magnet. Steel, on the other hand, is less strongly magnetized, but when it is removed from the magnet its magnetic domains do not become completely disordered again, so that some of the induced magnetism is retained, making it is possible to magnetize steel permanently.

Activity 15.6.1 provides more investigations of magnetic attraction and temporary magnets.

Children can make small permanent magnets from steel wire (e.g. paperclips straightened out with pliers) by stroking them with a 'strong' permanent magnet (Fig. 12.6c). Hold one pole of the magnet near to the wire, always stroke in the same direction and move the magnet well away from the steel object after each stroke. If the north pole is used for stroking, a north pole will be induced at the start of the stroke and a south pole at the end. The induced magnetism can be tested by repulsion (12.4). Because the wire is only weakly magnetized, a good way to test it is to fix it to a disc of cork with Blu-Tack and float it on water.

Activity 15.6.2 gives more ways of making small permanent magnets by induction and Activity 15.6.3 has ways of testing 'weak' magnets.

Demagnetizing   Magnetizing a material involves giving its many small magnetic domains an orderly arrangement (12.3). Anything which breaks down this order 'weakens' the magnet, making its magnetic field less intense. A metal magnet gradually becomes demagnetized if stored on its own, so bar magnets are stored in parallel pairs with pieces of soft iron (keepers) between pairs of unlike poles, and horseshoe magnets are stored with a single keeper. Demagnetization is quicker if metal magnets have mechanical shocks like being dropped, so they should be handled carefully. These problems do not affect ceramic magnets (12.7), though they also need to be handled carefully, because they are brittle and can easily be chipped or broken (12.7).

12.7   NON-METALLIC MAGNETIC MATERIAL

Non-metallic magnets of a manufactured ceramic material known as magnadur are black, hard and brittle. These special materials make 'strong' magnets which are unlikely to become demagnetized over time, so that they are easy to store. Their brittleness means they can be chipped or broken if dropped, so some magnets for school use have a row of ceramic magnets in a tough plastic case. These are very useful in simple investigations, being 'stronger', more robust and long-lasting, but they are not simple bar magnets and may give anomalous results in some investigations (12.3).

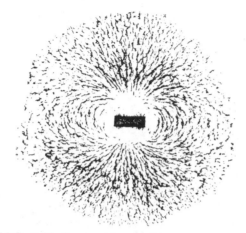

Field of a ring-shaped magnet standing on its edge. Its poles are its faces (contrast Fig.12.3). Cuboid ceramic magnets may be face- or end-polarized.

Figure 12.7 *Field of a ceramic magnet*

Materials similar to those used in ceramic magnets, in the form of a very fine powder, are bonded onto plastic tape and used for audio and video recording to store information as a complex pattern of magnetization. Storage of information in a computer memory, for example, can be done on a hard disk which is made of non-magnetic material coated with magnetic material; originally iron oxide. Modern magnetic coatings are made of cobalt alloys which have extremely small magnetic domains with which to store the information.

Ceramic magnets are made in a wide range of shapes and sizes, including discs and rings, so the location of the poles is not as obvious as in a bar-shaped magnet: at the ends. Many ceramic magnets are face-polarized: magnetized so that their poles are their flat faces. Place a piece of paper over the magnet and sprinkle iron 'filings' on to the paper to observe the shape of its magnetic field (Fig. 12.7).

Ring-shaped ceramic magnets show repulsion (12.4) and action-at-a-distance in a vivid and memorable way, when threaded onto an upright wooden dowel with their like poles opposed (Fig. 12.4). The upper magnet floats with no visible means of support, and will bounce in the air above the lower one if raised a little and then released. It is being supported by magnetic force acting upwards, balancing gravitational force acting downwards.

Section 15.7 has more investigations of non-metallic magnets.

SOUND AND LIGHT

INTRODUCTION

Sound and light are two more ways in which energy is transferred. Energy (9.1.1) is the property of material things or systems that enables them to change. It shows itself in different ways. When a change occurs, energy is transferred from one part of the system to another, often in a different form. This chapter is about understanding what sound and light are, and how they are transferred, as part of changes that take place in materials.

13.1 SOUND, WAVES AND VIBRATION

13.1.1 Observing wave motion

Sound consists of tiny movements in the environment to which the ear responds (3.10). We usually hear sound from movements in air, but sound is also transmitted through water and solids. The movements occur in a pattern which is described as a wave motion. In everyday life, there are many kinds of waves. Children are likely to be familiar with visible waves travelling outwards from a source of movement, such as ripples on water when an object is thrown into it. We see these waves are at right angles (perpendicular) to the direction in which the waves travel. This is similar to pulses in a rope when one end is moved up and down quickly (Fig. 13.1a). Sound waves also travel outwards from a source, but the movements are different.

We cannot directly see sound wave movements, but children can observe a similar pattern by moving a 'Slinky' spring as shown in Figure 13.1b and c. As the end of the spring is moved quickly back and forward, a series of pulses pass along it. Within each pulse the coils of the spring are momentarily squashed a little closer together than

Continued

Continued

normal, compressed, but between pulses they are stretched further apart and expand. The overall effect is the passage of a wave pattern. As the wave passes, each coil of the spring is moved forwards and then back again, so it ends up in the same position as before and the spring, as a whole, does not move.

Sound waves similarly involve forwards and backwards movements in the air, but they are very rapid and very tiny compared with the much slower waves in the 'Slinky' spring (Fig. 13.1c). As a wave passes, air molecules (6.4) are alternately compressed together then expanded and moved further apart than normal. Because the molecules are moving, they have kinetic energy (9.2.1). When sound waves enter the ear, some of that kinetic energy is transferred to the eardrum, making it vibrate. This vibration is detected by the ear, which transmits signals to the brain, so the sound is heard.

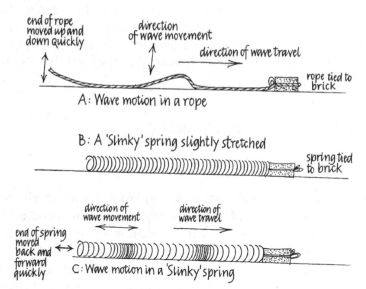

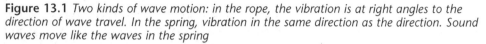

Figure 13.1 *Two kinds of wave motion: in the rope, the vibration is at right angles to the direction of wave travel. In the spring, vibration in the same direction as the direction. Sound waves move like the waves in the spring*

13.1.2 Sound waves and vibration

Sound waves are generated by objects which are moving rapidly to and fro: the kind of movement called **vibration**. A vibrating object makes the air around it vibrate, generating sound waves which travel outwards through the air. Musical instruments vibrate and produce sound waves in a variety of ways. If an object is not vibrating it cannot be producing sound waves, but most of the sounds we hear are produced by very small and rapid vibrations, which are difficult or impossible to see.

Children need to observe and gain evidence for themselves of the connection between vibration and sound in many different ways. A simple and popular way is placing grains of rice on a drum and observing their movement when it is struck and made to vibrate.

Activity 16.1.1 shows more investigations of vibration and sound.

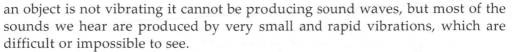

> A child can notice vibration in their voice by raising their chin, placing their finger-tips lightly on the lower part of the voice-box (larynx) in the throat and singing a single, prolonged note. Also, the vibration in stringed instruments (13.3), especially those with long or thick strings which produce a low note are interesting to observe.

13.1.3 Transmission of sound

Sound waves travel outwards from the vibrating object which is generating them. Sounds travel not only in air, but often more effectively in other materials. Water transmits sound very well, enabling whales and dolphins to communicate over long distances, and human technology to use echo-sounding (13.1.5). Many solids, particularly metals, are excellent transmitters of sound. A tap on a water-pipe can be heard by pressing an ear to a connected pipe in any part of a large building.

Activity 16.1.2 has more investigations of the transmission of sound.

Sound waves are transmitted by the material through which they travel, so if there is no material around a vibrating object, it cannot generate sound. This is not a situation we normally experience, since we live surrounded by air, but if all the air is pumped from a jar so that it contains a vacuum, a bell suspended inside it cannot make sound.

13.1.4 The speed of sound

Sound waves travelling outwards from the vibrating object, do so at a definite speed which is much less than the speed of light. This means that between generating a sound and its being heard by an observer, there is a delay, which over a short distance is not noticeable, but can be easily observed over greater distances. Light travels so fast (13.5.2) that light produced on Earth reaches an observer almost immediately. If something which generates sound can be seen by an observer some distance away, s/he notices the delay between seeing the event and hearing the sound. At a cricket match, the batsman is seen by spectators to hit the ball before they hear the sound. The speed of sound in air is about 340 metres per second, or 1 km every three seconds.

Knowing the speed of sound makes it possible to estimate how far away a lightning flash was, by timing the delay between seeing the lightning and hearing the sound it produces (thunder), then dividing the number of seconds by three to give the distance in km. The time taken for sound to travel to an observer also explains why thunder rumbles. A lightning-stroke may be several km long and is almost an instantaneous event, but its lower end is much nearer an observer on the ground than its upper end. The first sound heard, from the lower end, is usually a loud crack. This is followed by the rumbling thunder as sound waves arrive from more distant parts of the lightning-stroke.

13.1.5 Reflected sound: echoes

Children using a 'Slinky' spring to see the way that sound waves move (Fig. 13.1b and c), will notice that when a wave reaches the end of the spring, it bounces off the heavy object to which the spring is attached and travels back in the reverse direction. Sound waves can be reflected in the same way, and if the distances are great enough the reflected sound will be heard as a distinct echo. The human ear–brain system can hear two sounds as distinct only if they are one-tenth of a second or more apart, so to hear an echo of a sound they make themselves a person has to be at least 20 m away from the surface which is reflecting the sound. The most distinct echoes are made by short, sharp sounds directed at smooth, hard surfaces such as walls and rock-faces, which reflect sound rather than absorbing it (13.3). Some large, dome-shaped buildings, such as the Whispering Gallery in St Paul's Cathedral in London, have multiple echoes.

Echoes occur in water as well as air. Water transmits sound faster than air (about 1,400 metres per second) and more effectively. One technology which exploits this is echo-sounding. Short pulses of sound are produced by a device on the bottom of a ship. These travel to the sea-bed, are reflected back to the ship and detected by a microphone. The delay between sending the signals and receiving the echo depends on the depth of water. This is calculated to give the shape and depth of the sea-floor to be charted and to locate wrecks and shoals of fish.

13.2 DIFFERENCES BETWEEN SOUNDS: PITCH, LOUDNESS AND QUALITY

Children can learn to distinguish between and recognize a great variety of sounds. They can investigate basic differences and relate them to the concept of sound as waves and the properties of the objects which produce them, such as musical instruments.

13.2.1 Pitch and frequency

Pitch is the term used by musicians to refer to how high or low a sound is. Young children may initially confuse this meaning with high and low spatial positions. Usually, the pitch of a sound is determined by how rapidly the object producing the sound waves is vibrating (but not if the source of the sound is moving, see below). The number of vibrations in one second is the same as the number of sound waves generated, and is referred to as the **frequency**. The unit of frequency is the **Hertz** (symbol: Hz), 1 Hz being equal to 1 vibration each second. The higher the frequency of sound waves, the higher the pitch of the sound which is heard.

The normal range of human hearing is between about 20 Hz (a very low sound) to about 20,000 Hz in children. After childhood, there is a progressive loss of high-frequency hearing, so most adults cannot hear sounds above 16,000 Hz. Many animals can hear much higher-pitched sounds than humans. Dogs can hear sounds up to 35,000 Hz, and can be trained to respond to very high-pitched (so-called 'silent') dog whistles, which humans cannot hear. Bats use very high-pitched sounds to hunt and navigate in near-darkness using echoes for location. People who claim to hear bats squeak, are almost certainly hearing the bats' lower-frequency sounds: the high-frequency ones are far beyond the range of the human ear.

Children can investigate pitch using musical instruments. The guitar is useful as it has six strings, all of the same length (unlike the piano) and about the same tension, but of different thicknesses to produce sounds of different pitches. Thicker strings vibrate at a lower frequency when plucked and produce lower notes. The pitch of the note produced can be varied by changing tension or by changing length. The greater the tension on the string, the higher the pitch of the note it produces. Tension can be changed gradually by turning the tuning pegs, so that strings can be tuned accurately.

Activity 16.2.1 gives investigations of pitch and frequency.

Shortening the vibrating part of a string (on a guitar, pressing a string down on to the finger-board behind a fret) makes the pitch higher. The idea that '**the shorter the vibrating object, the higher the frequency**' applies not only to stringed instruments but also to woodwind and percussion.

Activity 16.2.2 has more investigations of controlling pitch in strings and Activity 16.2.3 has investigations of variable sounds made by blowing.

13.2.2 The Doppler effect

Children may have noticed a phenomenon which scientists call the Doppler effect. A stationary person listening to a siren on a vehicle passing by can hear a change in the pitch of the sound. The pitch seems to rise slowly until the vehicle passes, then suddenly falls, although the frequency at which the siren is vibrating does not actually change. This is because of the vehicle's movement in relation to the observer. The approaching movement of the vehicle means that more sound waves reach the observer every second than if it were stationary, so the frequency heard increases and the pitch rises. The passing movement reverses this effect. Fewer sound waves reach the ear each second, so the pitch of the notes heard is lower. The Doppler effect is also experienced when moving past a stationary sound source, for example when driving past a sounding alarm, but if the observer and the sound source are travelling at the same speed in the same direction, no change of pitch is heard.

13.2.3 Loudness

The loudness of a sound is related to how large a movement of air each sound wave causes. This in turn is related to how widely the object producing the sound waves is vibrating, a property known as **amplitude**. Plucking the bass string of a guitar lightly, producing a soft sound, the vibration has a small amplitude which is scarcely visible. Plucking it harder results in a greater amplitude, clearly visible vibrations and a louder sound. The movements are still very small, but create a larger movement of air, causing the eardrum to vibrate more violently, stimulating the ear more and making the sound louder. Loudness also depends on how far away the source of the sound is from the ear. The greater the distance, then the smaller the amplitude of the sound wave and the relatively quieter it sounds.

The loudness of sound is measured in **decibels** (symbol: dB). The softest sound which can be heard, such as the faint rustling of leaves, is 0 dB, a whisper is about 30 dB, normal conversation 50–70 dB, a pneumatic drill and a thunderclap 100–110 dB. Sounds over 140 dB may cause pain and permanent damage to the ears. A sound level of 140 dB represents an input of kinetic energy to the ear 10 million times greater than that of sounds at 0 dB, which can only just be heard.

Activity 16.2.4 has practical ideas about loudness and energy.

13.2.4 Quality of sound

Pitch and loudness are insufficient to describe accurately the great variety of sounds we hear, distinguish and recognize every day. There is a difference in the quality of sound between, say, a piano and a clarinet playing a note at the same pitch, and even more subtle distinctions between the voices of two people saying the same words. These differences in the quality of similar sounds are produced because sound waves, although it is useful to think of them as simple movements such as those we can see in a 'Slinky' spring, may be much more complex. Any sound waves from a voice or instrument have a basic frequency and loudness, but superimposed on this are subtle patterns which give the particular sound its quality. People with normal hearing are capable of learning to tell the difference between these patterns of sound waves to a very high degree.

13.3 NOISE POLLUTION AND SOUNDPROOFING

Unwanted noise intrudes on the lives and work of many people, including children and teachers in school and at home. Very high levels of sound can cause damage to the ears and loss of hearing (13.2.3), but even lower levels of noise increase stress and reduce concentration. Unwanted noise intruding into living space, for example from road traffic, aircraft or loud music, can make the most comfortable environment unbearable. Unwanted and intrusive noise should be regarded as a form of pollution which may not physically threaten people's well-being, but can seriously diminish their quality of life.

Children can learn about noise pollution by listening to noise around them and comparing noise levels indoors with those outdoors, and with doors and windows open and shut. Sound recorders can help to help make comparisons between noise levels at different places and times. If noise is a problem in the environment, its prevention is not easy, though there are legal limits on vehicle and aircraft noise.

Soundproofing Minimizing the effects of noise pollution usually means using some form of soundproofing. Sound waves have kinetic energy, and are transmitted through air. The basic principle of soundproofing is to ensure, as far as possible, that this kinetic energy is transferred to some object or system before it reaches our ears. This usually means placing a barrier between the source of the intrusive sound and the people whom it disturbs, which will absorb the sound waves rather than transmitting them. Workers in a noisy environment use ear-muffs (rather like large headphones) or ear-plugs made from plastic foam material to make a noise barrier. Noise pollution can be reduced by placing a soundproof barrier around the environment requiring protection. For example, a brick wall 250 mm thick reduces sound levels by about 50 dB, so the sound of a car 10 m away would be reduced to the level of someone whispering near the listener. A double layer (cavity) wall with insulating foam in the cavity is even more effective. Windows are much less effective as sound-proofing barriers than walls. A single glass window reduces noise only by about 15 dB but two sheets of glass tightly sealed with a small gap between them are used in windows of high-speed trains and aircraft as well as in buildings.

Activity 16.4.1 gives more ways of observing sound insulation in the classroom.

Children investigating soundproofing can compare the effectiveness of materials as noise preventers, for example by packing a material round a buzzer in a box (with the battery and switch outside), and finding out how far away the buzzer can still be heard in a quiet room. Using a variety of materials for the packing will give a rough comparison of their effectiveness as sound barriers. Alternatively, using a sound recorder with a detachable microphone, together with an audio system, place the microphone into a box and pack the material under test. Switch on the recorder while music is played at a certain volume, with the loudspeaker a measured distance from the box. Repeat the procedure for different packing materials but with all other conditions the same. The recordings then give a comparison of the soundproofing qualities of the different packing materials.

Activity 16.4.2 provides more ways of comparing materials as sound insulators.

13.4 LIGHT AND VISION

Light is the form of radiant energy (9.2) to which our eyes respond. The light we see is just one part of a very wide range or spectrum of radiant energy. Other forms of radiant energy which children are likely to encounter include radio waves in the form of signals for radio and television broadcasts, as well as: cell phones; microwaves used in cooking; infra-red radiation from hot objects which may be felt when it heats the skin; and X-rays used for medical diagnoses. Short range radio signals are increasingly part of domestic appliances such as remote controls. Although visible light is such a small part of the whole range of radiant energy, it is of great importance because we can respond to it through seeing, the sense through which most people gain the greatest amount of information about the world in which we live. Therefore the understanding and language we use to think about light are important not only in science but in the whole of the primary curriculum.

Children's investigations into light need to develop an understanding of two of its fundamental properties. First, the idea that **light is a form of energy which travels** underlies an understanding not only of *how* we see, but also much of *what* we see, including shadows, reflections and the bending of light (13.9). Second, **light varies in amount or intensity, and also in kind or quality**. The rainbow is a natural demonstration that there is a range of different kinds of light, which we perceive as colours (13.11).

Light as energy which travels   We do not experience light as something that travels outwards from its source, because its speed is much too great to be perceived: 300,000 km (over seven times the distance round the Earth) each second. Light from the Sun reaches the Earth across 150 million km of space in about eight and a half minutes. The very high speed of light means that normally on Earth, we cannot detect or measure the time taken for it to travel, so light seems to arrive at the same instant it is emitted. This is important in understanding the time-lag between seeing a flash of lightning and hearing the thunder which it causes (13.1.4).

Understanding vision   Scientists' general understanding of vision is that light (9.2.4) travels to and enters the eye, is focused by the curved front of the eyeball and the lens behind it, to form an image on the layer of light-sensitive cells (retina) inside the back of the eye. These cells respond to light falling on them by sending complex patterns of nerve signals to the brain, which uses this information to build up an image of what is seen (3.10).

This modern concept of vision, as a *passive* process, is essentially the same as that held by the School of Democritus in Ancient Greece. At the same period, the School of Pythagoras held an alternative idea which most children and a significant proportion of adults still intuitively use today, that vision is an *active* process. This usually centres around the belief that there is a kind of light in the eye and that in order to see an object it is necessary to send out a beam of light from the eye. This is usually coupled with the belief that the light which is sent out then comes back to the eye, so giving information about what is being looked at. Intuitive concepts of vision such as this one are important because they are very persistent and, if left unchallenged, make it much more difficult for children (and adults) to investigate and understand how light behaves.

Activity 17.1.1 explores ways of finding out about children's thinking about vision.

13.5   SOURCES, REFLECTORS AND TRANSMISSION OF LIGHT

13.5.1 Sources and reflectors

Everything we see can be classified into those things which emit light and those which do not. Light sources (**luminous** objects) transfer energy in the form of light to their surroundings (9.2.4), and they can be seen because some of the light they emit travels from them to the eye. Luminous objects use a variety of energy sources. The Sun uses nuclear energy; electric lamps use electrical energy; a candle-flame uses chemical-potential energy and sparks from steel on a grind-stone come from kinetic energy. Objects which do not emit light are **non-luminous**. A non-luminous object can be seen only because light from a luminous object reaches it and is reflected or scattered from it into the eye. Any non-luminous object which can be seen is therefore a reflector of light, and most objects which we see are reflectors of this kind.

Activity 17.2.1 gives ways of finding sources of light.

The difference between light sources and light reflectors is shown by the visible properties of the Sun and Moon (14.1), and by investigations using a dark-box (Fig. 13.2). When switched on, the lamp in the box is luminous, emitting light, some of which travels into the eye, so it can be seen. But a non-luminous object in the box, emitting no light, cannot be seen until light from a lamp or from outside is reflected from it into the eye.

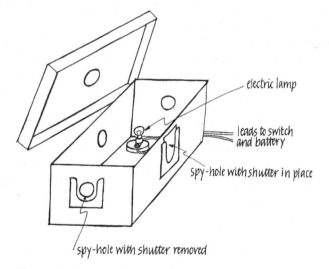

The inside of the box and lid should be painted matt black.

Figure 13.2 *Dark-box*

13.5.2 Transmission of light

Unlike sound waves (13.1), light needs no material medium in which to travel away from its source. Light from the Sun reaches the Earth across 150 million km of space, which is almost entirely empty of material. So light can be transmitted through a vacuum as well as through some materials.

Light travelling to the eye has passed through air, and often through other objects as well, such as glass windows. Children can classify materials into three groups, according to how light passes or fails to pass through them. Materials allowing no light to pass through are **opaque**: light falling on them is either absorbed (13.8) or reflected (13.10). Materials through which distant objects can be seen clearly are **transparent**. Those through which some light can pass, but distant objects cannot be seen clearly, are **translucent**.

These distinctions are useful, but do not always apply so simply. For example, it may be difficult to determine whether a material is opaque or not. Children may classify thin black polythene as opaque, but looked at closely in intense light, such as from an overhead projector, some light gets through. Also, the idea of transparency may not be as simple to children as to an adult, because they often confuse 'transparent' with 'colourless', and so may not regard clear but coloured plastic and glass bottles as transparent.

Activity 17.2.2 shows ways of investigating transmission of light through different materials.

13.5.3 Transparency, translucency and scattering of light

Light travels through transparent materials with a minimum of interference, enabling us to see a sharp image of what is on the other side of the material. The image may be distorted by refraction (13.9) but is still sharp. The transparent material may be coloured, but this means only that it absorbs part of the light passing through it (13.11), and it does not interfere noticeably with the remainder. However, translucent materials such as tracing paper or foggy air allow light to pass through them but scatter some or all of it in many different directions. The effect of slight scattering is that sharp images are lost and what we see appears fuzzy, with distant objects or light sources being affected most. More scattering means that distant objects cannot be seen at all, as when looking through tracing paper or walking in very dense fog.

Children can be confused by some translucent materials. When looking through a sheet of tracing paper, for example, distant objects cannot be seen at all, whereas images in contact with the tracing sheet can be seen clearly. This does not mean that the tracing sheet is transparent. It is translucent, but when it is in contact with the paper, scattering of light is greatly reduced and a more or less clear image can be seen through it.

13.6 THE DIRECTION IN WHICH LIGHT TRAVELS

A basic understanding of light uses the idea that light is a form of energy which travels away from its source in a particular direction. Children can notice a light beam passing through air looking from the side, because some light is scattered from suspended dust or smoke particles. Usually light travels in straight lines, as do sunbeams through gaps in cloud, car headlights in fog, theatre lights and the beam from a projector in a darkened room. Children should notice this evidence of the idea that unless prevented from doing so, light travels in straight lines.

Children can test the idea of light travelling in straight lines using simple logical thinking and careful observations of sighting-poles. Two thin, straight canes or dowels are placed on marks on the floor at either end of a large room. By sighting as near floor level as possible, a third cane is placed about halfway between and exactly in line with the first two, and its position marked. A thin string is then stretched taut between the two end marks, showing the shortest path and therefore a straight line between them. The third mark will, if the sighting and marking were accurate, lie on the same straight line. Since the sighting was done using light travelling from the distant cane to the near one and the observer's eye, the line of sight and therefore the direction of the light must itself have been a straight line.

Activity 17.3.1 describes ways of using a pin-hole viewer to investigate directions of light.

Children are interested in light when it is prevented from moving in this way. Apart from scattering this can happen when a material has properties affecting how light falls on it or passes through it. Some or all of the light may be **absorbed** by the material, and transferred as other forms of energy (13.8). The light may be bent from its straight line path by passing through different transparent materials, such as air and water, a change known as **refraction** (13.9). The light may be **reflected** from surfaces on which it falls and travel away in other directions (13.10).

13.7 SHADOWS

The idea that light travels in straight lines explains the formation and properties of shadows. A shadow is part of a surface on which less light falls than on the areas around it, because light travelling towards it has been obstructed, and either absorbed or reflected. An area in shadow appears darker than the area around it because less light is reaching it, so less light is reflected from it into the eye of the observer. Children investigating shadows may observe their size, shape, depth or intensity and how sharp or diffuse the edges are. As so often happens, the simplest kind of shadow formation is the most artificial, and most of the examples encountered in everyday experience are more complex.

13.7.1 Shadow formation using a point source of light

The most easily understood kind of shadow formation occurs when light is emitted from a very small or point source. The most convenient point source for primary science is a torch lamp in a holder and without a reflector, in a darkened room. Light from the lamp filament travels out in all directions. Placing an opaque object such as a shape cut from card between the lamp and a screen or wall casts a shadow with the same shape as itself and sharp edged. If either the lamp or the object is moved, the size of the shadow will change, but its sharpness will not. Figure 13.3 shows how this can be explained as light rays travelling in straight lines. Using diagrams drawn accurately to scale helps to predict the size of shadow an object will cast when it is at various distances from the lamp and screen.

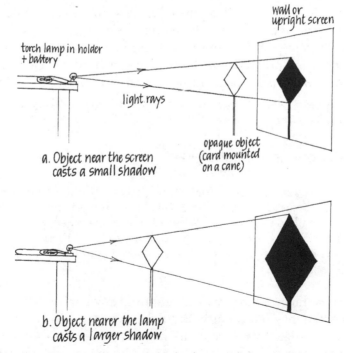

Figure 13.3 *Shadows from a point source of light: because light travels in straight lines, moving the object (or the lamp) causes the size of its shadow to change, but the edges of the shadow remain sharp*

Activity 17.4.1 shows more ways of observing shadow formation using a point source of light.

13.7.2 Shadow formation using an extended source of light

Most light sources are much larger than point sources such as torch lamps. They are known as extended light sources, and shadows of a different kind are produced when their light is obstructed. An ordinary electric lamp is a good extended light source for investigations. This should be used in a holder screwed to a baseboard, without a shade or reflector and taking care that children do not touch the lamp, which becomes hot in use.

Light from an extended source falling on an opaque object very near a screen or wall casts a fairly sharp shadow (Fig. 13.4a). As the object is moved away from the screen, the shadow increases in size and becomes blurred at its edges, producing a full shadow in the centre, surrounded by a less dark, partly shadowed zone (Fig. 13.4b). The paths of light rays from different parts cross each other because light travels out in straight lines from all parts of the lamp. As Figure 13.4a shows, when the object is very near the screen, light rays which cross at its edges have such a short distance to travel before they meet the illuminated surface that the partly shadowed zone is narrow and the shadow appears fairly sharp. When the object is moved away from the screen (Fig. 13.4b), the crossing rays have further to travel behind it, so the partly shadowed zone becomes wider and the shadow appears fuzzy and indistinct in outline.

Activity 17.4.2 gives further details on observing shadow formation using an extended source of light.

13.7.3 Shadows in sunlight

The Sun is a very large object, so that although it is very distant it acts as an **extended source of light**, not as a point source. Children can hold an object close to a sunlit wall and see its sharp shadow, then observe that as the object is moved further away (Fig. 13.5) the shadow becomes blurred as a zone of part shadow forms at its edges. However, the size of the full shadow in the middle does not change (contrast Figure 13.5 with Figure 13.4).

The Sun is so far away that rays of light from any part of it travel on almost parallel paths when they reach Earth. But the Sun is also a very large object, so rays of light from its edge (as we see it) are not travelling in *exactly* the same direction as those from its centre. Therefore the Sun is an extended light source, and moving an object away from a sunlit surface allows light rays moving in different directions to form a diffuse zone of part shadow, while the full shadow remains the same size (Fig. 13.5b). **Eclipses of the sun** are very large-scale examples of shadows in sunlight which also involve both full and part shadow.

Activity 17.4.3 describes ways of observing shadow formation in sunlight.

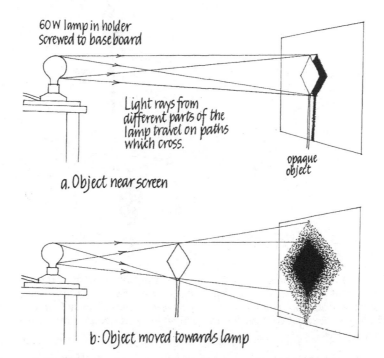

Figure 13.4 *Shadows from an extended source of light: when the object is near the screen there is little room for light rays to cross before they reach the screen, so the shadow is fairly sharp. When the object is further away the shadow is larger. There is much more room for the crossing rays to move apart so the shadow is fuzzy. The full shadow is surrounded by a zone of part shadow*

13.7.4 Shadows in classrooms

Children may see shadows in classrooms, which can be blurred and indistinct. Light entering through windows may come from many different directions, some of which will be reflected from the walls and ceiling. So any point in the room is being illuminated from many different directions at once.

Consequently, an opaque object has to be very near a surface to cast any full shadow. Even at the end of a room farthest from the window, shadows will be diffuse, and the nearer the observer moves to the window, the more indistinct they will become.

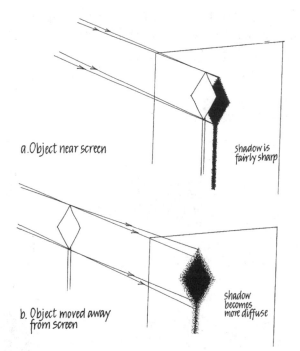

a. Object near screen

shadow is
fairly sharp

b. Object moved away
from screen

shadow
becomes
more diffuse

Figure 13.5 *Shadows in sunlight: the Sun is very distant but also very large, so light from different parts of it reach the Earth at slightly different angles. This means that the Sun is an extended light source, not a point source. As the object is moved away from the screen, the size of the full shadow does not change, but the part shadow caused by crossing light rays makes a diffuse zone round it*

Well-designed artificial lighting has exactly the same effect, even though most of the light comes from above rather than the side. Ideally, overhead lighting throws no shadows at all, because well-positioned fluorescent tube lights, coupled with reflection from the ceiling and walls, ensure that light reaches working areas from many different directions. In practice, any shadows that do occur are very diffuse.

13.7.5 Shadows, time and the seasons

On a sunlit day, children can investigate shadows noticing changes across time.

Children can fix a straight rod upright on a level surface, marking the end of its shadow throughout the day, noting the time of each record. A better method is to have an exactly vertical wooden dowel rod about 30 cm long, shaped to a point at its tip, glued into a hole near the middle of one side of a 50 x 50 cm square of blockboard. Permanent records of shadows can then be made on paper attached to the board.

As the Earth rotates (14.2), both the direction and the length of a shadow changes, providing evidence to explore the idea that it is the Earth which is moving, not the Sun. The relative lengths of shadows and the pattern they form throughout the day vary with the seasons, however the shadow is always longest in the morning and evening and shortest at about mid-day, when it always points due north.

At any time of year, plotting the pattern of shadow at fixed intervals during the day will produce a simple solar clock, which can be used for a while afterwards to tell the time if the weather is sunny and the board's position has not been changed. Over longer periods, however, it will begin to show an error, because the earth's orbit round the Sun (14.2) is not quite circular. A simple sundial, even when accurately made and set up, shows correct standard time on four days of the year only: 16 April, 14 June, 1 September and 24 December.

Activity 18.2.3 explores patterns of sun-shadows and the seasons.

13.8 ABSORPTION OF LIGHT

Any light falling on a material is either transmitted through it (13.5.2) or reflected from it (13.10), or absorbed by it. An opaque material that absorbs all the light falling on it, would reflect no light at all and be perfectly matt black, whereas one which absorbs very little light is white, and shades of grey are in between. If a material absorbs more of some colours than others, the light it reflects will appear coloured (13.11).

Light is a form of radiant energy, so when a material absorbs light, energy is transferred to it. In most materials all the radiant energy is transferred as thermal energy (9.2.2), so the material is heated and its temperature rises (9.3.2). In some materials, however, some of the light energy absorbed is transferred as other forms of energy. Children may encounter solar panels which transfer about 10 per cent of the radiant energy falling on them as electrical energy. They are used in so-called 'solar powered' watches and calculators, in satellites and space-stations, and increasingly as a renewable energy source.

Solar panels may in the future be an important source of energy, but far more important on a worldwide scale is the absorption of light by plants, in the process of photosynthesis by which they make their own food materials (4.4). In this process, some of the light energy absorbed is transferred as chemical-potential energy (9.2.8) in substances such as sugars. Plants are green because they absorb red and blue light for photosynthesis and reflect green light (13.11.2). Almost all life on Earth depends on photosynthesis and therefore on light energy from the Sun, because it is the only large-scale way in which energy can be transferred to the biosphere and food-chains (5.7). Fossil fuels such as coal and oil, formed by incomplete decay of plants and animals in the past, are also indirect products of light absorption by photosynthesis.

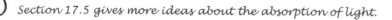

Section 17.5 gives more ideas about the absorption of light.

13.9 REFRACTION

The National Curriculum does not require children to learn about refraction of light until Key Stage 3. However, primary age children have many everyday experiences of things like spectacles, magnifying glasses, etc. which are scientifically understood using ideas about refraction. They can easily investigate ideas and evidence to learn interesting and valuable things about this aspect of light, which are presented here.

It is reasonable to suppose that a colourless and transparent material such as air or water would transmit light without changing it in any way. But everyday observations show that this is not so – see, for example, the shimmer in the air above a road or car on a hot day, and the distortion and appearance of movement seen when looking down through moving water. These are explained as bending of light by **refraction**.

Children encounter colourless and transparent materials such as air, water, glass and some plastics such as 'Perspex'. The speed of light changes as it travels from one transparent material to another, for example from water into air. Light is slowed most when it passes through glass and 'Perspex', water slows it down rather less and air very little.

This slowing down of light also causes it to change direction and be **refracted**. The only situation in which refraction does not result in bending is when light strikes the boundary between two transparent materials at a right angle, when it continues in the same straight line as before.

13.9.1 Basic observations

Just as with the formation of shadows (13.7), the simplest and most easily understood examples of refraction are the most artificial because real-life examples are usually more complex.

> Basic observations can be made using a cuboidal block of glass or 'Perspex' with smooth, flat sides. Good substitutes are a cuboidal box made of thin, transparent plastic partly filled with water to act as the main refracting material, or a water-filled, transparent plastic tank. Place the block (or box or tank) horizontally at eye level and look through two parallel faces. Notice the appearance of vertical edges such as the sides of a window or door which seem to be out of place. This displacement or distortion is caused by refraction.

13.9.2 Refraction between water and air

Children can explore different kinds of distortion when looking into water that are caused by refraction as light passes from water into air.

Looking down through water whose surface is not still we see what appears to be movement. This illusion of movement occurs because light passing from the water to the air above is refracted and bent in a continuously changing way. Consequently, the brain interprets seeing a stationary object as a moving one.

13.9.3 Refraction through lenses

Lenses are pieces of glass or transparent plastic, with curved surfaces specially shaped to refract light in particular ways. Most investigations involving lenses are beyond the scope of primary science, but some simple exploratory observations are relevant and useful.

Lenses have one or both faces curved. The most familiar kind has both surfaces curved outwards and is known as a biconvex lens as in simple magnifying glasses, which are good for children to play with and explore. Children can use a convex lens on sunny days, to project vivid images of windows and the scene outside onto paper or a white wall. The image is smaller than the real object, in full colour (children can be surprised by this), and upside down. A sharp image is formed only when the lens is at exactly the right distance from the screen or wall, and parallel to it.

The shape of the lens causes light passing through it to be bent inwards by refraction, and focused (Fig. 13.6a). A camera forms an image in exactly the same way. This can be shown with a disused film camera by putting tracing paper in place of the film, opening the shutter and pointing the camera, with its back open, towards a brightly lit scene.

A convex lens can also be used in bright sunlight as a burning-glass. The ease with which fires can be started in dry, sunny weather may make it inadvisable to introduce this topic, but if children play with lenses anyway, ignorance of the possible consequences may be more dangerous than understanding.

Children can use convex lenses as magnifying glasses, holding both the object and the lens close to the eye (Fig. 13.6b). Light from the object is bent inwards by the lens so that the object is seen as being much larger than it really is. The light rays from the top and bottom of the object do not cross, so the image is the right way up.

Activity 17.6.2 gives more ideas about observing refraction between glass and air in lenses.

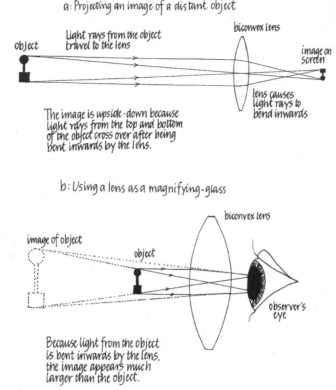

a: Projecting an image of a distant object

object

Light rays from the object travel to the lens

biconvex lens

image on screen

The image is upside-down because light rays from the top and bottom of the object cross over after being bent inwards by the lens.

lens causes light rays to bend inwards

b: Using a lens as a magnifying-glass

image of object

object

biconvex lens

observer's eye

Because light from the object is bent inwards by the lens, the image appears much larger than the object.

Figure 13.6 *Experimenting with convex lenses*

13.9.4 Refraction in the eye

In order to see clearly, the eye focuses a sharp image on the light-sensitive layer inside the back of the eyeball (3.10, Fig. 3.4). Light is refracted and bent inwards as it is in a camera, but in a different way. The eye has a flexible lens whose shape is changed to make fine adjustments of focus, but unlike the camera lens, it does not do all, or even most, of the necessary bending of light. This is achieved by the clear, curved front of the eyeball. Some defects in the eye causing a blurred or distorted image of near or distant objects, are corrected by wearing spectacles or contact lenses, which bend light, enabling eyes to focus light properly.

Children with both long and short sight defects may ask questions about, and enjoy experimenting with, the effects of looking through a very small hole such as a **pin-hole** in a piece of card held very close to the eye. In bright light, and without glasses or contact lenses, they will be able to see much sharper images than they can unaided. This happens because the hole in the card is making the eye work like a **pinhole camera**, which produces a sharp image without a lens. This effect is used to make pin-hole sunglasses which can be purchased quite cheaply. They reduce the intensity of bright light, and having many pin-holes in the glasses, instead of lenses, they help a person with long or short sight to see sharp images.

13.10 REFLECTION

Objects which do not themselves emit light (non-luminous objects) can be seen only because some of the light which reaches them is reflected by them into the eye. Reflection changes the direction of light in various ways which depend on the properties of their reflecting surfaces. A matt (non-shiny) surface under a microscope appears quite rough, even though it seems smooth to the unaided eye. Light falling on a matt or rough surface is partly absorbed (13.8) and partly reflected and scattered in many different directions. As a result the surface appears dull rather than shiny, and no 'picture' or image can be seen in it.

If the surface is very smooth, as in the case of water, glass or polished metal, there is very little absorption or scattering of light, so the surface appears shiny and images can be seen in it.

> The difference between diffuse and regular reflection can easily be shown by holding a mirror and a piece of white card upright on a sheet of white paper, and directing a narrow beam of light at each in turn. When the beam falls on the mirror it is reflected with very little scattering, still as a narrow beam. When the beam is directed at the card, however, scattering causes the reflected light to spread out widely and become diffuse.

Mirrors Children can investigates reflection with mirrors. Glass mirrors are made of a sheet of glass with a very thin layer of metal deposited on one side, which is protected by an opaque layer of paint or plastic material. Flexible mirrors are made of very thin metal foil between two layers of tough, transparent plastic. In both cases, the main reflecting surface is the metal foil: the glass or plastic is simply a transparent layer which supports and protects it.

13.10.1 Reflection in mirrors: angles

Light falling on a mirror is reflected in a very predictable way: the angle at which the light strikes the mirror and the angle at which it is reflected are the same.

This idea can be tested by pointing a narrow beam of light from a masked torch or a special ray-box onto a flat (plane) mirror, held upright on paper. However the mirror or light are moved, the two angles are always the same. This can also be recorded by drawing on the paper. The same can be observed by looking through narrow tubes (Fig. 13.7). Fixing a mirror in an upright position, move the tubes so that the object at A can be seen by looking from B, through both tubes and the mirror. The angles between the tubes and the mirror baseline will always be the same.

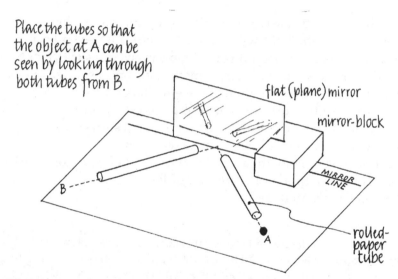

Place the tubes so that the object at A can be seen by looking through both tubes from B.

flat (plane) mirror

mirror-block

MIRROR LINE

rolled-paper tube

B

A

Figure 13.7 *How a mirror changes the path of light*

Activity 17.7.1 has further details about observing how a mirror changes the path of light.

It is normally impossible to see round corners because light travels in straight lines. But dentists use a mirror to overcome this problem when examining parts of the mouth which cannot be seen directly, such as a hidden side of a tooth. Mirrors can also be used to see what is behind the viewer, for example when driving, though many mirrors used in cars and lorries are not flat but curved, to give a wider field of view (see below). Children can devise various ways of seeing round obstacles while extending their understanding of reflection and the properties of mirrors. They can make mirror mazes using several mirrors. A mirror **periscope** is essentially a two-mirror maze used upright instead of on a flat surface.

Activity 17.7.2 shows how to make a mirror periscope for seeing round corners.

Children enjoy observing images of a small object placed between two upright mirrors, with their edges touching, at differing angles to one another. Two images are seen when the mirrors are at 90° and as the angle between the reflecting surfaces is reduced, the number of images increases. When the mirrors are at 60° to each other, five images can be seen, together with the real object, and the field of view is divided into six equal sectors; an effect used in the **kaleidoscope**.

a: The mirror is the line of symmetry between object and image.

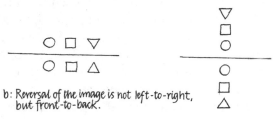

b: Reversal of the image is not left-to-right, but front-to-back.

Figure 13.8 *Mirror images*

13.10.2 Reflection in mirrors: images

When we look into a mirror, what we see is so familiar that it may seem to need no explanation, but mirror images are far from easy to understand. First, there is line symmetry: an object and its image are always symmetrical (Fig. 13.8a), with the mirror as the line of symmetry. Mirror images are reversed not parallel to the mirror, left-to-right, but at right angles to it, front-to-back. (Fig. 13.8b).

Write in front of a mirror and notice that your hand moves left to right, and so does its image in the mirror, which looks like the opposite hand. Place a mirror parallel with the needle of a magnetic compass and notice that in the mirror image, the north pole of the needle still points north, so left and right have not been reversed, even though front and back (east and west) have.

These observations explain a characteristic of mirrors which often puzzles children (and adults): that when a mirror is held vertically, the image appears to be reversed left-to-right, but is not upside-down. The answer is that the image is neither reversed left-to-right nor up-to-down, but back-to-front. To say that mirror images show left–right reversal is a misleading convention of language, which has developed because we are deeply aware of the distinction between left and right in ourselves. What mirrors in fact do is show us an image of an impossible world; of what would be seen if we could look in the opposite direction at a world in which everything had been reversed left-to-right. To check this, write a word such as LIGHT in large letters on a sheet of transparent acetate (OHP) film. Hold it up in front of a mirror so that the letters look the right way round to you, then look in the mirror.

Activity 17.7.3 has more ideas about observing reflection in mirrors as front-to-back, not left-to-right.

13.10.3 Curved mirrors

Flat (plane) mirrors form images which are reversed from front to back, but otherwise not distorted. Curved mirrors, on the other hand, form images in which the size, shape and orientation of the image may be quite different from reality. Children can look at flexible plastic mirrors and draw the distorted faces they see. They show that a very small amount of curvature affects the image, and also the different effects of bulging (convex) and hollow (concave) reflecting surfaces.

A shaving mirror is **concave** so that a near object makes an image that is upright and magnified. However, the image of a distant object in the same mirror is upside-down and reduced. A **convex** mirror forms an image of distant objects which is upright, reduced and somewhat distorted, with the disadvantage that objects seem much further away than they really are, but the great advantage of giving a wide field of view. Drivers may prefer a convex rear view mirror to a plane one, and large circular convex mirrors can be placed opposite concealed entrances to help drivers enter and leave safely. They can also be seen in buses to allow the driver to scan the whole of the inside of the vehicle without moving.

13.11 COLOUR

The National Curriculum does not require children to learn about colour of light until Key Stage 3. However, primary age children have many everyday experiences of colour which they can easily investigate to learn interesting and valuable things about this aspect of light, which are presented here.

White light is not one kind of light, but a band of radiant energy whose different parts have slightly different properties. Normally we do not see this, and become aware of it only when the white light is separated into narrower bands which we perceive as colours.

13.11.1 Dispersion and the spectrum

Children can observe white light separated to make the range of coloured light known as a spectrum, an effect called dispersion, by using prisms and by seeing a rainbow.

> Look through a prism made of glass or plastic (Fig. 13.9) or a water prism (Fig. 13.10) at a window or light source to notice coloured fringes: red to yellow on one side and blue to violet on the other. The spectrum always has the same colours in the same order: red, orange, yellow, blue and violet.

Activity 17.8.1 for more ideas about observing a spectrum.

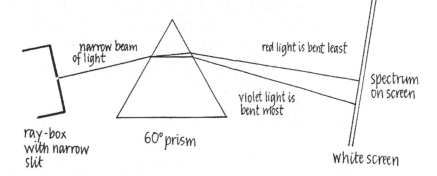

Figure 13.9 *Dispersion of light using a prism: a spectrum is produced because light we see as having different colours is bent through different angles as a result of refraction. This results in the spectrum which we see as bands of rainbow colours*

Dispersion of white light also occurs naturally when a rainbow is formed by a different transparent material causing refraction: the water of falling raindrops. A rainbow is seen only when the observer is standing between the Sun and rain falling in sunlight some distance away, facing towards the rain and away from the Sun. Raindrops are approximately spherical as they fall. White light entering a raindrop is subjected to refraction, reflection and dispersion to produce the spectrum. The reflection inside the raindrops directs light back to the eye of the observer. Red light is bent less than violet, so the red band of the rainbow is always on the outer side of the curve and the violet on the inner side. Sometimes a fainter, secondary rainbow is seen on the outside of the main one, with colours in the reverse order.

Colours created by reflection and interference Children are likely to experience many other natural and manufactured examples of objects which appear coloured because they create a spectrum in a different way. Examples include oil films on water, bubbles of soap or detergent solution, iridescent feathers of birds, hologram pictures and CD or DVD discs. They appear coloured when viewed from certain angles, because light is reflected from their surfaces in a complex way called **interference**.

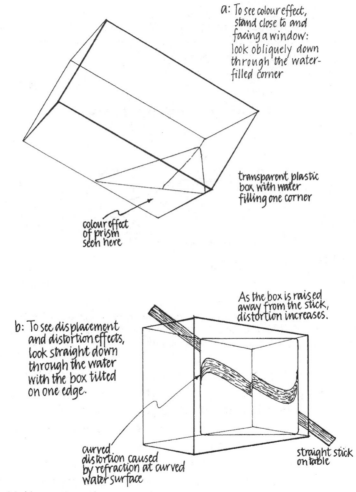

a: To see colour effect, stand close to and facing a window: look obliquely down through the water-filled corner

transparent plastic box with water filling one corner

colour effect of prism seen here

As the box is raised away from the stick, distortion increases.

b: To see displacement and distortion effects, look straight down through the water with the box tilted on one edge.

curved distortion caused by refraction at curved water surface

straight stick on table

Figure 13.10 *Making water prisms*

13.11.2 Colour by absorption: coloured objects

Most of the colour we see in everyday life is not produced by dispersion or interference but **absorption**. Objects and materials appear to have a colour of their own because some of the light is absorbed (13.8) and some is reflected by diffuse reflection (13.10). Light is absorbed from some parts of the spectrum and reflects other parts. A leaf uses red and blue light as the energy source for photosynthesis (4.4), so the red and blue parts of the spectrum are strongly absorbed and very little of them is reflected. Green and yellow light are not used in photosynthesis and so are reflected, giving the leaf its green appearance.

This is true of all coloured objects, regardless of whether they are opaque, translucent or transparent. The colours which we see are made up of the light which they do not absorb and which as a result is reflected if the object is opaque, or transmitted through if it is transparent.

Objects which absorb light from all parts of the spectrum more or less equally have no colour. If the object reflects a high proportion of the light falling on it and absorbs only a little, it appears white. If it absorbs a high proportion and reflects very little it will appear black, while materials with intermediate levels of absorption and reflection are seen as shades of grey.

13.11.3 Colour mixing: paints and dyes

When mixing paints and dyes, there are three colours which cannot be made by mixing other colours together, the so-called **primary colours**: red, blue and yellow. When they are mixed, other colours are produced because dyes and pigments reflect or transmit a mixture of colours, not a single pure colour. For example, a yellow paint absorbs violet, blue and red, and reflects yellow very strongly, but also reflects quite a lot of orange and green. A blue paint absorbs red, orange and yellow and reflects blue very strongly, but also reflects quite a lot of green and violet. The only colour which neither yellow or blue absorbs strongly and which both reflect is green, so the result of adding blue paint to yellow is green (Fig. 13.11).

Similarly, red mixed with yellow gives orange, and blue with red gives purple. Green, purple and orange are known as secondary colours. Mixing pigments and dyes produces different colours by absorbing and *removing* some colours from white light falling on the material. It is known as **colour mixing by subtraction**.

Children can investigate this by mixing paints, but mixing transparent dyes or inks, such as those used in felt- and fibre-tipped pens, may show more clearly how it works. Mix the dyes directly by applying a layer of ink, allowing it to dry, then adding a second colour layer on top. Each layer acts as a colour filter, removing light from the white light falling on it. Colour mixing by subtraction usually gives increasingly dark-toned colours as more layers are added.

Activity 17.8.2 has more ideas about investigating colour mixing with paint and dyes.

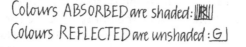

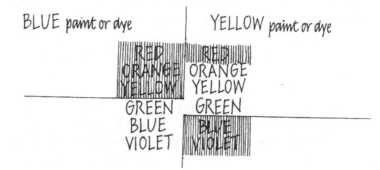

Figure 13.11 *Colour mixing by subtraction: green is the only colour reflected by both blue and yellow, so a mixture of blue and yellow appears green*

13.11.4 Colour mixing: coloured lights

Transparent colour filters look coloured for exactly the same reason that a dye does: they absorb some parts of the spectrum and transmit others. White light passing through a colour filter transmits the coloured light we see and absorbs the remainder. Mixing beams of coloured light, however, produces quite different results from mixing dyes or pigments.

The **three primary coloured lights**, which cannot be made by mixing other colours, are red, blue and green (not yellow). Blue and green together give a blue-green called cyan. Red and blue together give a purple-pink known as magenta. The surprise is that when red and green are mixed together they produce yellow.

Mixing coloured light can be investigated using a colour TV monitor and a large magnifying glass. Ideally, the TV monitor should be controlled by a computer using an art programme, so that areas of different colours can be put on screen and examined easily.

When mixing coloured lights, it is noticeable that the tone of the mixed (secondary) colours is lighter than that of the primaries which produce them, while white, which is produced by adding the three primaries, is the lightest of all. This is because light is being added as the colours are mixed, and more light is being reflected or emitted from the screen, so the process is called **colour mixing by addition**.

Activity 17.8.3 contains more ideas about mixing coloured lights.

13.11.5 Coloured lights and coloured objects

The colour which an object appears to be depends on the colour of the light which is reflected from it into the eye. If the light falling on an object is white, the colour of the object will be seen clearly, unless the light is very dim. If an object is lit with coloured light or viewed through a colour filter, however, its colour may appear to change.

13.11.6 Colours of the sky and sunset

Two things which are so familiar in our everyday lives that they are rarely questioned are the colours of the sky and the sunset. Both are remarkable phenomena brought about by the interaction between sunlight and the atmosphere. When the Sun shines on our planet from a particular direction, why do we receive light from the whole of the sky? And why is it blue?

To astronauts in space, the sky appears black: the only light they see is from the Sun and stars, or reflected from the Earth and Moon. But on the surface of Earth, we see the sky as blue because light must be coming from the atmosphere. This happens because very small dust particles and water-droplets suspended in the air intercept some of the sunlight passing through the atmosphere and **scatter** it in many directions. Some of this light is scattered downwards towards the Earth's surface and this is the light we see. The sky appears blue because the atmosphere scatters blue light more effectively than red, so more of the blue light is deflected downwards. A model of light-scattering by the atmosphere can be made by putting one or two drops of milk into a glass of water. The particles suspended in the milk are small enough to scatter blue light, so when lit from the side, the mixture has a bluish tint.

At mid-day, the colour of the Sun is yellow-white, but as it sets, this changes gradually to orange-yellow and often to a deep red-orange. This change of colour towards red as the Sun sets has exactly the same cause as the blue of the sky: the scattering of blue light by the atmosphere. At sunset, light from the Sun strikes the atmosphere at a very shallow angle, so light has to travel through the atmosphere for a much greater distance to reach the Earth's surface than at midday. The air tends to scatter blue light more than red, so more of the blue light is scattered and more of the red light gets through the air to the observer. The same effect can be seen in the milk-water mixture, by looking directly through the liquid at a light source. The light reaching the eye will appear much redder than normal because more of the blue light is being scattered.

14 THE EARTH AND BEYOND

14.1 THE SOLAR SYSTEM

The planet we live on, which we call the Earth, is one of nine planets which are in orbit round a star, which we know as the Sun. Although they vary greatly in size, see Table 14.1, all of these bodies: Sun, planets and moons, have similar, approximately spherical forms. The only one whose form can be observed directly by children is the Moon. The curved edge of the shadow on the Moon's surface shows that it is spherical. Earth is too large for us to be able to observe easily the curvature if its surface, but photographs of Earth, the other planets, and their moons taken from spacecraft show curved shadows and spherical forms clearly. The Sun, its planets, their moons and other bodies such as comets make up the Solar System. The Sun is an unremarkable star: observations suggest that even in our own star cluster (galaxy), which we see across the night sky as the Milky Way, there are thousands of millions of stars like it. On the scale of the galaxy, therefore, the Sun is small and ordinary, but in comparison with the planets it is huge and dominant: its mass is more than 750 times greater than that of all the planets added together. To put it another way: the Sun contains over 99.8 per cent of all the material in the Solar System.

The Sun is the only large light source (luminous object, 13.5) in the Solar System. In the innermost part of the Sun, at temperatures of around 15 million degrees Celsius, nuclear fusion occurs, in which matter is transformed into very large amounts of nuclear energy (9.2.9) by fusing pairs of hydrogen atoms to form atoms of helium. This is basically the same process as occurs in hydrogen bombs, and results in the transfer of very large amounts of energy to the surface of the Sun and, partly in the form of radiant energy, to the space around it. The radiant energy transferred from the Sun to the space around it includes light which we can see (13.4), which is the major energy source for the Earth. Unlike the Sun, the planets and their satellites are non-luminous. With the very minor exceptions of volcanoes on Earth, they emit no light of their own and are visible only because they reflect sunlight falling on them.

Table 14.1 Some basic information on the planets of the Solar System

Name	Diameter (km)	Mass (Earth = 1)	Distance from Sun (millions of km)	Time taken to circle Sun	Number of moons
Mercury	4,878	0.06	60	88 days	0
Venus	12,104	0.82	108	225 days	0
Earth	12,756	1.00	150	365.25 days	1
Mars	6,794	0.11	228	687 days	2
Jupiter	142,800	318	778	11.9 years	16+
Saturn	120,000	95	1,430	29.5 years	22+
Uranus	50,800	14.5	2,870	84 years	15+
Neptune	49,100	17.2	4,500	165 years	8
Pluto	2,280	0.002	5,900	248 years	1

14.1.1 Planets in orbit

The planets are in orbit round the Sun. To understand how they remain in orbit, it is useful to make a simple model by attaching a soft ball to a length of thread or thin string and swinging it in a circle around one's head. The ball is then moving much as an object in orbit does, but if the string breaks or is released, it flies out of its circular path. This shows that for an object to stay in orbit, there must be a force acting inwards on it, preventing it from flying off in a straight line. In the model, this force is exerted by the inward pull of the thread, but in the Solar System the force keeping the planets in orbit is gravitational. The Sun is so massive that its gravitational field (12.2) can keep planets from flying off into space even when they are thousands of millions of kilometres away from it.

If the Solar System could be viewed by an observer completely outside it, it would be seen that the planets move in orbit in a very particular way. With one exception (Pluto) all the planets move as if they were on a huge flat disc with the Sun at its centre. The orbits of most of the planets have only a slight tilt to this imaginary disc, and it was because of this, and the particular positions of the planets, that the Voyager spacecraft could make close encounters with Jupiter, Saturn, Uranus and Neptune between 1979 and 1989. Astronomers call this imaginary disc around the Sun the plane of the **ecliptic**. The way the Earth spins in relation to the ecliptic causes the seasons we experience every year (14.4). An observer outside the Solar System would also notice that all the planets move in their orbits in the same direction: anti-clockwise when viewed from above the North Pole of the Earth.

14.1.2 Modelling the Solar System

It is very difficult to gain an idea of the scale of the Solar System, not only because the sizes of the Sun and planets are so different, but also because the distances between the planets are very large in comparison with their diameters. Therefore tables showing the actual dimensions of planets and their distances from the Sun (Table 14.1) may be of limited use in helping children gain any concept of the scale of the Solar System. What may be more helpful is to make a model of the Sun and at least the inner planets by scaling down the Solar System enormously. (Table 14.2)

Table 14.2 Modelling the Solar System (scale: 1 to 5,000 million); at this scale the Sun is 28 cm in diameter and can be represented by a beach-ball

Planet	Scaled-down diameter (mm)	Suggested model	Scaled-down distance from Sun (m)
Mercury	1.	poppy seed	12
Venus	2.4	peppercorn	22
Earth	2.5	peppercorn	30
Mars	1.3	mustard seed	45
Jupiter	28.5	(clay ball)	156
Saturn	24.	(clay ball)	285
Uranus	10.3	small glass marble	574
Neptune	10.	small glass marble	900
Pluto	0.5	poppy seed	1,180

Activity 18.1.1 contains more advice about modelling the Solar System.

14.2 THE EARTH IN ORBIT

14.2.1 The orbit of the Earth

The Earth's orbit round the Sun is an almost circular ellipse (an oval shape), with the Sun at the centre. The Earth moves round this orbit at a very high speed: about

107,000 km per hour, or nearly 30 kms–1, but we are usually unaware of this, because we and the Moon (14.3) are carried along with the Earth, anchored to it by gravitational forces, and have no object near enough to act as a point of reference by which to judge our speed through space.

14.2.2 Years and days

The Earth completes one journey in its orbit round the Sun every year, and this is how our year is defined. However, as it travels in orbit, the Earth also spins. To an observer in space, the Earth would appear to be spinning slowly around an imaginary axis whose outer ends are at the North and South Poles. The observer would also notice that this axis of spin is tilted to the Earth's orbit round the Sun (the plane of the ecliptic, 14.1): which is important in understanding the seasons (14.4). As the Earth spins, different parts of its surface are turned towards the Sun. We call the time taken for one complete spin a day, although over most of the Earth this also includes the dark time we call night.

Activity 18.2.1 has more advice about modelling the Earth in orbit.

Night and day can easily be modelled using a terrestrial globe mounted at the correct angle of spin, with the beam from a projector to represent the Sun. It is important when using this model to ensure that the light source is level with the middle of the globe. At any time, it is day over the half of the Earth which is illuminated by the Sun, and night over the half in shadow. As the Earth spins, in an anti-clockwise direction when viewed from above the North Pole, different parts of the Earth are carried into the path of light from the Sun, while others are carried into the Earth's own shadow and the darkness of night. For purposes of telling the time, the day is divided into 24 hours, but unlike years and days, the hour is an artificial time unit which has been in use since the fourteenth century, when mechanical clocks came into use.

Activity 18.2.2 provides more advice about modelling day and night.

14.2.3 Leap years and the calendar

Because they arise from the movement of the Earth in orbit and its spin, years and days are natural units of time, but there is no simple relationship between them, and a year is not made up of an exact number of days. One year is 365 days, 5 hours, 48 minutes and 46 seconds. The result is that in order to have a usable dating system or calendar, we need a system which allows for the 'extra' length of each year over and above the 365 days. The calendar in general use today is the Gregorian Calendar, introduced by Pope Gregory XIII in 1582, though not adopted in England until 1752.

This is itself a refinement of the Julian Calendar introduced by Julius Caesar in 45 BC. The Julian Calendar uses the rough correction which we know as the leap year: one day (29 February) is added to the calendar every fourth year, when the number of the year can be divided by four (e.g. 1992, 1996). This slightly over-corrects the error, so the Gregorian Calendar introduced a second correction: a leap year does not occur in a centurial year (e.g. 1900, 2000) unless it is still divisible by four when two zeros have been removed (e.g. 2000, 2400).

14.2.4 The apparent motion of the Sun

Unless an observer on Earth makes very accurate measurements of the stars, there is nothing to show that our planet is in orbit round the Sun. The effects of the Earth's spin, however, are visible at any time of the day or night, whenever the sky is clear. The most obvious effect of the Earth's spin is the apparent movement of the Sun across the sky during the day and the resulting changes in length and direction of shadows, which are discussed in section 13.7. Careful observation of stars over a period of some hours shows that they too appear to move (14.5).

In relation to the rest of the Solar System, the Sun is a fixed, central point. It appears to move across the sky because the spinning Earth carries an observer round with it, exactly as a roundabout or carousel carries a rider. The angle from which a rider sees fixed objects distant from the carousel is constantly changing, but the angle from which the moving carousel is viewed remains the same. The result is often the illusion that the world is moving round the carousel, which seems to remain still. During a sunny day we experience the same illusion, but in a much stronger form, because the Sun seems to move in relation to all the fixed objects which we use as landmarks to orient ourselves within the world around us. Our usual experience is that if something changes position when we ourselves have not, it has moved, and the only exceptions to this we ever see are the Sun and, if we observe them carefully, the stars.

Children's learning that the apparent movement of the Sun is an illusion may take a long time, but models can be helpful. A good one is to use a terrestrial globe lit by a horizontal beam of light from a projector. The first thing to determine is which way the Earth spins. The Sun appears to move from east to west, so the Earth must be moving in the opposite direction, i.e. anti-clockwise when viewed from above the North Pole. Position the globe so that the children's home country is on the boundary between light and shadow. Turn the globe a little in the correct direction. Has the place moved into light or into shadow? If into light, it was at the point of sunrise; if into shadow, at the point of sunset. Now ask the children to imagine that they are tiny people on the globe. Where would the light seem to come from, and how far above the horizon would the Sun appear to be? At sunrise and sunset, light strikes the Earth at a shallow angle: the Sun is low in the sky. As a particular place on the globe is turned from a sunrise position to a mid-day position, the angle at which light strikes that part of the Earth becomes steeper: the Sun would appear higher in the sky, and this is exactly what is observed in reality. In addition, the Sun appears due south at noon to an observer in the Northern Hemisphere, but due north to one in the Southern Hemisphere. On a large globe lit in this way, observations can also be made with very small shadow-sticks (short pieces of thin wire attached with masking tape), which mimic the variation in length and direction of shadows formed in sunlight using full-size shadow-sticks (13.7).

14.3 THE EARTH AND THE MOON

14.3.1 The Moon as a satellite

All the planets of the Solar System except Mercury and Venus have one or more satellites or moons in orbit around them (Table 14.1). The Earth has one satellite, which we simply call the Moon, and which is unusual in that it is very large in relation to its planet, having a diameter (3,476 km) nearly a quarter that of the Earth. The moon is held in orbit round the Earth by the Earth's gravitational field (12.2), much as the Earth and Moon together are held in orbit round the Sun. Although the Moon is large for a satellite its mass is much less than that of the Earth, so its gravitational field is much less intense: 1 kg on the Moon weighs only 1.6 N, whereas on Earth it weighs 9.8 N (12.2). One result is that the Moon has retained no atmosphere and is completely lifeless.

The average distance between the Earth and the Moon is 384,000 km, so the Moon is far closer to us than either the Sun or the nearest planet, Venus. The Moon is by far the smallest of all the objects we can see in the night sky without a telescope, but because it is so close to us it is, when it can be seen, by far the most prominent. Its nearness also means that the Moon has other effects on the Earth which children may observe: eclipses and tides (see below).

14.3.2 The Moon in orbit

The Moon moves in orbit round the Earth once in about 28 days, a period known as a lunar month. It travels in the same direction as the Earth itself orbits the Sun: anti-clockwise when viewed from above the Earth's North Pole. During each lunar month the Moon's appearance undergoes a series of progressive changes known as the phases of the Moon (see below). The Moon also spins on its axis, but it takes exactly the same time to spin once as to move once round in its orbit, so it always has the same face towards the Earth. A simple model can help to show this. Place a large ball on a table to represent the Earth. Put a mark on a small ball, which is to represent the Moon, and move it round the large one, always keeping the mark on the 'Moon' facing the 'Earth'. In travelling once round the 'Earth' the 'Moon' will also have rotated once on its axis. When using this model, care is needed to avoid suggesting that the Moon moves through space in a circular path. The Moon's orbit round the Earth is almost circular but, as Figure 14.1 shows, its path through space is quite different because the Earth itself is in orbit round the Sun.

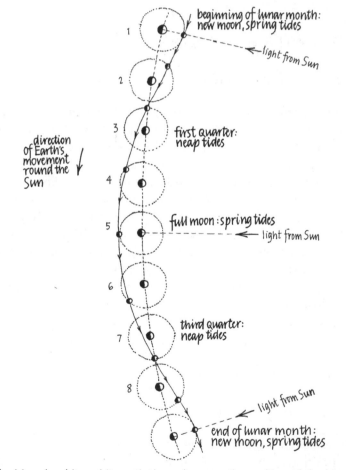

Figure 14.1 *The Moon's orbit and its path through space: the position of the Moon is shown at eight points during the lunar month. These correspond to the phases of the Moon shown in Figure 14.2. The path of the Moon through space is shown by the solid arrowed line*

14.3.3 Phases of the Moon

During a lunar month the Moon's appearance, if it is visible, changes in a regular and predictable way. The beginning and end of the lunar month are taken to be the short period when the side of the Moon facing the Earth is wholly in shadow. Even during this period the Moon may be faintly visible if the sky is very clear, because light reflected from the Earth travels to the Moon and some of it is reflected back again as 'earthlight'.

As the Moon moves in its orbit round the Earth, the angles between the Moon, the Earth and the Sun are continually changing (Fig. 14.2). As a result, the proportions of the Moon's face in light and shadow change throughout the lunar month.

This can be modelled by acting out Figure 14.2 , using a ball painted half black and half white as the 'Moon', with a window to represent the Sun. One child, acting as the Moon, carries the ball in a circle around observers who represent the Earth, but so that the white half of the ball is always directly facing the window. When the 'Moon' is nearest the window, the observers will see only the black half of the ball: this represents the new moon phase. As the 'Moon' moves round them, the observers turning to look at it will see more and more of the white face of the ball, until the 'Moon' is at its farthest from the window, when only the white half of the ball will be seen: this represents the full moon phase. Here again it may be relevant to remind children that although the Moon's orbit is nearly circular, its path through space is not (see Fig. 14.1).

This activity can also help children to understand that the curved edge of the shadow that is visible on the moon, except at the half moon phase, is evidence that it is a sphere.

14.3.4 Eclipses and tides

There are three complex kinds of event, two rare and one which occurs every day, which are the result of the Moon moving in orbit round the Earth. These are eclipses of the Moon, eclipses of the Sun, and tides in the seas. A comprehensive understanding of any of these events is far beyond the scope of primary science, but for children who observe them, simple explanations, though incomplete, are useful and interesting.

Eclipses of the Moon (lunar eclipses) occur only at full moon, on the rare occasions when the Earth moves into line between the Sun and the Moon. Because light travels in straight lines, this causes the Earth's shadow to fall on the Moon, darkening it. If only part of the Moon's face is darkened the eclipse is said to be partial, whereas if the whole face is in shadow the eclipse is total. Total eclipses of the Moon can last for several hours, unlike total eclipses of the Sun (see below). When an eclipse of the Moon occurs, it can be seen from any part of the Earth from which the Moon itself is visible, but because the Moon's orbit is tilted in relation to that of the Earth, the exact lining-up of the Earth, Moon and Sun which causes it is a rare event.

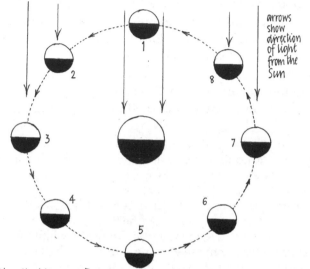

a: How the Moon and Earth would appear to an observer in space (not to scale).

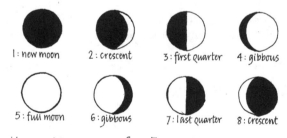

1: new moon   2: crescent   3: first quarter   4: gibbous

5: full moon   6: gibbous   7: last quarter   8: crescent

b: How the Moon appears from Earth.

Figure 14.2 *Phases of the Moon*

Activity 18.3.1 contains advice about modelling phases of the Moon.

Eclipses of the Sun are more common than those of the Moon, but because each one can be seen only from a fairly small part of the Earth, they are very rare events in any one place. They occur only at new moon, when the Moon moves between the Sun and the Earth. Seen from the Earth, the Moon is just large enough to obscure the Sun completely and make a total eclipse for a few minutes. When this happens, a bright halo of light (the corona) can be seen around the dark disc of the Moon. When a total eclipse is seen in one part of the Earth, observers a few hundred kilometres to the north or south will see only a partial eclipse, in which the Moon does not obscure the Sun completely. The last total eclipse of the Sun visible in Northern Europe was on 11 August 1999 and the next one visible in the UK is not until 2090, though a partial eclipse will be visible from north-west Scotland on 20 March 2015.

Tides are the twice daily rise and fall of the sea, which can be observed on the seashore and in harbours. Tides are caused by the changing balance between a complex set of three forces acting on the water of the Earth's oceans: the gravity of the Moon and Sun, together with an outward force caused by the way in which the Moon and Earth move around each other. The forces combine to make the water in the oceans bulge out slightly, both on the side of the Earth nearest the Moon and on the opposite side. These bulges in the water are only a few metres high, and therefore very slight in comparison with the size of the Earth, but they are like two very broad, shallow waves which seem to travel round the shorelines of the world as the Earth spins, causing the water level to rise and fall. What actually happens is that the tidal bulges stay in more or less the same place during a 24-hour period while the Earth spins underneath them, so most shorelines have two high tides a day as they are carried past the bulges, and two low tides as they are carried past the slight troughs between them.

There is a longer-term pattern of tides over and above the twice-daily rise and fall, which is linked to the phases of the Moon (Fig. 14.1). At full moon and new moon, when the Moon, Earth and Sun are almost in line with each other, the range of the tides is wide: they rise higher and fall lower than the average. These are called spring tides. At the first and third quarters, when the Moon and Sun are at right angles in relation to the Earth, the range of tides is narrow, so their rise and fall are smaller than average. These are called neap tides.

14.4 THE MOVEMENT OF THE EARTH AND THE SEASONS

The Earth moves round the Sun in an orbit which is like the edge of a huge, imaginary and almost circular disc (the plane of the ecliptic, 14.1). This imaginary disc is also the direction in which light travels to the Earth from the Sun. As it moves in orbit, the Earth spins once a day on an imaginary axis through the North and South Poles. The Earth's axis is not at right angles to its orbit: it is tilted by almost 23½°, which is why terrestrial globes are usually mounted on a tilted stand. This means that the spin of the Earth is tilted in relation to the light reaching it from the Sun. This in turn causes changes in the length of day and night during the year, as well as very important effects on climate, especially in the temperate and polar regions, which we call the seasons.

Even though it is moving in its orbit round the Sun, the direction in which the Earth spins does not change. This is shown by the way in which the North Pole always points towards the Pole Star whatever the season of the year (14.5). Because the direction of the Earth's spin does not change, there is a time in the year when the North Pole is as far away from the Sun as possible, as shown in Figure 14.3a. This always happens on 21 December, the Winter Solstice, which in the Northern Hemisphere is the shortest day of the year, whereas in the Southern Hemisphere it is the longest. Figure 14.3a compares sunlight falling at maximum intensity with that falling at a north temperate latitude, about that of southern Europe or the northern USA. It shows that the angle between the sunlight and the Earth's surface is shallow at the temperate latitude: the Sun is low in the sky, even at mid-day. This means that, to put it very simply, the same amount of light is spread over a much larger area (X) in the temperate zone than it is in the tropics (Z). The result is that the intensity of light (i.e. the amount of radiant energy reaching each square metre of the Earth's surface each second) is much lower in the temperate zone, so the rate of energy transfer and heating by the Sun is low. A low rate of energy transfer and short days result in cold weather: it is winter.

When the North Pole is tilted as far as possible towards the Sun, which happens on 21 June, the Summer Solstice, it is the longest day in the Northern Hemisphere and the shortest day in the Southern (Fig. 14.3b). At mid-day, sunlight reaches north temperate latitudes at a much steeper angle than in winter, so that the same amount falls on a much smaller area (Y). As a result, sunlight is much more intense, so energy transfer and heating occur at a much faster rate than at the Winter Solstice. Long days and a high rate of energy transfer result in the weather being much hotter: it is summer in the Northern Hemisphere. All these changes occur in the reverse way in the Southern Hemisphere, where the summer solstice is on 21 December and the midwinter solstice on 21 June.

Activity 18.2.3 provides more investigations into patterns of Sun shadows.

These changes, and others such as equinoxes which occur in between them, can be modelled using a terrestrial globe and an overhead projector. This can show very clearly the changes in both day-length and the angle of sunlight at mid-day during the year. It also makes it possible to see why polar regions have 24 hours of daylight around mid-summer and of darkness around midwinter. In addition, it can help to overcome the very commonly held but quite mistaken belief that temperate regions are hotter in summer because they are tilted towards the Sun *and are therefore nearer to it*, rather as a person moves nearer to a fire to keep warm.

As the model outlined in Table 14.2 shows, the distance between the Sun and the Earth is so huge in relation to the size of the planet that the tilt cannot make any significant difference to it. The overall pattern of our seasons is caused, not by our moving nearer to or farther away from the Sun, but by changes in the length of daylight and the angle at which light reaches the surface of the Earth.

Activity 18.4.1 provides more advice about modelling energy input to the Earth.

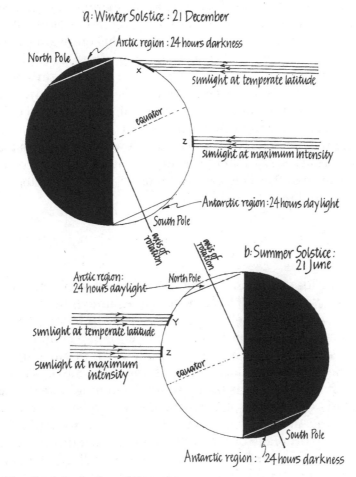

Figure 14.3 *The tilt of the Earth and the seasons*

Midsummer and midwinter Although the overall pattern of the seasons in temperate parts of the earth is determined by changes in energy input from the Sun, there are variations which are not. In Britain, for example, the summer solstice is popularly known as 'Midsummer Day' and the winter solstice as 'Midwinter Day'. This can be confusing for children because neither solstice coincides, in most years, with the hottest and coldest weather. Midsummer Day is only about one-third through the season thought of as 'summer' in Western Europe. The popular naming of the solstices is arbitrary, a historical accident, but the question remains as to why in Britain the extremes of temperature lag significantly behind the periods of maximum and minimum input of solar energy.

This delay between energy input and climatic response occurs because the sea and, less significantly, the land surface, act as thermal energy reservoirs, rather like gigantic 'night storage' heaters. Sea temperatures of North-West Europe continue to rise well beyond the summer solstice so that our warmest weather usually occurs in July and August, when the sea temperature and solar input are both high. The annual cycle of temperature change is, however, further complicated by warm water from the North Atlantic Drift. This not only causes the seas around Britain and Ireland to be much warmer overall than they would otherwise be, giving these islands a very mild climate in relation to their latitude, but also makes them warm up more quickly than they cool down. The result is that the time-lag between the Winter Solstice and the coldest weather (typically eight to 10 weeks) is much longer than that between the Summer Solstice and the hottest weather (typically four to six weeks).

14.5 STARS

The Sun is our local star; one of billions in the huge star-cluster or galaxy we call the Milky Way, and which can be seen as a faintly luminous band across the night sky. Even without a telescope it is possible to identify many bright stars and major star groups or constellations. Observing the night sky just above the horizon gives confirmation of the spin of the Earth in much the same way that observing the Sun by day does: the stars appear to move across the sky, from east to west if the observer is facing south. Even more interesting are the stars around Polaris or the Pole Star, which always appears in the same direction (due north) and at the same angle above the horizon (the latitude of the observer). The North Pole of the Earth points almost directly towards this star whatever the season of the year, so that it alone of all the stars in the sky never seems to move. The stars around it appear to move, but unlike those just above the horizon their apparent path is not across the sky but in a circle whose centre is the Pole Star. This can be shown (though not easily by children) by pointing a camera on a tripod at the Pole Star on a clear, moonless night and leaving the shutter open for several hours. The curved tracks of the stars on the resulting photograph are a record of the spin of the Earth.

All stars are luminous objects (13.5) and most, like the Sun, give out light and other forms of radiant energy as a result of the nuclear fusion inside them (9.2.9). This is the same kind of reaction which results in the explosion of hydrogen bombs, but stars like the Sun do not explode because they are so massive: they are held together by their intense gravitational fields. Most stars are very large, many much bigger than the Sun, but they are so far away that they appear very small.

The star nearest to the Solar System is so far away that light from it (travelling at 300,000 km each second) takes 4½ years to reach us, and most stars are very much more distant than that.

Stars and planets Stars are so far away, and the distances between them are so great, that to us they seem to have fixed positions in relation to each other. Their positions are in fact changing, but from Earth the changes appear so gradual that they cannot be detected without very accurate measurements.

Groups of stars in the sky (constellations) have suggested mythological beings or animals to peoples all over the world, who have given them names. From one such set of names we have inherited our Signs of the Zodiac. Because the stars do not seem to change their positions in relation to one another, they were known to many ancient astronomers as fixed stars, to distinguish them from other bright objects in the sky, which appear to move quite quickly against the background of unchanging constellations. These were known as the wandering stars, which today we know are not stars at all, but planets. Venus, Jupiter and Mars can all be seen from Earth without a telescope and often appear larger and brighter than stars because, although they are very much smaller than any star and only reflect light from the Sun, they are also very much nearer to us.

The twinkling of stars Without a very large telescope, stars appear as no more than tiny points of light. Their apparent size from Earth is so small that they show a familiar but interesting property: they twinkle. A twinkling star not only seems to vary in brightness but may also seem to move about slightly. One clue to the cause of twinkling is that stars directly overhead on a clear, warm night often seem to twinkle less than those near the horizon or in very cold or windy conditions. Twinkling is, in fact, an effect of the Earth's atmosphere, because when seen from a space station or the Moon, the stars shine steadily. Light from the stars has to travel through the atmosphere to reach us, but the atmosphere is never still. Movement and temperature differences in the air cause very small amounts of refraction and bending of the light passing through it (13.9). Normally we are unaware of this, but from the Earth the stars appear so small that even a tiny amount of refraction makes them look as if they were moving slightly and varying in brightness. The same effect can sometimes be seen when looking at distant street lamps on a windy night. In contrast to the stars, the planets do not twinkle, and this is usually the easiest way to distinguish between a planet and a bright star. The reason is simply that the planets are near enough to us to appear larger than the stars, so that they shine steadily while the much greater but much more distant stars appear to dance.

INDEX